teach yourself...
QUARK XPRESS 3.1

DOUGLAS H. SNYDER

A Subsidiary of
Henry Holt and Co., Inc.

▼ Dedication ▲

I'd like to dedicate this book to my beautiful wife Deb, who has helped to keep me on track through the process of writing this book, as well as through everything else that has happened over the past eleven years.

▼ Acknowledgments ▲

While my name goes on the cover of this book, it was in fact a group effort. I'd like to thank the people who made this book a reality. Special thanks goes to:

John Sullivan, president of the Task Force, who gave me the opportunity and parented me through the process.

Veronica Hubbard, L. West Nelson, and JonJo Suliban, for helping me get to this point through friendship and inspiration, and by keeping me on my toes. I would be a much poorer person if I hadn't met them.

Copyright © 1991 by Management Information Source, Inc.
a subsidiary of Henry Holt and Company, Inc.
115 West 18th Street
New York, New York, 10011

All rights reserved. Reproduction or use of editorial or pictorial content in any manner is prohibited without express permission. No patent liability is assumed with respect to the use of the information contained herein. While every precaution has been taken in the preparation of this book, the publisher assumes no responsibility for errors or omissions. Neither is any liability assumed for damages resulting from the use of the information contained herein.

First Edition—1991
ISBN 1-55828-129-0
Printed in the United States of America
10 9 8 7 6 5 4 3 2 1

MIS:Press books are available at special discounts for bulk purchases for sales promotions, premiums, fund-raising, or educational use. Special editions or book excerpts can also be created to specification.

For details contact: Special Sales Director
MIS:Press
a subsidiary of Henry Holt and Company, Inc.
115 West 18th Street
New York, New York 10011

Adobe Illustrator, Adobe PhotoShop, and Adobe PostScript are trademarks of Adobe Systems Inc.
Claris MacDraw is a trademark of Claris Corporation.
Deneba Canvas is a trademark of Deneba Software.
MacIntosh is a trademark of Apple Computer.
Microsoft Excel and Microsoft Word are trademarks of the Microsoft Corporation.
Quark and QuarkXPress are trademarks of Quark Inc.

CONTENTS

▼ CHAPTER 1 1
You Will Learn 2
What Is QuarkXPress? 3
What's in a Publication? 3
Installing QuarkXPress 4
Starting QuarkXPress 7
Program Attributes 11
Working with a Document 15
Summary 25

▼ CHAPTER 2 27
You Will Learn 28
Entering and Importing Text 29
Text Attributes 33
The Measurement Palette of a Text Box 51
Style Sheets 53
Formatting Paragraphs 58
Tabs 64
Summary 69

▼ CHAPTER 3 71
You Will Learn 72
Adding Graphics 73
The Picture Style Menu 87
The Picture Usage Dialog Box 89
Modifying Picture Box Shapes 94
Runaround Options 98
Summary 104

▼ CHAPTER 4 105
You Will Learn 106
Moving Around a Document 107

Flowing Text 108
Master Pages 110
Automatic Text Chain 110
Inserting and Arranging Pages 112
The Document Layout Palette 115
Automatic Page Numbering 119
Jump Commands 119
Grouping 120
Locking 121
Summary 122

▼ CHAPTER 5 123
You Will Learn 124
The Printing Process 125
The Traditional Printing Press 126
Halftone Screens 129
Manipulating Colors 132
The Separation Process 137
An Example 138
Summary 141

▼ CHAPTER 6 143
You Will Learn 144
Preferences 145
Summary 168

▼ CHAPTER 7 169
You Will Learn 170
Additional Utilities and Commands 171
File Menu Extras 171
Edit Menu Extras 174
Item Menu Extras 184
Page Menu Extras 191
View Menu Extras 192
Utilities Menu Extras 197
Summary 204

APPENDIX 205

INDEX 207

In This Chapter

- ▼ What Is QuarkXPress?
- ▼ What's in a Publication?
- ▼ Installing QuarkXPress
- ▼ Starting QuarkXPress
    - Opening an Existing File
    - Creating a New File
- ▼ Program Attributes
    - The Menus
    - Keyboard Equivalents
    - Submenus
    - Dialog Boxes
- ▼ Working with a Document
    - Windows
    - Viewing the Document at Different Magnifications
    - The Tool Palette
    - Moving and Manipulating Items
    - The Measurement Palette
- ▼ Summary

You Will Learn

▼ How QuarkXPress combines text and images into a single document.

▼ How to Install QuarkXPress.

▼ How to open an existing file or create a new one.

▼ How to access commands through the Menu bar and dialog boxes, and using keyboard equivalents.

▼ How to change the scale at which the document is viewed.

▼ How to use the Item tool to move and manipulate items.

▼ How to use the Measurement palette to view and manipulate an item's location, dimensions, and attributes.

What Is QuarkXPress?

QuarkXPress is desktop, or electronic, publishing software that is designed to help you create and combine text and/or images into a layout. It is called "desktop" because you can do it all at your desk, "publishing" because you can go all the way from idea to printed page. A program like QuarkXPress gives you a place to gather all of the text and images into one document, and the tools to manipulate and control the way the text and images are presented.

It doesn't really matter what you are laying out—whether it's a matchbook cover, a forty-foot billboard, or anything in between, QuarkXPress can help you put it together.

Creating a document traditionally involves many different people—a graphic artist, a copywriter, a typesetter, a paste-up person, and possibly a photostat operator—each with specific talents and a specific task. Though QuarkXPress doesn't magically give you the talents and experience of the different people involved in a traditional publication, it does allow you to perform many of their tasks without needing to learn the manual operations involved. You won't need an X-acto knife or the steady hand of a traditional paste-up artist. Using today's high-quality clip-art, you needn't be able to draw to include powerful, appropriate images to strengthen your message. You don't even need to know what a photostat camera looks like to be able to resize or rotate an image.

QuarkXPress gives you the tools and assistance you need to put together any type of publication using just common sense, good judgment, and a little planning.

What's in a Publication?

The steps taken to create any type of publication are similar, no matter what the publication is. The first step, and usually the first overlooked, is planning and preparation. A carpenter doesn't go to the lumberyard and buy a bunch of two-by-fours before knowing what the house is going to look like. The same is true when you build a document in QuarkXPress. You should know what your final goal is before you open a page and start throwing things around on it. A little planning in the beginning will save you a lot of time throughout the project.

If you are using QuarkXPress to design a document, one of the first choices you have to make is what the page size will be. This can be determined by the cost of available paper, mailing considerations, and the content of the document. There are many other decisions to make, and each of these may affect the others. Issues like margin width, number of columns, type fonts and sizes, color or black and white, bi-fold or tri-fold, number of pages—all of these decisions are based on the message you are trying to present. To determine the answer to these questions you need to do some preliminary design and research.

For example, imagine that you're responsible for creating publications for Uncle Freddy's Franks-N-Fun—a fun place to take the kids. The menus for such an establishment should use colorful images and a large, fun typeface. The menu might have balloon and clown clip-art and be a nonstandard size, possibly shaped like an elephant.

Uncle Freddy's Franks-N-Fun might be a mini-circus for the patrons, but I'm sure the stockholders are interested only in making money. You would probably use charts, graphs, and columns of numbers rather than clowns and balloons in the financial report at the end of the year. You would also use a font that is easy to read and inspires confidence. And this report would probably be printed in a standard size.

Whatever type of document you wish to create, QuarkXPress can help you assemble it.

Installing QuarkXPress

Insert the first QuarkXPress disk into your floppy drive and find the QuarkXPress Installer program. Its icon will look like the one shown in Figure 1.1.

The Installer will inform you if there are any other programs running. If there are, just click on the OK button, quit all other programs, and try again.

Figure 1.1. The QuarkXPress Installer program icon.

If no other programs are running when you launch the Installer program you will be presented with a dialog box. If at this point you decide you don't want to install QuarkXPress, you can bail out by clicking on the Quit button. Clicking on the OK button will continue with the installation process.

The first decision that you must make is where you want to install the program. If you already have created a folder in which the program and all of its companion files may reside, you can use the dialog box shown in Figure 1.2 to navigate to that folder, then press the Install button.

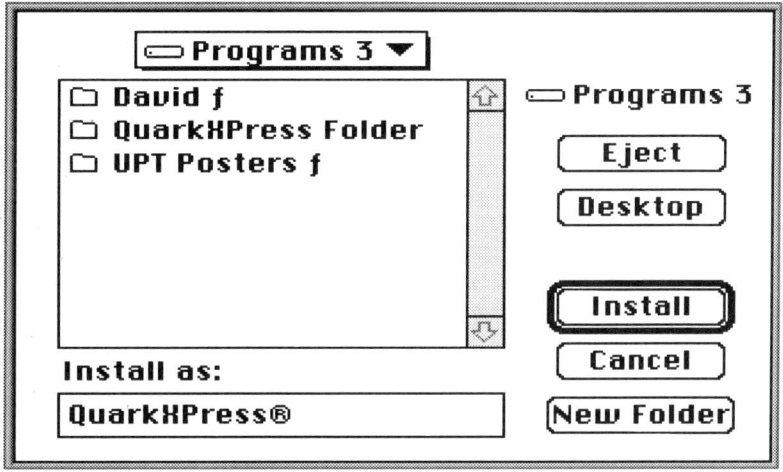

Figure 1.2. Click on the Install button to place QuarkXPress in an existing folder.

If you need to create a folder for QuarkXPress and its companion files, click on the New Folder button, which will bring up the dialog box shown in Figure 1.3.

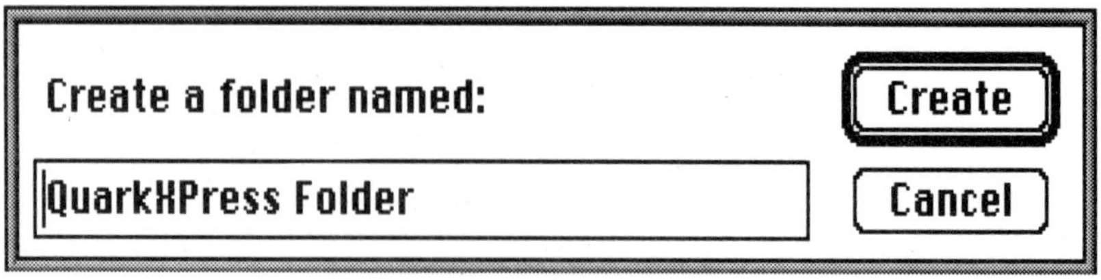

```
Create a folder named:          [ Create ]
[QuarkXPress Folder        ]    [ Cancel ]
```

Figure 1.3. The Create a Folder dialog box.

A name for the new folder may be entered into the field in this dialog box; clicking on the Create button will create the folder. Clicking on the Cancel button will take you back to the previous dialog box. The Cancel button on that dialog box allows you to abort the installation process.

Once you have indicated where you want the program installed, you will be asked what files and XTensions you want installed with the program. The options will be listed in a dialog box like the one shown in Figure 1.4, with the XTensions on the left and files along the right.

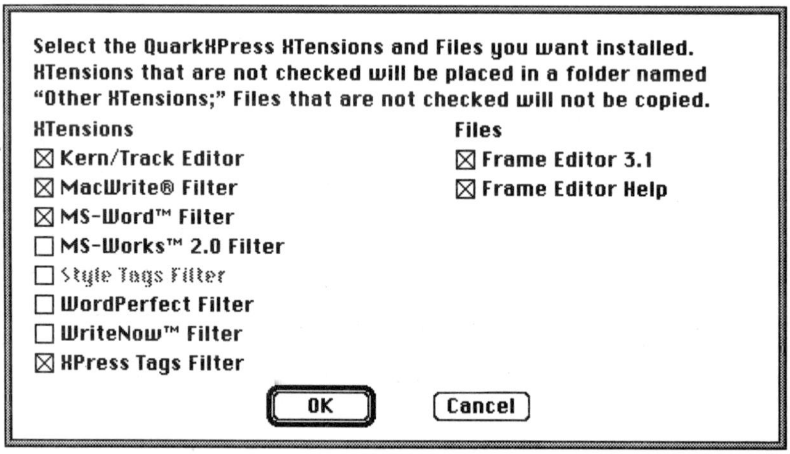

```
Select the QuarkXPress XTensions and Files you want installed.
XTensions that are not checked will be placed in a folder named
"Other XTensions;" Files that are not checked will not be copied.
XTensions                        Files
☒ Kern/Track Editor              ☒ Frame Editor 3.1
☒ MacWrite® Filter               ☒ Frame Editor Help
☒ MS-Word™ Filter
☐ MS-Works™ 2.0 Filter
☐ Style Tags Filter
☐ WordPerfect Filter
☐ WriteNow™ Filter
☒ XPress Tags Filter
                    [  OK  ]   [ Cancel ]
```

Figure 1.4. Files and XTensions must be placed in the folder that holds the QuarkXPress program.

Use the check boxes to indicate your choices. Since these files are all relatively small, it's not a bad idea to install them. It's usually better to have them and not need them than to need them and not have them.

Clicking on the OK button in this dialog box will actually start the installation procedure. You will be informed about the progress with the Copying File dialog boxes like the one shown in Figure 1.5.

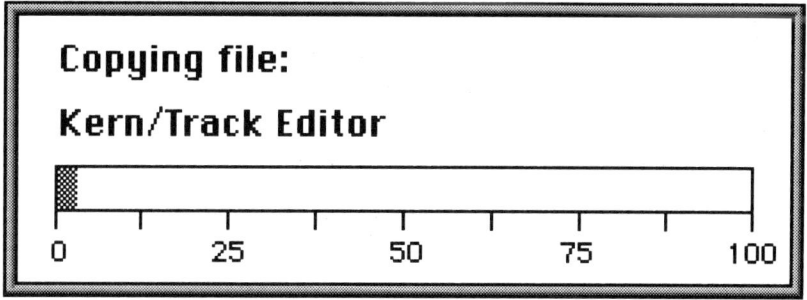

Figure 1.5. A Copying File dialog box.

When the Install program requires additional floppy disks to read files from, it will spit out the current disk and ask for another.

When you have been prompted for all the necessary disks, you will be informed whether or not the program has been installed successfully. If it has, you are ready to begin.

Starting QuarkXPress

When the installation process is complete, you can launch QuarkXPress either by double-clicking on its icon or by clicking once on the icon and choosing Open from the File menu. The Title screen will appear, as shown in Figure 1.6. If you have any XTensions in the folder with the QuarkXPress program, their icons will scroll past in the bottom-left corner of the Startup screen. Don't worry about XTensions for the moment; they will be discussed in Chapter 2. Once the program is loaded, it waits for you to make a choice: you can open an existing document, or start a new one.

8 ▼ *Teach Yourself QuarkXPress 3.1*

Figure 1.6. The Title screen.

Opening an Existing File

There are two types of files you can open in QuarkXPress: templates and documents. *Templates* are used to hold layouts for future use; *documents* are individual projects.

To open an existing file, select Open from the File menu. This brings up the dialog box shown in Figure 1.7.

Along the bottom of the dialog box are three check boxes labeled All Types, Documents, and Templates. The box that is checked will determine what type of files will appear in the Document field. The first check box is really misnamed; if this box is checked you will not, in fact, see all types of files. You will see only the files that can be opened in QuarkXPress. When Documents is checked you will only see QuarkXPress documents; templates will not be shown. When Templates is checked you will see only QuarkXPress templates; documents will be hidden. A file is defined as a document or a template when it is saved. As with all Macintosh dialog boxes, you can double-click on folders to open them and see if there are any available documents or templates inside, and you can click and hold on the shadowed box above the Document field to exit folders.

Chapter One ▼ 9

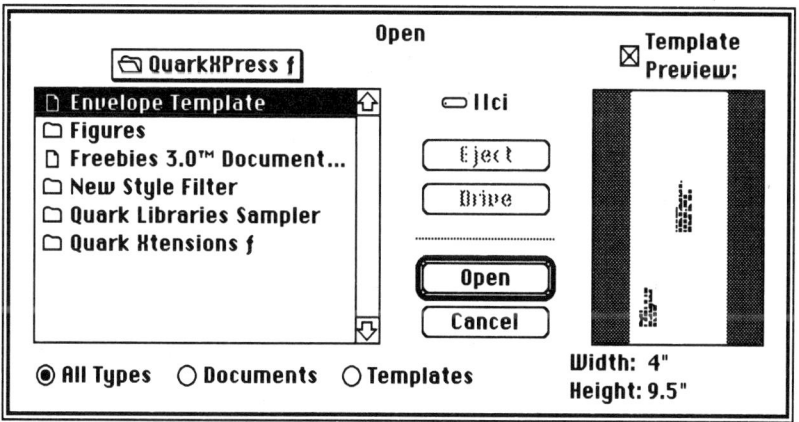

Figure 1.7. The Open dialog box.

In Figure 1.7, the Template Preview check box has been selected. It shows a preview of the selected template, in this case an envelope template. If you click this check box off, the preview will not be shown. The Template Preview setting you choose will be remembered for future sessions.

You can click on the Open button to open the highlighted file, or you can double-click on any other file name to open that file.

Creating a New File

If you wish to open a new document, select the New command from the File menu. This will bring up the New dialog box, as shown in Figure 1.8.

There are several choices you must make in the New dialog box that will control the size of the page, its margins, and how columns will be handled.

The top-left portion of the New dialog box contains the Page Size controls. There are five options that pre-set the size of the page to a standard size.

- US Letter creates a page that is 8.5" wide by 11" tall.
- US Legal creates a page that is 8.5" wide by 14" tall.
- A4 Letter creates a page that is 210mm wide by 297mm tall.

- B5 Letter creates a page that is 182mm wide by 257mm tall.
- Tabloid creates a page that is 11" wide by 17" tall.

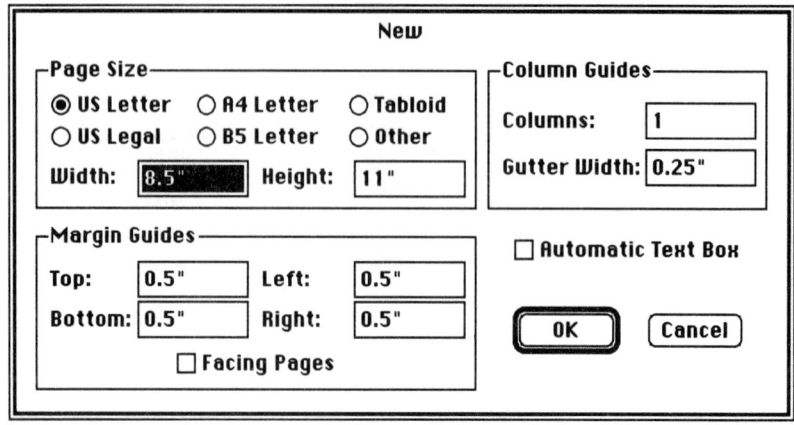

Figure 1.8. The New document dialog box.

If you check the Other option, you can enter the desired measurements into the Width and Height fields to specify a page size. The minimum page size is 1" x 1", and the maximum page size is 48" x 48".

Next to the Page Size options are two fields into which you enter the desired number of columns (up to thirty) and the desired gutter width. The *gutter* is the space between columns, and can range from 3 points (0.042") to 288 points (4").

▼ **NOTE** ▲ There are several types of measurements used in desktop publishing in addition to the common inch. One of the most often used alternatives is points. There are seventy-two points to an inch. Measurements will be discussed in greater detail in Chapter 2.

The bottom-left corner of the New dialog box contains the Margin Guides field, into which you enter the margin width. Next to this field is the Automatic Text box. If the Automatic Text box is checked, a text box will be placed on every newly created page conforming to the page size minus the margin guides. For example, if you choose US Letter (8.5" x 11") with 0.5" margins all around, then an Automatic Text box will be created that is 7.5" x 10".

Clicking on the OK button creates a new document with the parameters you've chosen. Clicking on the Cancel button closes the New dialog box without creating a document.

If you change any of the pre-set options in the New dialog box, those changes will be retained and will appear the next time you select New from the File menu. For example, if you enter "2" for the number of columns and create a new document, the next time you select New from the File menu, "2" will be in the Column Number field.

Program Attributes

The following sections describe some basic elements that make up the QuarkXPress interface. If you are not familiar with the Macintosh Operating System and the Macintosh interface, refer to the manuals that came with your Macintosh. QuarkXPress conforms to Apple's recommended interface standards.

The QuarkXPress screen has three major elements: menus, windows, and palettes.

The Menus

The Menu bar titles remain the same regardless of the task you are performing in QuarkXPress, but the contents of some of these menus change depending on your current activity. For example, Figure 1.9 shows the way the Style menu appears when a picture box has been selected, and the completely different set of options it contains when a text box is selected.

When there is no image, or the image is uneditable, the Style menu bar will appear in grey letters rather than the usual black. When the menu is greyed you cannot access its options. Menus may be greyed for different reasons. When a picture box is selected, the Style menu holds options for manipulating how that picture will print. If the image in the picture box is in a format that QuarkXPress can't manipulate, the Style menu will be greyed. You may also find that while a certain menu is accessible, individual commands under that menu are greyed. This indicates that a particular option is not currently available. For example, if only one object is selected, the Group command will be greyed, since you can't group one object.

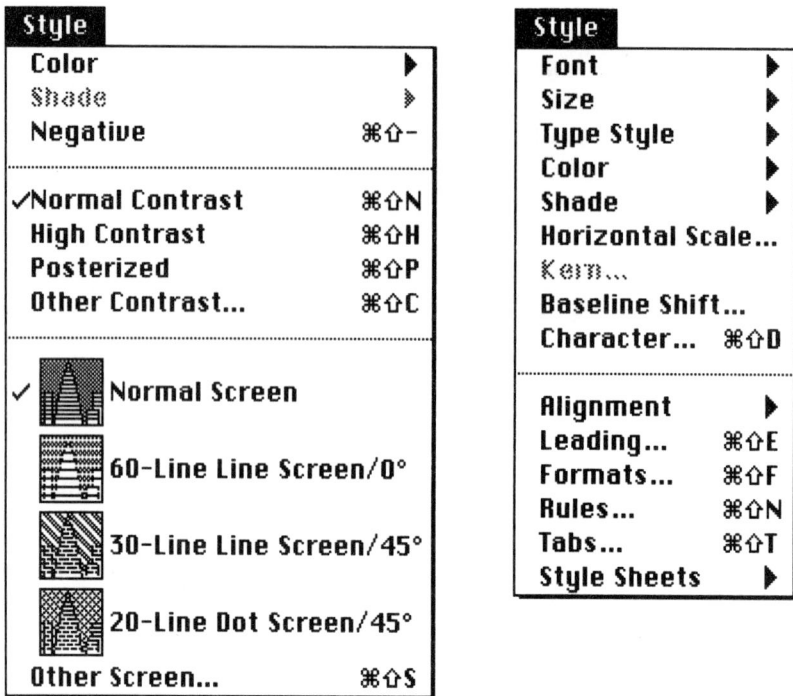

Figure 1.9. On the left is the Style menu when a picture box is selected. On the right is the Style menu when a text box is selected.

Keyboard Equivalents

To the right of many menu commands you will find symbols that represent *command-key equivalents,* which allow you to access menu commands using the keyboard rather than the mouse. For example, in Figure 1.10, next to the Copy command is a symbol that looks like a cloverleaf followed by the letter "C." The cloverleaf represents the Command key; therefore, this indicates that holding down the

Command key and pressing "C" has the same effect as selecting Copy from the Edit menu.

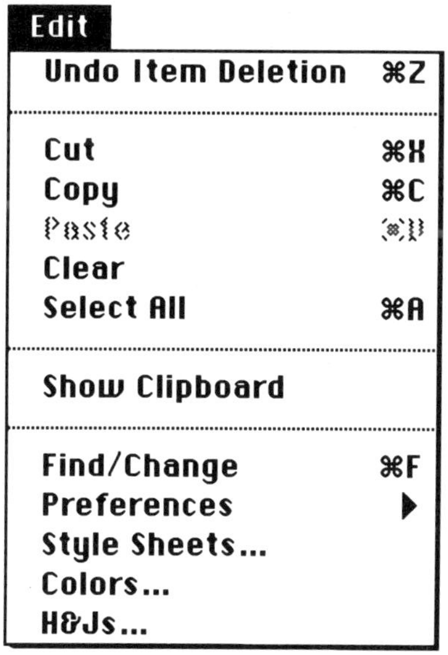

```
Edit
Undo Item Deletion    ⌘Z

Cut                   ⌘X
Copy                  ⌘C
Paste                 ⌘V
Clear
Select All            ⌘A

Show Clipboard

Find/Change           ⌘F
Preferences           ▶
Style Sheets...
Colors...
H&Js...
```

Figure 1.10. The Edit menu options showing the command-key equivalents.

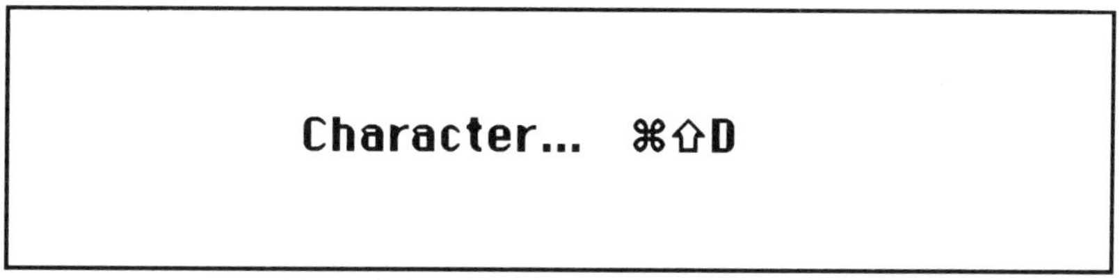

```
Character...    ⌘⇧D
```

Figure 1.11. Command-Shift symbols.

    Figure 1.11 shows a variation on the command-key equivalent. This is the Character command from the Style menu when a text box is selected (you can see this in the Style menu on the right in Figure 1.9). The Character command is followed by the cloverleaf symbol, an arrow pointing up, and the letter "D." The arrow represents the Shift key. Thus, the command-key equivalent in this example indicates that holding down the Command key and the Shift key while pressing "D" is the same as selecting Character from the Style menu.

14 ▼ *Teach Yourself QuarkXPress 3.1*

The Command, Shift, and Option keys are used for many key combinations. Figure 1.12 shows these three key symbols.

⌘ Command Key
⇧ Shift Key
⌥ Option Key

Figure 1.12. Key equivalence symbols.

Submenus

In Figure 1.9, to the right of many of the menu items are small black triangles pointing to the right. When you click and hold the mouse button on a menu item with this symbol next to it, a submenu will pop out listing the choices you can make. Figure 1.13 shows the Size options accessed by clicking and holding on the Size command under the Style menu.

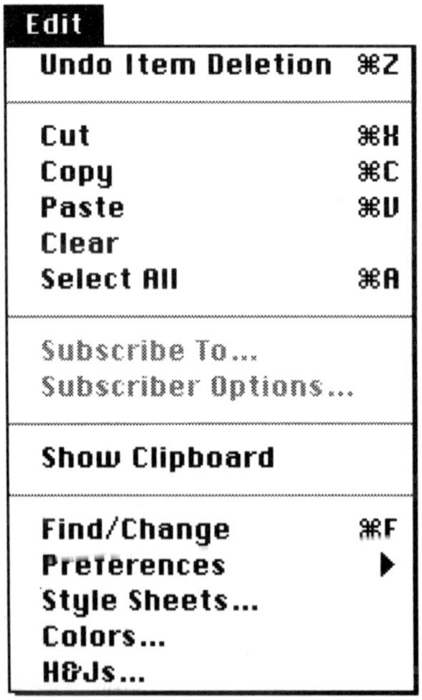

```
Edit
Undo Item Deletion    ⌘Z

Cut                   ⌘X
Copy                  ⌘C
Paste                 ⌘V
Clear
Select All            ⌘A

Subscribe To...
Subscriber Options...

Show Clipboard

Find/Change           ⌘F
Preferences           ▶
Style Sheets...
Colors...
H&Js...
```

Figure 1.13. The Style menu's Size submenu.

Dialog Boxes

An ellipsis (...) after a menu item indicates that when you select that item a dialog box will appear. A dialog box contains the options and commands relevant to that menu item. For example, when you start QuarkXPress you must select the New command from the File menu to create a new document. This command presents you with the New dialog box that lets you describe how you want the pages of the new document to look. Figure 1.8 shows what that dialog box looks like.

In a dialog box there are three basic ways to indicate the parameters to be chosen. There are *fields* into which you enter data, *check boxes* that you click on to select and unselect, and *buttons* that either open an additional dialog box or accept or cancel your choices. The New dialog box shown in Figure 1.8 has all three of these devices. You select the page size by clicking on one of the check boxes in the Page Size area. If you select Other you must then enter the desired dimensions into the Width and Height fields. When you have made all of your selections you use the OK button to accept them or the Cancel button to forget them.

Working with a Document

Windows

Create a new document using the New command from the File menu, and enter the following options in the New dialog box: U.S. Letter, one column, 0.25" gutter, 0.5" margins all around, and an Automatic Text box. The screen will appear as shown in Figure 1.14.

On this screen you can see the Menu bar along the top, the Main window containing the document and the arrow cursor, the Tools palette on the far left, and the Measurement palette along the bottom.

16 ▼ *Teach Yourself QuarkXPress 3.1*

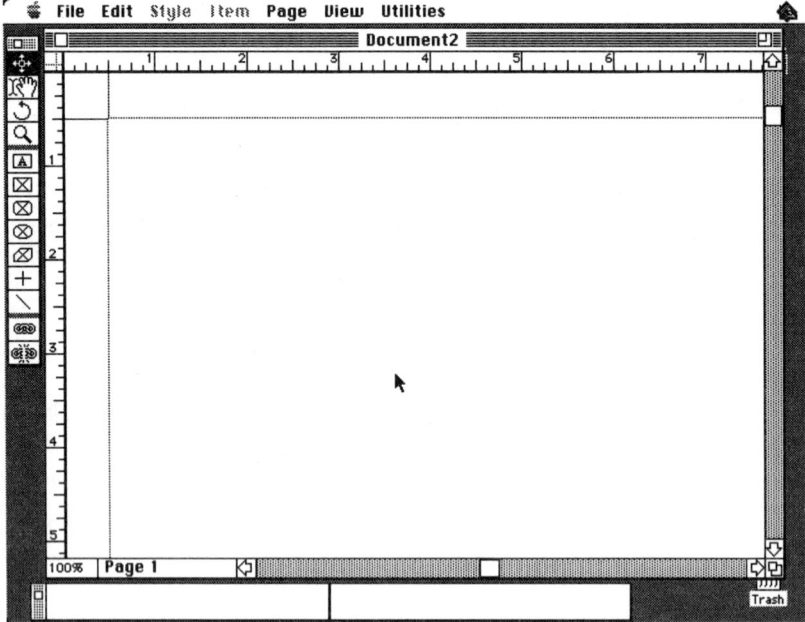

Figure 1.14. The first look at a new document.

Viewing the Document at Different Magnifications

The Main window contains the document you just created. Since it is being displayed at actual size, you can see only the top-left corner on a standard monitor. You can view the document in the Main window at several different magnifications. The normal view is Actual Size. If you were to select Fit in Window from the View menu, the document page would shrink to a size that would fit in the current Main window. This is shown in Figure 1.15.

You can see that the ruler scales down to show the measurement with respect to the page.

Several viewing sizes are available through the View menu, including 50%, 75%, and 200%. There are other ways to set the viewing size also. In Figure 1.15, the box in the bottom-left corner of the Main window says "46.7%." This is the magnification, or *viewing percentage,* that was required to fit the document in the window. In Figure 1.14, this box says "100%." You can double-click on this box and type in any magnification between 10% and 400%. The window will change to show the entered viewing percentage when you press the Return key.

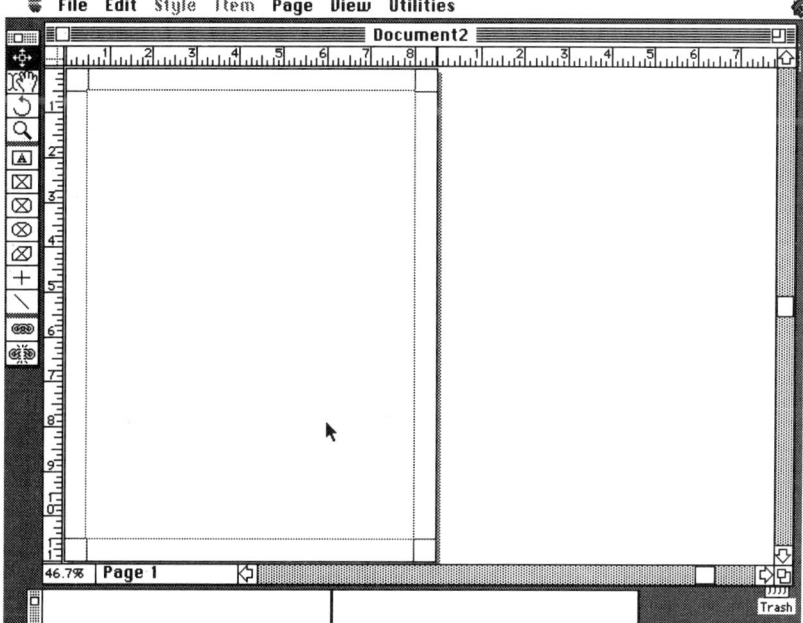

Figure 1.15. A standard U.S. Letter page with the Fit in Window view selected. Notice the viewing percentage in the bottom-left corner.

You will probably switch magnifications depending on the task you are performing. When you are placing items on the page you will probably want a magnification that shows you the whole page and how the elements relate to one another. When you are editing text or fine-tuning graphics, you may find it easier to work in actual size or larger.

The Tool Palette

Figure 1.16 shows the Tool palette, which is located along the left side of the Document window.

18 ▼ *Teach Yourself QuarkXPress 3.1*

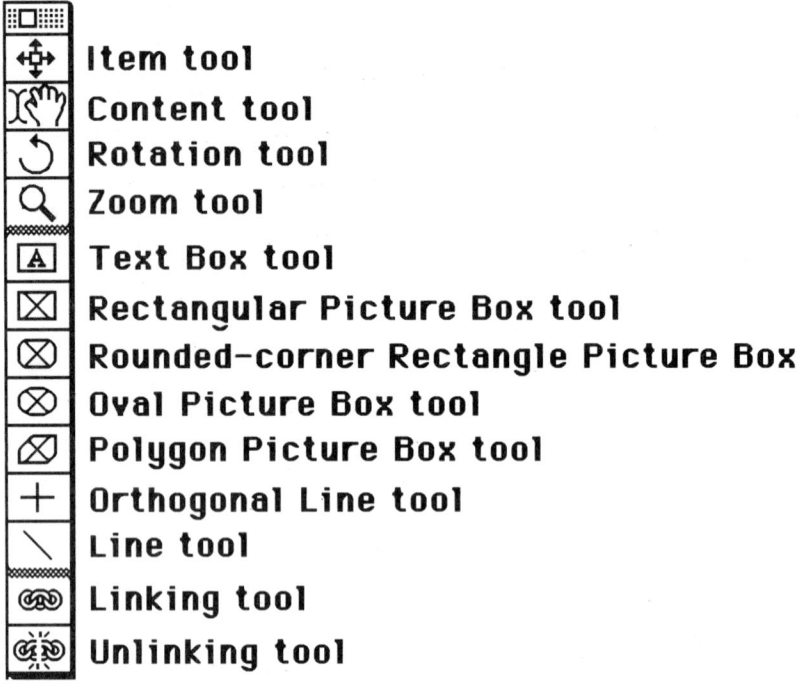

Figure 1.16. The Tool palette.

You can move the Tool palette, and any other palette or window, by clicking and dragging on its Title bar, which is the striped bar above it.

We're going to discuss these tools in a different order than they appear in the palette. You can refer to Figure 1.16 to see where each tool resides on the palette.

The Zoom Tool

The tool that is shaped like a magnifying glass is the Zoom tool, and it gives you another way to adjust the viewing size of your document. When you click on this tool to select it, the cursor changes to a magnifying glass with a plus sign in it. If you click on the Document window with this tool, the view will magnify by 25%. For example, if you are viewing your document at 100% (actual size), clicking with the Zoom tool will increase the view to 125%. This can be confirmed by looking at the number in the Viewing Percentage field shown in Figure 1.15. Clicking a second time would increase the magnification by another 25%, to 150%, and so on.

If you hold down the Option key while the Zoom tool is selected, the plus sign changes to a minus sign. Clicking with the Zoom tool while holding down the Option key causes the document magnification to reduce by 25%.

The Line Tools

So you have a page that's the right size, and you know how to change its scale. At this point you probably want to put something on your page. There are only three things you can put on a page: lines, text boxes, and picture boxes. Every letter of text must be inside a text box, and every image must be in a picture box. Even if you are going to use a simple line that was drawn in another program, you must have a picture box for it to be imported into. The only thing you can put on a page that doesn't have to be in some kind of box is a line drawn with one of the Line tools on the QuarkXPress Tool palette.

There are two Line tools: the Orthogonal Line tool and the Line tool. Don't let the term "Orthogonal" scare you—all it really means is that the line is straight, either vertically or horizontally. If you want to draw a line that runs exactly vertically or exactly horizontally, use the Orthogonal Line tool. If you want to draw a line that runs at any other angle, use the Line tool.

To draw a line with either Line tool, click on the desired tool in the Tool palette, and your cursor will change to a plus sign. The lines of the plus sign cross at the active point of the line cursor. Place the cursor on the Document window where you wish to start the line, and click and hold the mouse button. While holding the mouse button down, move the mouse to drag the cursor in the direction you wish the line to be drawn. Remember that if you have selected the Orthogonal Line tool, the cursor won't move in any direction but straight up, straight down, directly to the left, or directly to the right. If you selected the Line tool you can drag the mouse in any direction and a line will be drawn in that direction. Releasing the mouse button places the endpoint of the line at the current location of the cursor.

Don't be concerned if you don't place the starting point or endpoint of a line in exactly the right position in your document. A line's length, location, and angle can be changed at any time using the Item tool.

Moving and Manipulating Items

The first two tools in the Tool palette are used to move and manipulate items. The type of item and what you wish to do with it determine whether you use the Item tool or the Content tool.

The Item Tool

The first tool on the Tool palette is the Item tool. The Item tool is for items other than text, and has two main uses: moving items around the page, and resizing items.

To get a feel for how this tool works we need an item to play with. In the document you've created, use the Line tool to draw a line a few inches long, as shown in Figure 1.17.

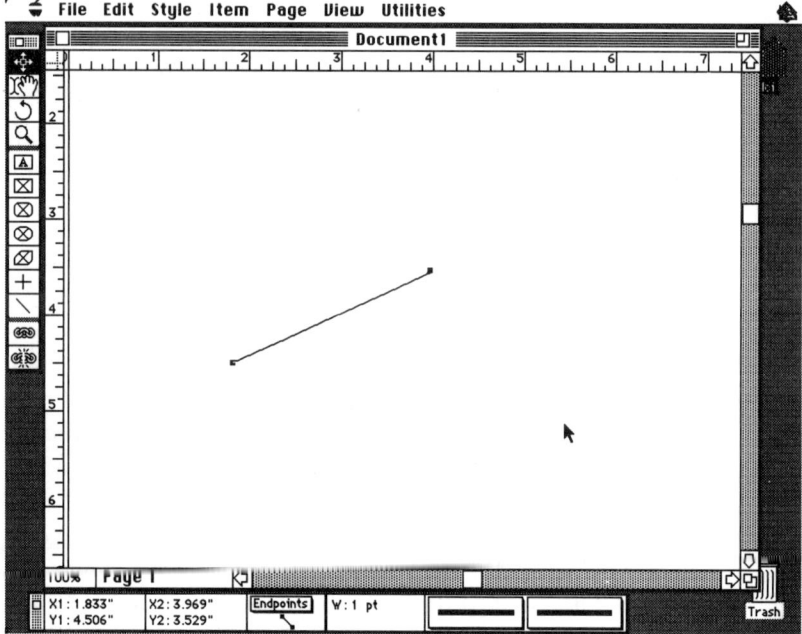

Figure 1.17. A line created with the Line tool. Notice the Measurement palette located below the Document window.

Notice that at both ends of your line are small, black squares. These are called *control handles*, and will be visible only when the line is selected. When you draw an item it remains selected until you select something else. To select an item, click on the Item tool to activate it, then click on the item you wish to select. As long as the cursor is away from your selected line it will look like the standard arrow cursor. When you move the cursor over the selected line it will change to the shape of the Item tool.

Move the cursor away from your line and click the mouse button. The line will be deselected and will lose its control handles. Now when you move the cursor over the line, the cursor doesn't change to look like the Item tool. You can tell that the Item tool is still selected because it is still highlighted in the Tool palette.

To select the line, place the tip of the pointer cursor over the line and click once. The control handles reappear, and if you leave the cursor over the now-selected line, it will change to the Item tool icon. While the cursor is over the selected item, you can click and drag with the mouse to move that item.

With the line selected, move the cursor over one of the control handles and you will notice that the cursor changes to a hand with a pointing finger. When the cursor is shaped like a hand, use the tip of the pointing finger to click and drag on the control handle to resize the line and/or change its angle. Dragging along the length of the line resizes the line. Dragging on an arc changes the angle of a line drawn with the Line tool. The angle of a line drawn with the Orthogonal Line tool can be changed only in 90° increments.

You've seen how you can use the Item tool to move and resize a line. The Item tool can also be used to move and resize text boxes and picture boxes, as you will see later.

The Measurement Palette

Figure 1.17 shows a document with a line drawn on it. Below the Document window is the Measurement palette, shown in detail in Figure 1.18. To make the Measurement palette appear and disappear, you use the Hide Measurements/Show Measurements command from the View menu.

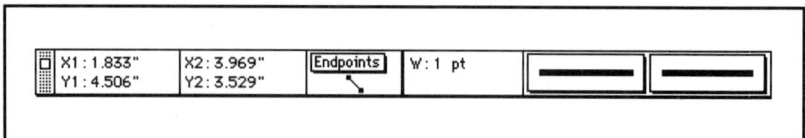

Figure 1.18. The Measurement palette for the line shown in Figure 1.17.

The Measurement palette gives information about the currently selected item. The type of information shown in the Measurement palette depends in part on what type of item is selected. If an object other than a line were selected, the Measurement palette would display different information. As we discuss other items we will look at the types of information the Measurement palette displays about them.

Location, Angle, and Length

The first two fields in the Measurement palette when a line is selected indicate the endpoints of that line in relation to the ruler. The X1 measurement tells you how far the left endpoint of the line appears from the left edge of your page. In this case, it is at 1.833" along the horizontal ruler. The Y1 measurement tells you the left endpoint's location on the vertical ruler. The X2 and Y2 measurements indicate the location of the right endpoint.

The third field in the Measurement palette allows you to choose the reference point(s) along the line for these measurements. As with other shadowed boxes in QuarkXPress, if you click and hold on the shadowed box that says Endpoints, a pop-up menu appears, as shown in Figure 1.19. This pop-up menu gives the possible reference-point positions; the current reference point is indicated by a check-mark.

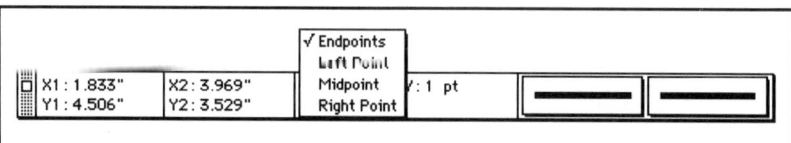

Figure 1.19. The Measurement palette's endpoint marker options.

Figure 1.20 shows how the displayed measurements for the line in Figure 1.17 differ depending on which reference point is chosen.

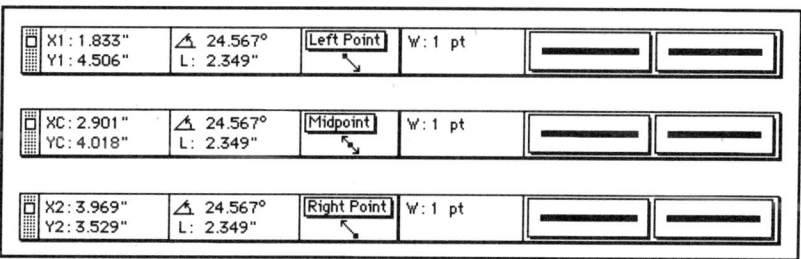

Figure 1.20. The Left Point, Midpoint, and Right Point reference measurements.

- When Left Point is chosen, the first field shows the line's left point (X1 and Y1) location. The second field shows the line's angle and total length.
- When Midpoint is chosen, the first field indicates the location of the center of the line (XC and YC). The second field shows the angle and length.
- When Right Point is chosen, the first field shows the location of the right end of the line. The second field again shows the angle and length.

Width

The fourth field in the Measurement palette, when a line is chosen, displays the width of the line in points. The line in Figure 1.17 is one point thick. You can double-click on this number and enter a new width in points. Press the Return key to change the line to the newly entered width.

Line Style and Endcaps

When a line is selected, the last two fields in the Measurement palette are the Line Style and Endcaps fields. When you click and hold on the Line Style field you are presented with a number of different types of lines that can be applied to the currently selected line. Figure 1.21 shows the options available. To apply a style to the currently selected line, hold down the mouse button and place the cursor over the desired line style, then release the mouse button.

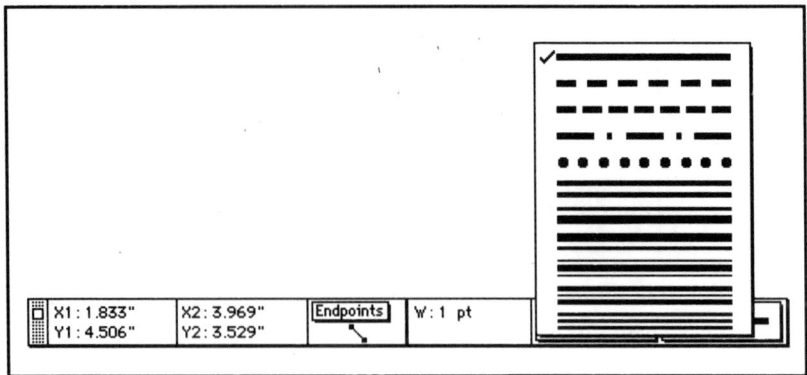

Figure 1.21. Available line styles.

Clicking and holding on the Endcaps field presents a list of arrow options that can be placed at the end of the currently selected line. Figure 1.22 shows the available options. Placing the cursor over the desired endcap and releasing the mouse button causes that endcap to be applied to the currently selected line.

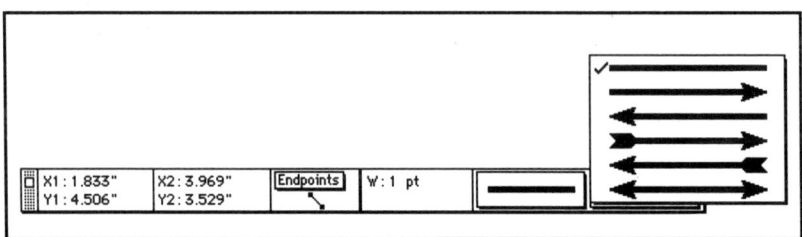

Figure 1.22. Endpoint marker styles.

As we discuss other types of items we will look at the information the Measurement palette gives us about those items.

Summary

▼ QuarkXPress allows you to put text and images together into documents with the standard sizes US Letter, US Legal, A4 Letter, B5 Letter, and Tabloid, or any size dictated by the user.

▼ Existing files can be opened for modification and new documents can be created.

▼ Menu commands along the top of the screen can be accessed by clicking on them with your mouse. Most can also be accessed using keyboard equivalents.

▼ When you click and hold on a menu item, its options are presented in a drop-down list. Some items in these drop-down lists present further options in a pop-out list. Other menu items present dialog boxes from which options can be chosen.

▼ A QuarkXPress document can be viewed at any magnification between 10% and 400%.

▼ The Tool palette contains the tools used to move and manipulate items, create text and picture boxes, draw lines, link and unlink text boxes, and change the magnification of the document.

▼ The selected item's location, dimensions, and some attributes can be viewed and changed in the Measurement palette.

CHAPTER 2

In This Chapter

- ▼ **Entering and Importing Text**
  - The Text Tool and the Content Tool
  - The I-Beam Cursor and Highlighting Text
  - Importing Text
- ▼ **Text Attributes**
  - Type Fonts and Styles
  - Type Width and Spacing
- ▼ **The Measurement Palette of a Text Box**
  - Controlling Text Using the Measurement Palette
- ▼ **Style Sheets**
  - The Style Sheets Dialog Box
  - Creating a New Style Without Existing Text
  - Importing Style Sheets
  - Editing a Style Sheet
  - Saving a New or Edited Style Sheet
  - Appending Style Sheets
  - Deleting a Style
- ▼ **Formatting Paragraphs**
  - The Formats Command
  - Control Characters (Invisibles)
  - Line Indents
  - Line Spacing
  - Paragraphs and Pagination
  - Drop Caps
  - Alignment
- ▼ **Tabs**
  - Setting Tabs
  - Moving and Removing Existing Tabs
- ▼ **Summary**

You Will Learn

- ▼ How to use one tool to control text boxes and another to control the contents of the boxes.
- ▼ How to select text for manipulation.
- ▼ How to import text.
- ▼ How to control text attributes such as font, style, leading, alignment, kerning, and tracking.
- ▼ How to use the Measurement palette to control text attributes.
- ▼ How to create and use style sheets.
- ▼ How to use the Formats command to control margins and tabs.
- ▼ How to set tabs and manipulate existing tabs.

Entering and Importing Text

The Text Tool and the Content Tool

Let's move up the Tool palette to a tool you will probably use a lot more often than either of the Line tools: the Text tool. The Text tool is the fifth one down in your tool box; its icon is a square containing a capital "A." You use the Text tool for one thing only: creating text boxes. Once you have made a text box, you use another tool to enter and edit the text. But let's not get ahead of ourselves.

Click on the Text tool to select it and the cursor will become a plus sign, just as it did for the Line tools. This time, though, when you click and drag on the Document window, a box will be created instead of just a line. When selected, a text box has eight control handles instead of just two. Figure 2.1 shows a screen with a text box and the Measurement palette for that text box. Let's talk about the text box first, then we'll see what the Measurement palette does.

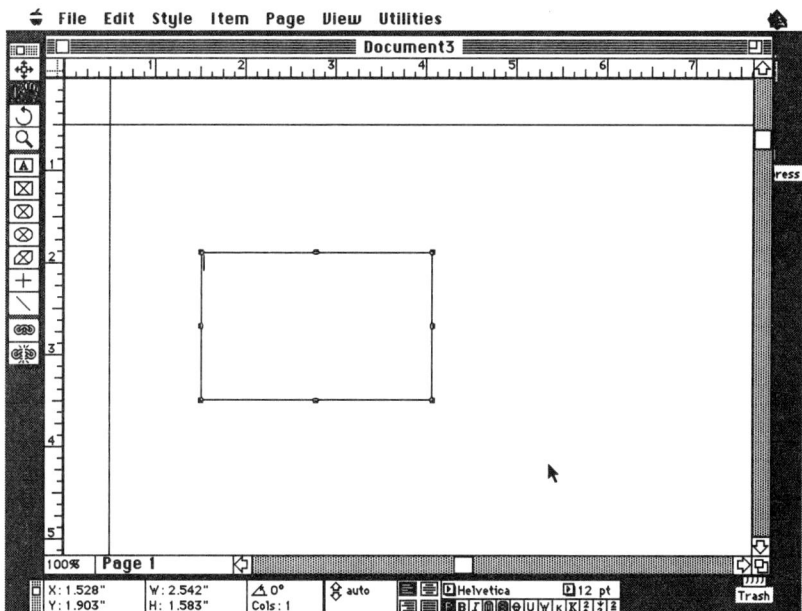

Figure 2.1. A text box.

The first thing to note is that after you release the mouse button, the Text tool is no longer selected. The Content tool—whose icon depicts a hand next to an I-beam cursor—is now highlighted, indicating that it is the active tool.

When you release the mouse button after creating a text box, the cursor changes to look like a hand with a pointing finger. This is because the cursor is over one of the control handles. The pointing hand means the same thing for a text box that it did for a line; if you click and drag the mouse while the hand is pointing to one of the control handles on your text box, the text box will be resized.

When you move the cursor off the control handle and away from the text box, it changes to the standard pointer icon.

The I-Beam Cursor and Highlighting Text

When you create a text box, the text insertion point always appears in its upper-left corner until text is created or imported. When there is text in the text box, the insertion point can be moved around it with the arrow keys. The forward and reverse arrow keys move the insertion point within a line; the up and down arrow keys move the cursor from line to line. To highlight text, use the arrow keys while holding down the Shift key.

If you press any key when text is highlighted, the highlighted text will be replaced with the characters typed. This includes the Spacebar, the Return key, the Backspace key, and the Tab key. If you wish to deselect a section of highlighted text, place the I-beam cursor anywhere in the text box and click the mouse button once.

> ▼ **NOTE** ▲ Don't leave text highlighted unless you are in the process of manipulating it. One accidental keystroke could cause you to lose the selected text. You can usually recover lost text, but why take the chance? If you accidentally lose text, immediately hold down the Command key and press "Z." This activates the Undo command.

For ease of textual manipulation, you can also move the mouse cursor into the text box. When you do this, the mouse cursor changes to an I-beam cursor, which works much the same as the text cursor would in any word processing program. You use this cursor to place the text insertion point, or to select existing text by dragging the I-beam over it:

- Clicking once places the text insertion point at that location.
- Double-clicking on a word highlights that word.
- Triple-clicking highlights an entire line of text.
- Clicking and dragging over text highlights that text.

If the clipboard contains text, you can use the Paste command from the Edit menu to replace highlighted text with the text in the clipboard.

Importing Text

You can enter text into a text box simply by typing, or you can import text from other programs.

To import text, make sure your cursor is in a text box, then select the Get Text command from the File menu. This opens a standard Open dialog box, whose File field will contain the names of all of the files you can import into QuarkXPress from the current drive or folder.

QuarkXPress can import ASCII text files as well as fully formatted files from many word processors. The formatting of these files is translated by either a filter or a Quark XTension.

Filters are utilities that Quark provides with the main program, and to function they must be in the same folder as the QuarkXPress program. When you select Get Text from the File menu, the Get Text dialog box will display files that are saved in the format of the available filters. For example, if the Microsoft Word filter is in the proper folder, you will see the names of all files that have been saved as Microsoft Word files in the Get Text dialog box. When you open one of those files, its text will be placed in the selected text box and will include all formatting that was applied in Microsoft Word when it was saved.

In the dialog box shown in Figure 2.2, the highlighted file is a text file saved in Microsoft Word. Since I have the Microsoft Word filter in the same folder as my QuarkXPress program, I can import this file.

32 ▼ *Teach Yourself QuarkXPress 3.1*

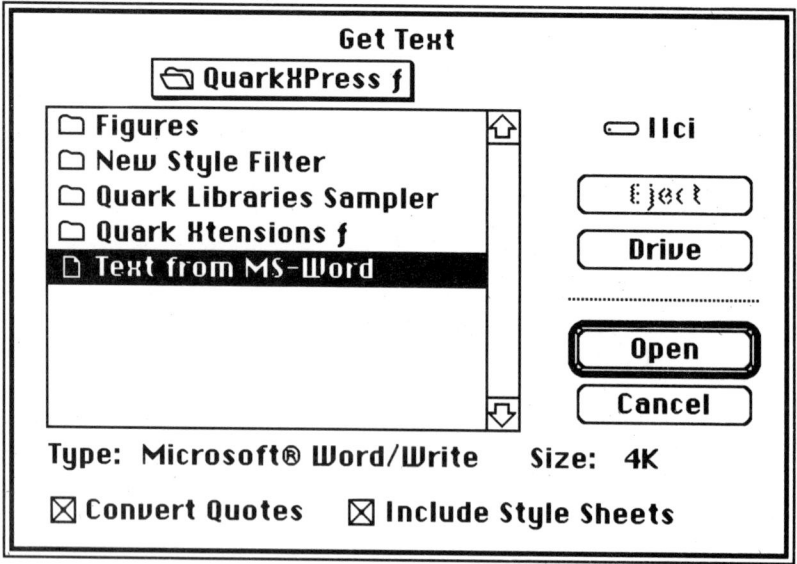

Figure 2.2. The Get Text dialog box.

Quark XTensions are software modules that add features to QuarkXPress; they are written by many companies and do many things, but the ones we are concerned with now are those that are included in the Quark program and act as filters. Many XTensions have been written that allow you to import text created in programs that run in other operating systems, such as MS-DOS. For example, there is an XTension that allows you to import files that were created in WordPerfect on an IBM compatible computer. These files would not show up in the Get Text dialog box because XTensions don't work like filters. Each has its own function, and they are accessed through the Utilities menu; for example, if you place the Kern/Track Editor XTension in the QuarkXPress folder when loading the program, the Tracking Edit and Kerning Table Edit commands are available in the Utilities menu.

Convert Quotes

At the bottom of the Get Text dialog box (Figure 2.2) are check boxes for Convert Quotes and Include Style Sheets.

Two types of quotation marks may be used: regular and typesetter's quotes. Figure 2.3 shows the difference between these.

> "Non-typesetter's Quotes"
> "Typesetter's Quotes"
> 'Internal Quotes'

Figure 2.3. Regular and typesetter's quotes.

Notice that in the regular quotes, the beginning and ending quotation marks are the same—straight up and down. The apostrophe is also straight. Regular quotes are usually used to designate feet (') and inches ("). In the typesetter's quotes, beginning double and single quotation marks are different from end marks, making them less ambiguous. Similarly, the typesetter's apostrophe is curved.

If you check Convert Quotes in the Get Text dialog box, typesetter's marks will automatically appear in place of any regular quotation marks or apostrophes.

Include Style Sheets

The second check box in the Get Text dialog box is the Include Style Sheets option. When this box is checked and you import a file saved in a format for which you have a filter, the styles defined in the word processor will be added to the Style Sheet list at the bottom of the Style menu. Style sheets will be discussed in greater detail later in this chapter.

When the Include Style Sheets option is not checked, the imported file retains the formatting if the proper filter is present. The styles will not be available for you to apply to other text.

Text Attributes

Text comes in all types, styles, sizes, spacings, and colors. QuarkXPress gives you control over every imaginable variation of these—but before you can control them you have to know what they are.

Type Fonts and Styles

Figure 2.4 shows several different kinds of typefaces, called fonts.

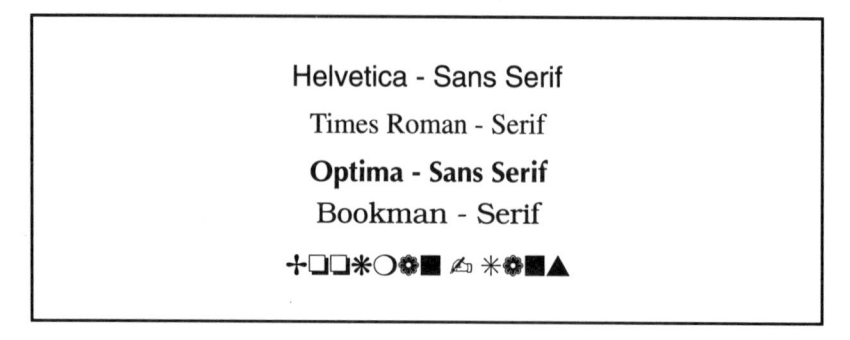

```
              Helvetica - Sans Serif
              Times Roman - Serif
              Optima - Sans Serif
              Bookman - Serif
              ✣▫▫✳○✿■ ✎ ✳✿■▲
```

Figure 2.4. Several different fonts.

    The first four fonts contain letters and numbers, and are alphanumeric fonts; the last contains pictures, and is called a *dingbat,* or symbol, font.

    Letter fonts are generally broken down into two families: *serif* and *sans serif.* A serif font has small extensions on the ends of the lines that make up letters. Serifs are pointed out in Figure 2.5.

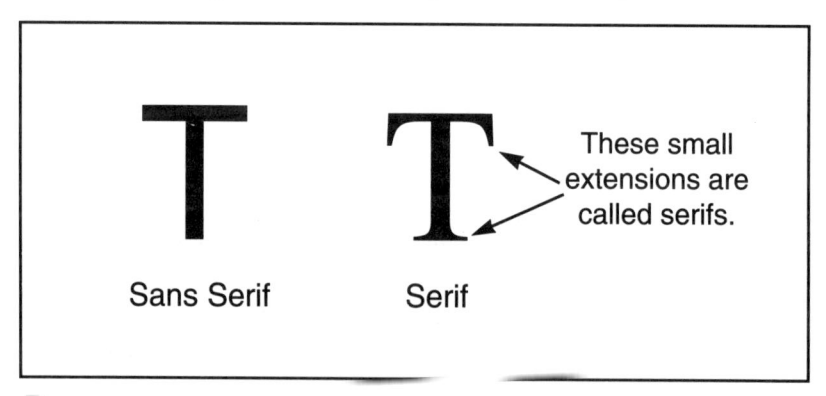

```
         T           T  ← These small
                        extensions are
                        called serifs.

       Sans Serif      Serif
```

Figure 2.5. Parts of a font.

    A sans serif font is one that doesn't have these extensions. As a general rule, sans serif fonts are used for titles, headings, and other elements in large type, while serif fonts are used for body text. The serifs make it easier to read the text as words and phrases rather than as individual letters.

The dictionary defines a *font* as a complete assortment of type in one size and style, but there is a bit of confusion in the computer world about how to use this word. To avoid confusion, when the term "font" is used in this book it refers to a typeface only, not its size. For instance, 12 point Times will be considered the same font as 14 point Times, even though they are different sizes.

Within a particular typeface you can have several different styles. These styles can be part of the font itself or can be added by QuarkXPress. That may sound a little confusing so let's look at it more closely.

The first thing we should establish is that we are talking about PostScript fonts being printed on a PostScript printer. PostScript is a *page description language* (PDL), which means that it "describes" the contents of a page (text and graphics) to the printer. If you aren't using a PostScript printer, this discussion won't apply.

▼ **NOTE** ▲ There are two font standards in effect for the Macintosh since the introduction of System 7. The new font standard is called TrueType, and will not be discussed in this book. All references to fonts, how they are used, how they are accessed, and how they print refer to Adobe Type 1 PostScript fonts.

On the Macintosh you need two sets of information for each font: one for the printer and one for your screen. The printer information is called the font outline, and is contained either in the printer itself or in a file in your System folder. The information for your screen is the screen font, or *bitmapped font,* which is a font made up of a series of dots. This bitmapped font must be installed in your system. When you access the Font submenu through QuarkXPress's Style menu, you are seeing the names of the bitmapped fonts that have been loaded into your system. Figure 2.6 shows what this submenu looks like with a typical selection of fonts.

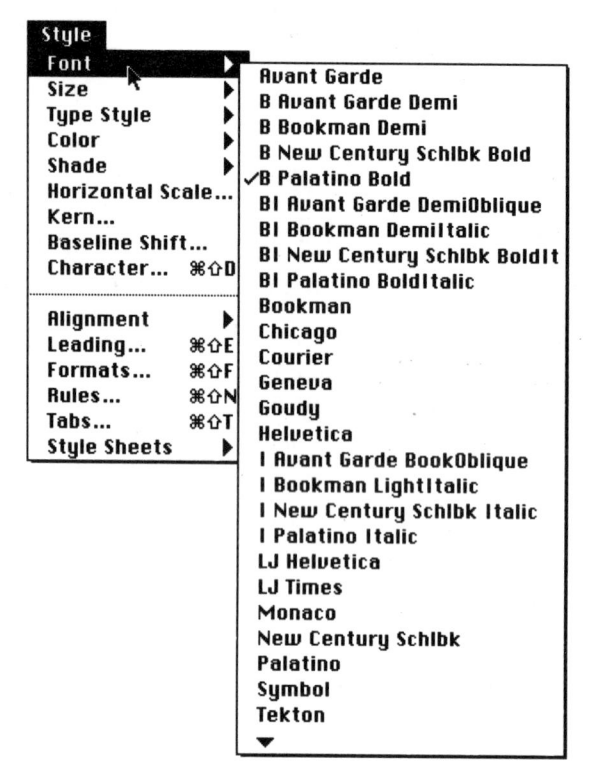

```
Style
Font          ▶   Avant Garde
Size          ▶   B Avant Garde Demi
Type Style    ▶   B Bookman Demi
Color         ▶   B New Century Schlbk Bold
Shade         ▶   ✓B Palatino Bold
Horizontal Scale...  BI Avant Garde DemiOblique
Kern...           BI Bookman DemiItalic
Baseline Shift... BI New Century Schlbk BoldIt
Character... ⌘⇧D  BI Palatino BoldItalic
                  Bookman
Alignment     ▶   Chicago
Leading...   ⌘⇧E  Courier
Formats...   ⌘⇧F  Geneva
Rules...     ⌘⇧N  Goudy
Tabs...      ⌘⇧T  Helvetica
Style Sheets  ▶   I Avant Garde BookOblique
                  I Bookman LightItalic
                  I New Century Schlbk Italic
                  I Palatino Italic
                  LJ Helvetica
                  LJ Times
                  Monaco
                  New Century Schlbk
                  Palatino
                  Symbol
                  Tekton
                  ▼
```

Figure 2.6. The Font submenu showing the bitmapped fonts installed in the system.

▼ **NOTE** ▲ If you are using a font management program such as Adobe's Type Reunion, your menu will look different. Refer to the manual that came with your font management program to see how it affects your font family listings.

Basic Type Styles

There are four basic *styles,* or variations on a typeface, although some fonts have more and some have fewer. They are plain, bold, italic, and bold italic. And, just to make things more confusing, each of these four styles has more than one name. For example, plain is also called roman or book, bold is also called demi, and italic is sometimes called oblique.

Consider Palatino, shown in Figure 2.7. The plain version is called simply "Palatino." The bold version is called "Palatino Bold"; the italic is "Palatino Italic," and the bold italic is "Palatino Bold Italic."

> This is Palatino Plain.
> **This is Palatino Bold.**
> *This is Palatino Italic.*
> ***This is Palatino Bold Italic.***

Figure 2.7. Some style options.

All text has both a font and a type style applied to it at all times. To put a sentence into Palatino Bold, you would drag the I-beam cursor over the desired text to select it, then either:

- Select Palatino from the Font submenu and Bold from the Type Style submenu, or
- Select B Palatino Bold from the Font submenu.

No matter which method you use, the printed results will look the same. One caution: if you apply the Bold command from the Type Style submenu to a bold typeface, you will get extra-bold. How this extra-bold will print varies widely, so if you really want a text that is very bold, it is recommended that you use a font that is designed to be extra-bold.

Italics work in the same manner. If you want italic text you can either select an italic typeface or apply the Italic command from the Type Style submenu to a normal font. If you apply the Italic command to an italic typeface you will get extra-italic, which is usually unreadable.

Other Styles

QuarkXPress offers many type styles in addition to bold and italic. When a text box is selected, these are accessed through the Style menu's Type Style submenu, shown in Figure 2.8. Not only can you apply any of these styles to any font, you can also apply several styles to the same section of text. For example, you could have bold text with Strike Thru, or text that is shadowed and superscripted.

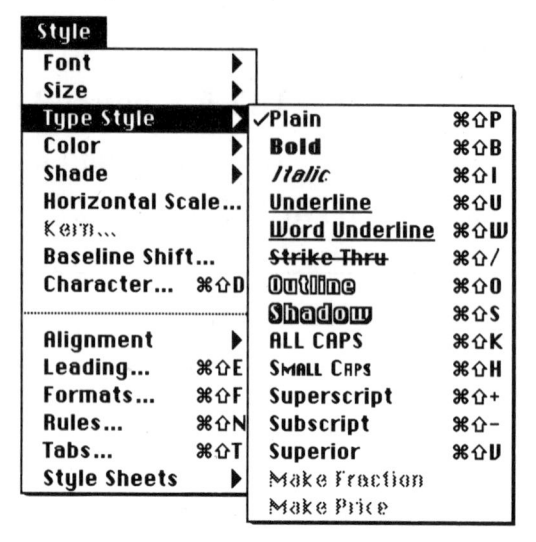

```
Style
Font              ▶
Size              ▶
Type Style        ▶  ✓Plain              ⌘⇧P
Color             ▶  Bold                ⌘⇧B
Shade             ▶  Italic              ⌘⇧I
Horizontal Scale...  Underline           ⌘⇧U
Kern...              Word Underline      ⌘⇧W
Baseline Shift...    Strike Thru         ⌘⇧/
Character... ⌘⇧D     Outline             ⌘⇧O
                     Shadow              ⌘⇧S
Alignment         ▶  ALL CAPS            ⌘⇧K
Leading...   ⌘⇧E     SMALL CAPS          ⌘⇧H
Formats...   ⌘⇧F     Superscript         ⌘⇧+
Rules...     ⌘⇧N     Subscript           ⌘⇧-
Tabs...      ⌘⇧T     Superior            ⌘⇧V
Style Sheets      ▶  Make Fraction
                     Make Price
```

Figure 2.8. The Type Style submenu.

- Plain removes all previously selected styles.
- **Bold** makes the strokes of the letters thicker.
- *Italic* places letters on a slight angle and softens the letters' curves.
- Underline places a continuous underline beneath the selected text.
- Word Underline places an underline under each word in the selected text.
- ~~Strike Thru~~ places a continuous line through the middle of the selected text.
- Outline places a line around the outline of each letter and changes the stroke of the letter to white. If you apply a color to the text (discussed in Chapter 5), the outline will change to that color and the centers of the letters will remain white.
- Shadow gives the selected text a "drop shadow," which makes the text look slightly three-dimensional.

- ALL CAPS places the selected text entirely in capital letters.
- SMALL CAPS changes the selected text to all caps and reduces the size of all but the first letter in each word. How much these letters are reduced is determined by the Typographic Preferences dialog box (discussed in Chapter 6).
- Superscript raises the baseline of the selected text. The amount of the baseline shift is determined in the Typographic Preferences dialog box, where you can also specify the letter size of the superscripted text.
- Subscript lowers the baseline of the selected text. Again, the amount of this shift is determined in the Typographic Preferences dialog box, where you can also specify the letter size of the subscripted text.
- Finally, the *Superior* option reduces the size of the selected text to that specified in the Typographical Preferences dialog box, and raises that text so that its top is aligned with the top of the capital letters in the surrounding text.

As you can see in Figure 2.8, there are some options at the bottom of the Type Style menu that haven't been discussed here. These and other type styles can be added as XTensions.

Alignment

Alignment refers to how the edges of a paragraph line up. There are four options described below and illustrated in Figure 2.9:

- Left aligned text lines up along the paragraph's left edge, leaving the text along the right edge *ragged,* which means that it stops at different lengths for each line.
- Right aligned text lines up along the paragraph's right edge, leaving the left edge ragged.
- In justified text, space and hyphens are automatically inserted where needed to make the text line up along both the right and left edges.
- When text is center aligned, each line in the paragraph is placed equidistant from the left and right edges of the page, causing both edges to appear ragged.

```
Once upon a time in a land far, far    Once upon a time in a land far,
away there lived a beautiful           far away there lived a beautiful
Princess in a large, ivy covered       Princess in a large, ivy covered
castle. Around that castle was a       castle. Around that castle was a
deep mote and the only way to get      deep mote and the only way to
into or out of the castle was over a   get into or out of the castle was
small drawbridge.                              over a small drawbridge.
           Left Aligned                             Right Aligned

Once  upon  a time in a land far, far   Once upon a time in a land far,
away  there  lived  a  beautiful        far away there lived a beautiful
Princess in a large, ivy covered        Princess in a large, ivy covered
castle. Around  that  castle  was  a    castle. Around that castle was a
deep  mote and the only way to get      deep mote and the only way to
into or out of the castle was over a    get into or out of the castle was
small drawbridge.                              over a small drawbridge.
              Justified                             Center Aligned
```

Figure 2.9. Alignment examples.

Size

Text size is the measure of the letter's height in points. One point is 1/72nd of an inch. Figure 2.10 puts this in perspective. It shows text in 12, 32, and 72 point Helvetica.

```
                    12 Point

                  32 Point

         72 Point
```

Figure 2.10. Relative font sizes.

Even though there are 72 points to an inch, a letter shown in a 72 point font won't necessarily be one inch high. This is because these measures were defined back when typographers used individual letters carved in blocks of metal. They would measure the height of the block, and since the letter was smaller than the block, a 72 point font would be on one-inch blocks with letters smaller than one inch. Figure 2.11 helps to demonstrate this.

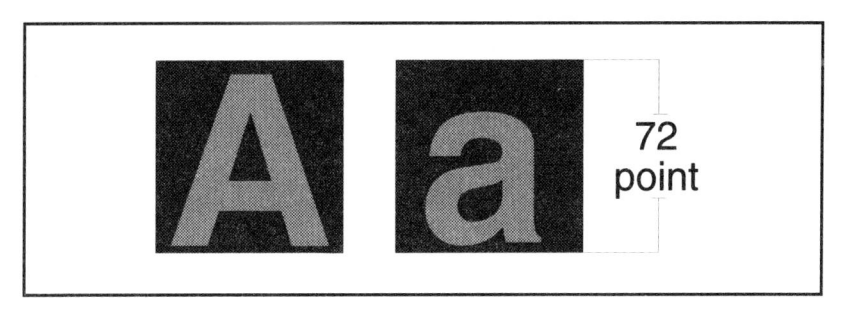

Figure 2.11. Font sizes as they relate to letter height.

What Is Leading?

Another term that originated in the days of movable type is *leading,* also known as *line space.* Leading is the distance from the baseline of one line of text to the baseline of the next. To achieve this difference in baseline distance, typographers would put strips of a lead alloy between lines of type. Thus the term leading (pronounced "ledding").

Today, of course, it is much easier to change the leading of text. QuarkXPress has a Leading command under the Style menu, which presents you with a dialog box that allows you to enter a number indicating the amount of leading desired. If you enter "auto" into the Leading dialog box, the line spacing will be set to the amount entered into the Auto Leading field in the Typographic Preferences dialog box. You can enter a specific number to set the line spacing to that number of points, or you can enter a percentage that will cause the line spacing to be relative to the font size. For example, if you enter 50% into the Leading dialog box, the line spacing will be half again as large as the current font size; for 12 point type the leading would be 18 points, for 24 point type the leading would be 32 points, and so on.

The default amount for automatic leading is 20%, which is fine for most applications. As you get more experienced using QuarkXPress you may wish to fine-tune this for different sizes and applications. A general rule of thumb is the larger the font size, the greater the leading.

In addition to applying leading manually, you can apply it using your mouse cursor and the Measurement palette, which is discussed later in this chapter. Figure 2.12 shows 9 point text with different leadings.

In this comic spoof of swashbuckling films, Hawkins (Danny Kaye), a weak, inept flunky for a Robin Hood-like band of benevolent outlaws, becomes involved in a plot to restore a deposed infant king, the Purple Pimpernel, to the throne	In this comic spoof of swashbuckling films, Hawkins (Danny Kaye), a weak, inept flunky for a Robin	In this comic spoof of swashbuckling films, Hawkins (Danny Kaye), a weak, inept flunky for a Robin Hood-like band of benevolent outlaws, becomes involved in a plot to restore a deposed infant king, the Purple Pimpernel, to the throne that is rightfully his.
Auto Leading	**24 Pt. Leading**	**10 Pt. Leading**

Figure 2.12. 9 point type with different leadings.

What Leading Affects

If no text is highlighted when you select Leading from the Style menu, then the amount you enter into the Leading dialog box will apply only to the line that the cursor is in at that time. If you have highlighted text, the leading amount you enter will be applied to all highlighted lines. Remember, that is all *lines,* not all sentences. The leading will be applied to the edge of the text box for every line that contains highlighted text, even if only one word of that line is highlighted. If the sentence wraps to a line that has no highlighted text it will retain its original leading.

Type Width and Spacing

Proportional and Nonproportional Fonts

Now that we've talked about the height of text, let's talk about its width. The width of a font falls into one of two categories, proportional or nonproportional (also called *monospace*). The horizontal spacing between letters is determined by *kerning* (the space between any given pair of letters) and *tracking* (the space between all letters of a selected text).

In a nonproportional font, each letter in a particular font size has the same width; for instance, even though an "i" is much thinner than a "w," they each take up the same amount of horizontal space. The top example in Figure 2.13 is in Courier, a common nonproportional font.

```
Willow
```
Willow

Figure 2.13. On the top is Courier, a nonproportional font. On the bottom is Helvetica, a proportional font.

The bottom example is in Helvetica, a proportional font. Single-stroke letters, such as "i," are given less room than letters with multiple strokes, such as "w." Although it is the same word in the same type size, in Courier the line appears longer.

Kerning

Kerning is the space between any one pair of letters in a proportional font. Kerning information is built into every font, and stored in a table included called the kerning table. QuarkXPress allows you to change the amount of space between letter pairs through the Kern command in the Style menu.

44 ▼ *Teach Yourself QuarkXPress 3.1*

▼ **NOTE** ▲ The Kern command will be visible in the Style menu only when a text box is active and the cursor is between two letters. If text is highlighted or the cursor is at the beginning of the text, the Kern command will not appear in the Style menu.

In QuarkXPress, an *em space* is equal to two zeros in any given font (00). You can adjust the kerning to 1/20,000 of an em space.

One way to kern a letter pair is to place the cursor between the two letters, in the space you wish to adjust, and select the Kern command from the Style menu. You will be presented with the dialog box shown in Figure 2.14.

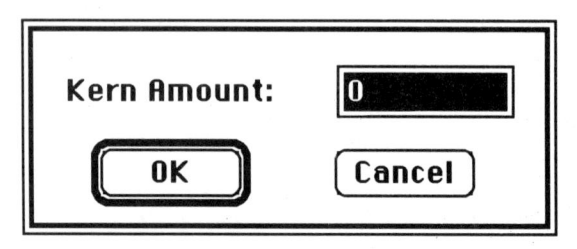

Figure 2.14. The Kern dialog box.

You enter a positive number into the Kern Amount field to increase the distance between the two letters, and a negative number to decrease the distance. Entering "1" into this field would increase the distance by 1/200th of an em space. Entering "-1" would bring the two letters 1/200th of an em space closer together.

On the left in Figure 2.15, "Road" appears in the Times font with normal letter spacing; notice that the distance between the "R" and the "o" appears to be too large. By placing the cursor between the two letters, selecting the Kern command from the Style menu, and entering "-12," the distance is reduced by 12/200ths of an em space, as shown in the middle example in Figure 2.16. The example on the bottom shows the effect of kerning every letter pair. The distance between the "o" and the "a" has been reduced by 4/200ths of an em space, and the distance between the "a" and the "d" has been increased by 2/200ths. This also demonstrates that you can overkern. Judge for yourself, but I think the middle example looks best.

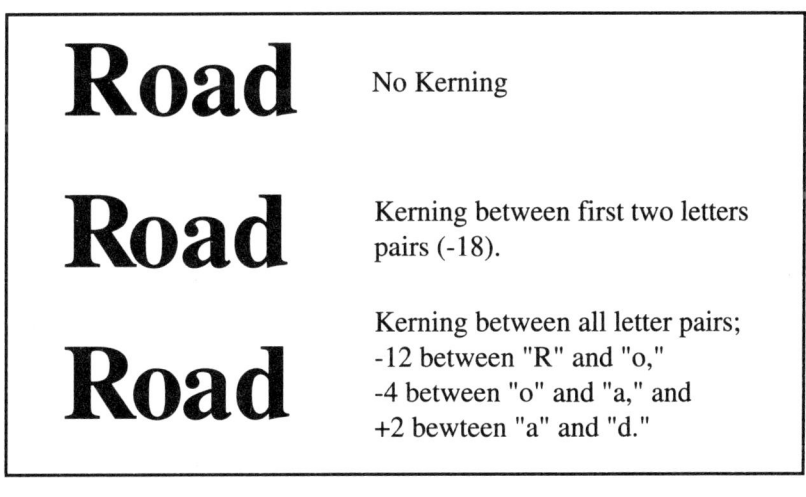

Road No Kerning

Road Kerning between first two letters pairs (-18).

Road Kerning between all letter pairs; -12 between "R" and "o," -4 between "o" and "a," and +2 bewteen "a" and "d."

Figure 2.15. Kerning examples. The amounts indicated are in 1/200ths of an em space.

Editing Kerning Tables

When you are using QuarkXPress's Automatic Kerning function (accessed through the Typographic Preferences dialog box), you can edit the kerning tables of a font directly. This allows you to enter, change, and record kerning pairs that will automatically be applied when you type or import text into QuarkXPress. You edit Kerning tables using the Kern/Track Editor accessed through the Utilities menu.

▼ **NOTE** ▲ The Kern/Track Editor file must be in the QuarkXPress folder when you open the program for it to be displayed in the Utilities menu.

Figure 2.16 shows the dialog box that is presented when you access the Kern/Track Editor.

46 ▼ *Teach Yourself QuarkXPress 3.1*

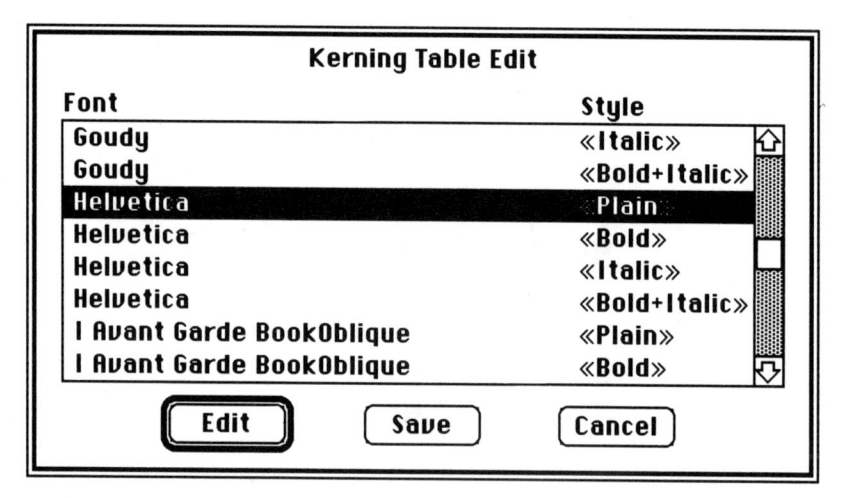

Figure 2.16. The Kerning Table Edit dialog box allows you to choose which font to edit.

From this dialog box you select the font you wish to modify, and click on the Edit button. The kerning table, as shown in Figure 2.17, will display the current letter pairs and their kern amounts listed on the left.

Figure 2.17. The Kerning Table for Helvetica Plain.

To change the value of a listed pair, click on that pair to select it. The current kerning value will be listed in the Value field and the first button will change to a Replace button, as shown in Figure 2.18.

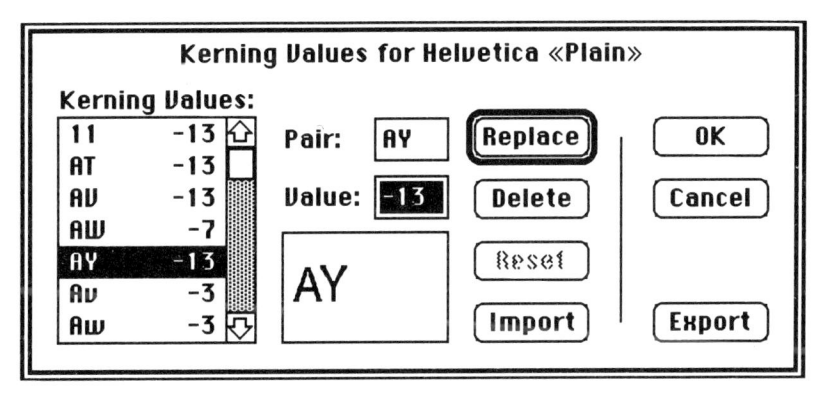

Figure 2.18. The kerning value of a listed pair.

Enter the desired amount and click on the Replace button to enter the change. You could click on a letter pair and the Remove button if you didn't wish that letter pair to be automatically kerned in the future.

To add a letter pair that doesn't already exist, click on the Pair field to place the cursor, and type the desired letters. Then click on the Value field and enter the desired value. Figure 2.19 shows how the buttons change when you are adding a letter pair.

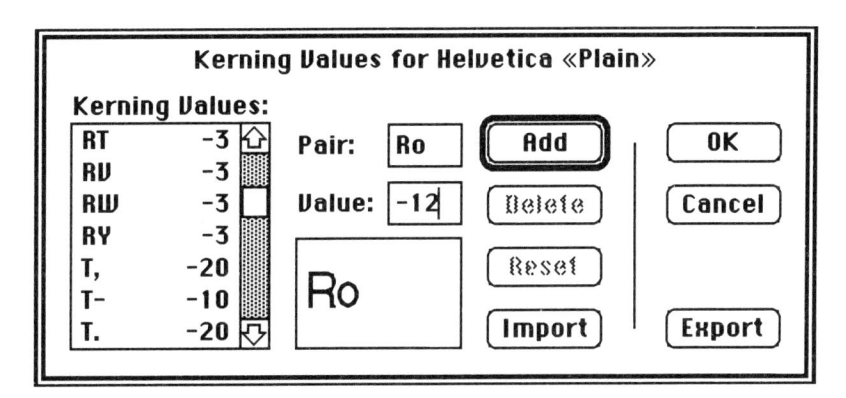

Figure 2.19. Adding a new letter pair to a kerning table.

Click on the Add button to record the new letter pair. These commands are case-sensitive; that is, you can create a different kerning amount for the letter pair "Ro" than for "ro," so be sure to type exactly the pair you want.

When you have finished adding new letter pairs and editing existing kerning values, click on the OK button to return to the Kerning Table Edit dialog box (Figure 2.16), which contains a Save button. You must save your changes in order for them to take effect.

Saving/Importing a Kerning Table

If you click on the Export button in the Kerning Table Edit dialog box, you will be presented with a standard Save dialog box, as shown in Figure 2.20, from which you can name the kerning table, indicate a path, and save the kerning table to use with other fonts.

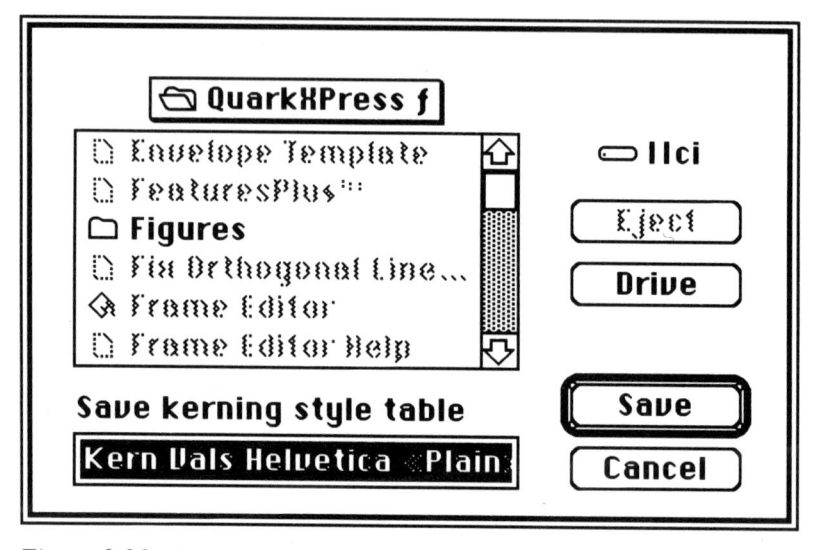

Figure 2.20. A standard Save dialog box, for the kerning style table.

You can edit kerning pairs for only one font style at a time. For example, if you edit the plain version of a font, your changes will not affect the bold or italic versions. You must open and change each style separately. To do this:

1. Open one version of a font family (such as Helvetica Plain);
2. Make the desired changes;
3. Click on the Export button and save the kerning table as a separate file (give it a name you will recognize, and place it in a folder you'll easily recall);

4. Click on the OK button to exit the Helvetica Plain Kerning Table;
5. Click on the Save button in the Kerning Table dialog box to save the changes;
6. Use the Kerning Table Edit dialog box to open another version of that font family (or any font to which you wish to apply that kerning table);
7. Click on the Import button and open the kerning table you saved earlier;
8. Click on the OK button to close the Kerning Table Edit dialog box;
9. Click on the Save button to record the changes;
10. Repeat for the rest of the styles in that font family.

Tracking

Tracking refers to the spaces between all the letters in the selected text. When you highlight a section of text (usually by dragging the I-beam cursor over it), the Kern command under the Style menu changes to Track, and will present you with a dialog box. The values for tracking are the same as for kerning. Tracking can be adjusted to within 1/20,000th of an em space. Entering "1" into the amount field increases the distance between every letter in the selected text by 1/200th of an em space. Entering a "-1" reduces each letter space by 1/200th of an em.

Tracking has two main uses, copyfitting and creating typographical effects. Copyfitting is the act of making text fit into a specific space. For example, sometimes at the end of a paragraph, one word will wrap to a new line; the hanging word is called an *orphan*. To correct this, you can apply negative tracking to the last sentence to reduce the length of the line and bring the orphan up one line. Figure 2.21 demonstrates this. The two paragraphs are the same except that in the bottom one, the last line and the second-to-last line were selected and -8 tracking was applied. This reduced the space between each letter in the last line by 8/200ths of an em space, enough to eliminate the orphan.

> The term sincere comes from two Italian words. When artists in ancient Italy would carve a marble statue and make a mistake they would sometimes apply a certain type of wax, or "cere" to the blemish to cover the error. If a statue was "sincere" it was without wax or sin-cere.

> The term sincere comes from two Italian words. When artists in ancient Italy would carve a marble statue and make a mistake they would sometimes apply a certain type of wax, or "cere" to the blemish to cover the error. If a statue was "sincere" it was without wax or sincere.

Figure 2.21. Using tracking to eliminate orphans.

Figure 2.22 shows an example that used tracking for artistic reasons rather than for copyfitting.

> HYPOCHONDRIA
> POWER

Figure 2.22. Tracking used for artistic purposes.

To create this logo for the Hypochondriacs of America, the Tracking function was used to make the width of "power" equal to that of "hypochondria," which has many more letters. "Hypochondria" is in 32 point Avant Garde with normal letter spacing; "power" is in 48 point Times with a tracking of 100 (100/200ths of an em space).

You can use the Kern function to adjust letter-pair spacing in a word that has been tracked. For instance, in Figure 2.22, you could place the insertion point between the "P" and "O" of "Hypochondria" and use the Kern command to bring these two letters closer together.

In addition to applying tracking manually, you can apply it using your mouse cursor and the Measurement palette, which is described in the next section of this chapter.

The Measurement Palette of a Text Box

You may have noticed that the contents of the Measurement palette of the text box in Figure 2.1 look different than the contents of the Measurement palette for the line we created earlier. This is because the Measurement palette gives information about the currently selected item, and there are many more things to know about a text box than there are to know about a line. For example, a text box has both a height and a width; there are four corners instead of two endpoints; a text box has text while a line doesn't; and so forth.

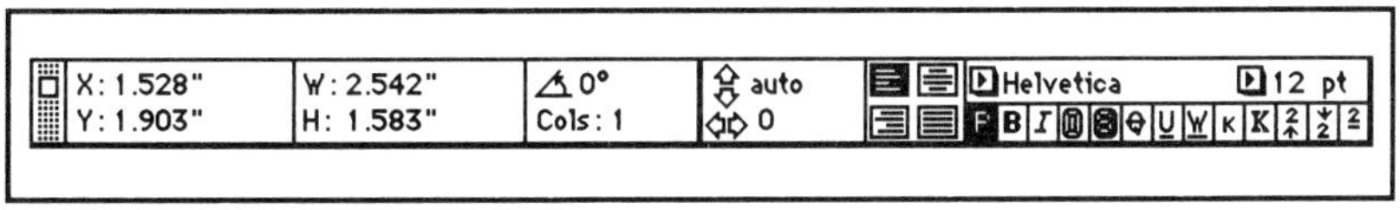

Figure 2.23. The Measurement palette for the text box shown in Figure 2.1.

Figure 2.23 is an enlargement of the Measurement palette for the text box in Figure 2.1. Let's examine it more closely.

The first field in the text box Measurement palette tells us that the top-left corner of the text box is located at 1.528 inches along the horizontal ruler, and 1.903 inches along the vertical ruler. The second field tells us that the text box is 2.542 inches wide and 1.583 inches high. The third field tells us that the box is rotated zero degrees, and that it contains one column of text. These first three fields are separated from the last part of the Measurement palette by a slightly darker line, which indicates that the next fields are about the contents of the text box, rather than about the box itself.

If no text is highlighted (as is the case with a new, empty text box) these content indicators tell us what the default text characteristics are, or how text will appear when it is typed. If there is highlighted text, then these indicators tell us the properties of that text.

The first of these content fields tells us two things: the number next to the up and down arrows indicates the amount of leading, and the number next to the left and right arrows indicates the amount of kerning/tracking. In this case both are set to zero. If the insertion point is between two letters, the bottom number indicates the amount of kerning applied to this letter pair. If there is text highlighted, the bottom number indicates the amount of tracking applied to the highlighted text. If the insertion point is at the beginning of a new paragraph, the kern/track indicator is not visible.

As we know from the section on text alignment, there are four alignment possibilities; the next field in the Measurement palette uses images to indicate these. The upper-left box indicates left alignment, beneath it is right alignment; the upper-right box indicates centered alignment, and the remaining box, justified.

The final field in the Measurement palette tells us the text's font, size, and style. In this case, it is 12 point Helvetica Plain.

Controlling Text Using the Measurement Palette

You know how to control leading, tracking, alignment, font, size, and type style using commands in the Style menu. The menu commands aren't the only way to control these functions. All of the indicators in the Measurement palette also control new or highlighted text.

- To increase or decrease the amount of kerning in increments of ten, place your text insertion point between the letter pair you wish to kern, and click on the left or right arrow in the fourth field of the Measurement palette. To increase or decrease the amount of kerning in increments of one, do the same thing while holding down the Shift and Option keys. You can increase or decrease the amount of tracking in the same way, by simply selecting the text you want to track. You may also kern or track by double-clicking on the number next to the horizontal arrows in the Measurement palette to select it, typing in the new amount, and pressing the Return key.

- When the Leading indicator says "auto," clicking on the arrows won't affect the leading amount, but you can double-

click on "auto" and enter a new amount. When the leading amount is a number rather than "auto," you can use the arrows to increase/decrease the leading by two-point increments.
- You can click once on any of the alignment icons to select the desired option.
- To select a type style, simply click on the desired indicator.
- Next to the font and size indicators are small boxes containing arrows. If you click and hold the mouse button on one of these boxes, you will be presented with a pop-up menu of available fonts or sizes. While holding down the mouse button, place the cursor over the desired font name or point size and release the mouse button to activate that option.

You can also manipulate the size, location, rotation, and number of columns of a text box using the Measurement palette. Double-clicking on the number of any of these parameters in the Measurement palette will highlight that parameter. You can then enter a new amount and press Return. The results will be applied to the active text box.

Style Sheets

So now you know how to apply attributes to text. You can select the text in a paragraph and make it 24 point Palatino, shadowed italic, center aligned, with 48 point leading and tracked -2. To apply each of these attributes one at a time to a section of highlighted text requires seven steps. No big deal.

But to apply each of these attributes separately to four different sections of text would require twenty-eight steps. Doing this paragraph by paragraph throughout a large document could become bothersome in a hurry.

Fortunately, you don't have to. You can format one example of text and then record that formatting into a style sheet. A style sheet isn't really a sheet at all—it is formatting information that is included in the document. Style sheets can be transferred between QuarkXPress documents, and also from documents imported into QuarkXPress from a program for which you have a filter.

When a text box is active, the Style Sheets command appears at the bottom of the Style menu. When you place the cursor over this command, a list of available styles pops out. Placing the cursor over one of these styles applies that style to the paragraph that contains the text insertion point.

The Style Sheets Dialog Box

To create or edit style sheets, use the Style Sheets command under the Edit menu. This command brings up the Style Sheets dialog box shown in Figure 2.24.

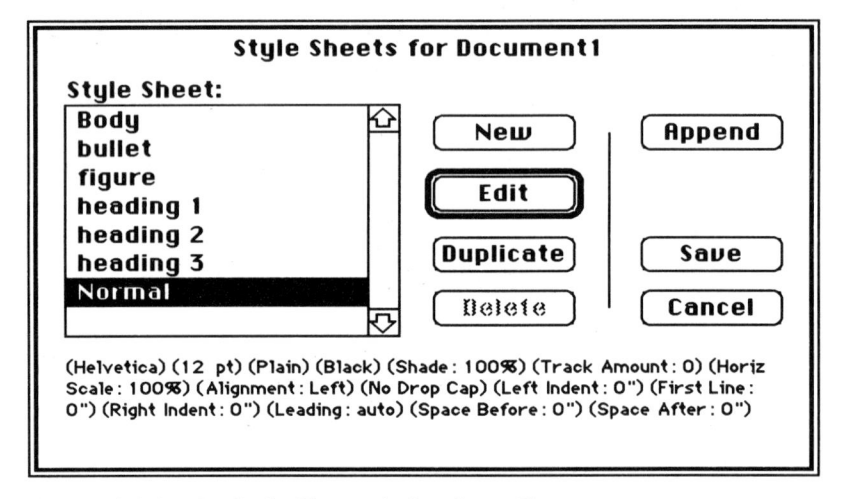

Figure 2.24. The Style Sheets dialog box allows you to create new style sheets or edit existing ones.

In this example, the last style in the menu, Normal, is highlighted and the attributes that make up this style are listed at the bottom of the dialog box. Normal is the default style and all text attributes that can be affected are listed here. Figure 2.25 shows the style Body selected. The attribute listing is much smaller since the only attributes shown are those that are different from Normal. Thus, in this example, text that has the Body style applied to it will be the same as Normal except that the font will be Times, the first line will appear 0.306 inches from the left margin, and the paragraph will have 0.111 inches of space above it.

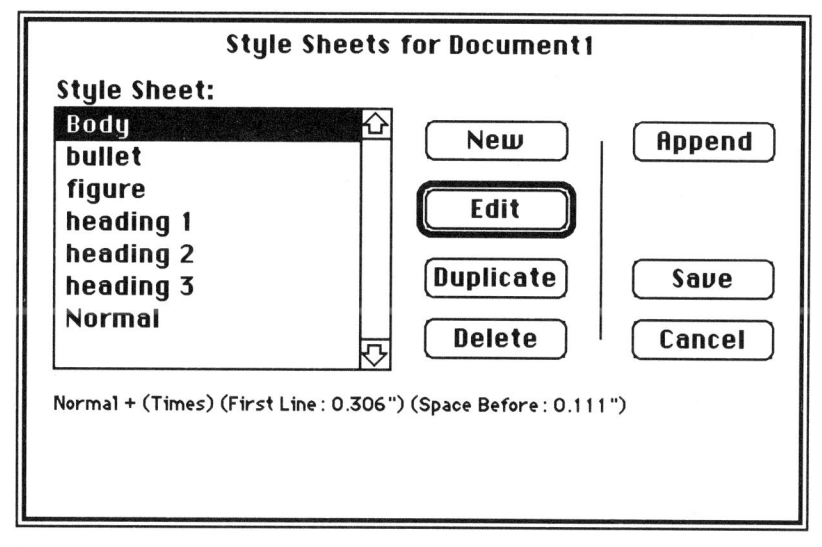

Figure 2.25. The Style Sheets dialog box showing the attributes that have been changed to create the style Body.

When you click on the New button you are presented with the Edit Style Sheet dialog box shown in Figure 2.26.

Figure 2.26. The Edit Style Sheet dialog box.

If a text box is active when you select Style Sheets from the Edit menu, the text attributes at the insertion point will be listed in the Edit Style Sheets dialog box. So to create a new style, simply apply the desired attributes to your text using the Measurement palette or menu choices, open the Style Sheets dialog box, and click on the New button. The attributes will be set. You just need to give the new style a name, and a keyboard equivalent if you want.

To do this, place the insertion point in the Name field in the Style Sheets dialog box and enter a name for the new style. Then place the insertion point in the Keyboard Equivalent field and press any combination of Shift/Option/Command and another key to define it. You can also use function keys and numeric keypad keys if your keyboard has them. If you define a key combination that is already defined as another action, you will hear a beep and nothing will be entered into the Keyboard Equivalent field.

When you highlight text to select it and apply a Style Sheet, the styles in that Style Sheet are applied only to the selected text. If you apply a Style Sheet when no text is selected, then that style will be applied to the entire paragraph that contains the cursor.

Creating a New Style Without Existing Text

You don't have to create a new style around existing text. You can use the Based On pop-up menu in the Edit Style Sheet dialog box to select an existing style or to select No Style. When you select No Style, the default attributes are selected. After you have selected a style on which to base the new style, you can use the four buttons on the right side of the Edit Style Sheet dialog box (Character, Formats, Rules, Tabs) to adjust the style's attributes. Clicking on these buttons is the same as selecting these options from the Style menu, and will bring up the appropriate dialog box for that option.

Importing Style Sheets

When you import a text file through a filter with the Include Style Sheets option checked in the Get Text dialog box, the style sheets for that file are interpreted and placed in the Style Sheets submenu in the Style menu. Figure 2.27 shows the Style Sheets submenu with a listing of styles that were imported with a document created in Microsoft Word. I can highlight text anywhere in this QuarkXPress document and select one of these style sheets, and all of the formatting contained in that style sheet will be applied to the highlighted text.

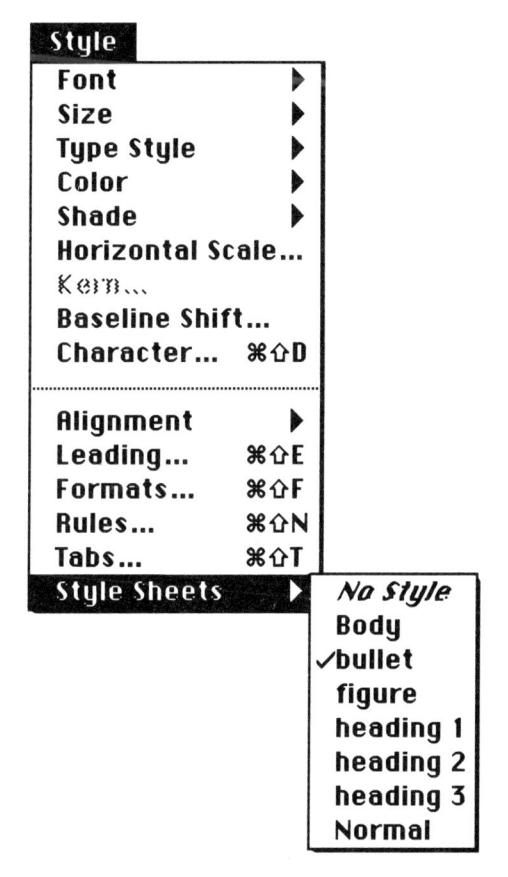

Figure 2.27. The Style Sheets submenu.

Editing a Style Sheet

To edit an existing style sheet, select the desired style sheet name from the list in the Style Sheets dialog box (Figure 2.24) and click on the Edit button. This brings up the Edit Style Sheet dialog box

(Figure 2.26) containing the attributes of the selected style. You can then use the Character, Formats, Rules, and Tabs buttons to access and edit the desired attributes.

Saving a New or Edited Style Sheet

Once you have made the desired attribute selections for a new style, or have edited an existing style, click on the OK button to return to the Style Sheets dialog box, and click on the Save button to record these changes. If you made changes that you don't wish to keep, you can click on the Cancel button at any time.

Appending Style Sheets

Click on the Append button in the Style Sheets dialog box to open a standard Open dialog box through which you can access any QuarkXPress document and append its style sheets to the current document. The appended styles will appear, and can be applied and edited just like styles created in the current document.

Deleting a Style

You can click on a style name in the Style Sheets dialog box and click on the Delete button to delete any unused or unwanted style sheets, but since style sheets don't take up much space, you might want to keep unused ones for possible future use.

Formatting Paragraphs

Aside from the typographical control that we have already talked about, QuarkXPress also contains many of the same paragraph formatting controls available in a word processor. There are commands that allow you to indent the first line of a paragraph, set the right and left offset margins of a paragraph, set tabs, create drop caps, and anchor *rules,* or lines, above and/or below a paragraph. The next few sections examine these commands.

The Formats Command

When a text box is selected, the Formats command appears in the Style menu. When you select this command you are presented with the Paragraph Formats dialog box shown in Figure 2.28. When this dialog box is active, a text ruler is placed at the top of the active text box (see Figure 2.29). This text ruler contains the margin and tab controls for the active paragraph.

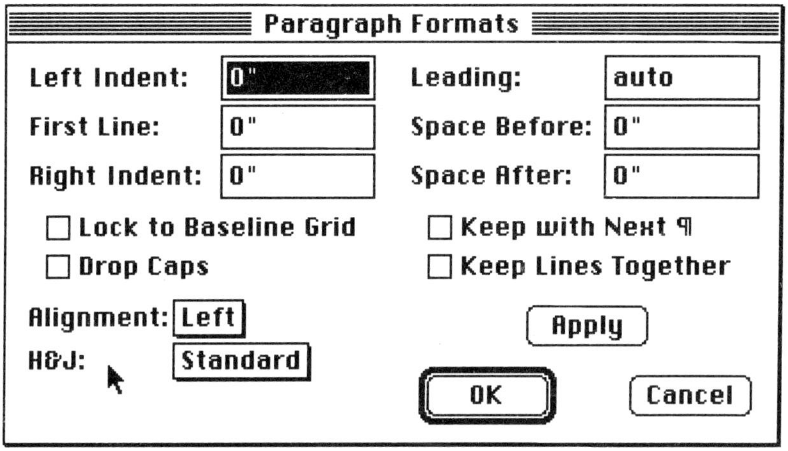

Figure 2.28. The Paragraph Formats dialog box.

If the text insertion point is within a paragraph of text, that is the active paragraph. If text is highlighted, anything you specify in the Paragraph Formats dialog box will apply to all paragraphs that have highlighted text. If the text insertion point is after the last paragraph control character in a text box, then the attributes you indicate in the Paragraph Formats dialog box will apply to text entered after that point.

Control Characters (Invisibles)

Usually when you press a key on the keyboard the character shown on that key appears on the screen. There are some keys that don't represent characters, but are control keys. When you press control keys, such as the Return, Tab, or Space keys, no alphanumeric character is displayed, but a control character is inserted into the text. The Show Invisibles command under the View menu allows you to see these invisible characters. Figure 2.29 shows some text with the Show Invisibles command turned on.

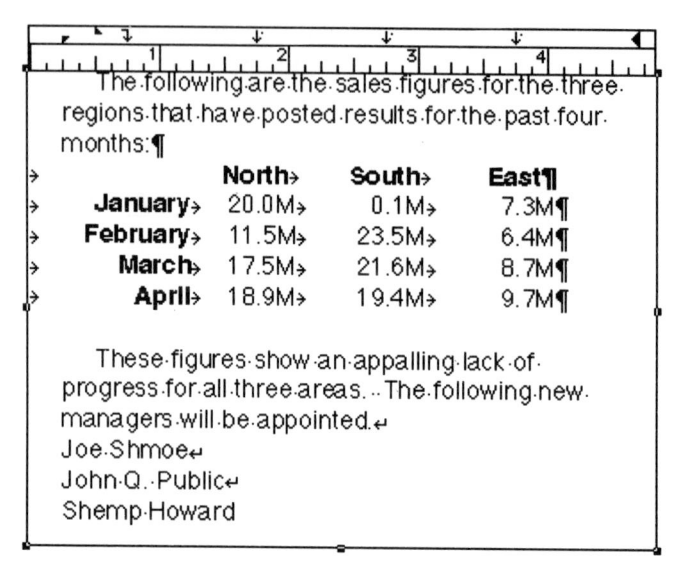

```
           The following are the sales figures for the three
           regions that have posted results for the past four
           months:¶
                    North→    South→    East¶
           January→ 20.0M→    0.1M→     7.3M¶
           February→ 11.5M→   23.5M→    6.4M¶
           March→   17.5M→    21.6M→    8.7M¶
           April→   18.9M→    19.4M→    9.7M¶

           These figures show an appalling lack of
           progress for all three areas... The following new
           managers will be appointed.↵
           Joe Shmoe↵
           John Q. Public↵
           Shemp Howard
```

Figure 2.29. A text box showing the text ruler and with invisible characters showing.

In this figure, arrows indicate tab stops, which are inserted every time you press the Tab key. (Tabs will be discussed in greater detail at the end of this chapter.) Dots centered between words indicate spaces.

The backward, double-stemmed "P" that appears in Figure 2.29 represents a paragraph mark, or hard return. This is inserted every time you press the Return key, and indicates the end of a paragraph.

The lines that come down and point to the left represent soft returns, which simply move the cursor to the next line without starting a new paragraph. This allows you to control wordwrap without inserting before-paragraph spacing, first-line insert, or any other beginning paragraph formatting. To insert a soft return, hold down the Shift key while pressing Return.

If text is highlighted, anything you specify in the Paragraph Formats dialog box will apply to all paragraphs that have highlighted text. If the text insertion point is after the last paragraph control character in a text box, then the attributes you indicate in the Paragraph Formats dialog box will apply to text entered after that point.

Line Indents

Let's consider the first three fields in the Paragraph Formats dialog box—Left Indent, First Line, and Right Indent. The numbers you enter into these fields control where the lines in the selected paragraph begin and end. The first field, Left Indent, controls how far from the left edge of the text ruler the text will start. The second field, First Line, allows you to set a different left indent for the first line in a paragraph. This is normally used to indent the first line three to five characters more than the following lines, but it can also be used to indent the first line less than the following lines.

The third field, Right Indent, determines how far from the right side of the text box the text is when it wraps to the next line. Figure 2.30 shows a paragraph with three different sets of parameters entered for its indents.

Tropical forests are located between the Tropic of Cancer and the Tropic of Capricorn, 20 degrees above and below Earth's equator. Once they formed a lush green belt around the planet, but most of these forests have been destroyed.

   Tropical forests are located between the Tropic of Cancer and the Tropic of Capricorn, 20 degrees above and below Earth's equator. Once they formed a lush green belt around the planet, but most of these forests have been destroyed.

Tropical forests are located between the Tropic of Cancer and the Tropic of Capricorn, 20 degrees above and below Earth's equator. Once they formed a lush green belt around the planet, but most of these forests have been destroyed.

Figure 2.30. Three paragraphs with different paragraph-indent parameters.

The first paragraph in Figure 2.30 has "0" entered for each field, causing all lines to start at the extreme left of the text box and continue as far to the right as the wordwrap allows. The second paragraph has the Left Indent set to 0.25" and the First Line set to 0.5", which causes all of the lines except the first to start 0.25" from the left side of the text box. The location of the first line is relative to the amount entered into the Left Indent field. Thus the first line in the middle paragraph is indented 0.5" further than the following lines, which are indented 0.25". This places the first line 0.75" from the left side of the text box. To place the first line 0.5" from the left side of the text box, 0.25" must be entered into the First Line field for the second paragraph. The Right Indent has been set at 0.5", which causes the lines to wrap 0.5" before the right side of the text box.

The third paragraph has the Left Indent set at 0.5" and the First Line set at -0.25". The negative number causes the first line to be set to the left of the Left Indent position. This is called *hanging text,* and is mainly used in bulleted or numbered lists.

Line Spacing

The three fields on the right side of the Paragraph Formats dialog box (Figure 2.28) allow you to control the line spacing in a paragraph. The amount entered into the Leading field sets the leading amount for the entire paragraph. The Space Before and Space After fields allow you to indicate the amount of separation between the active paragraph and those that precede and follow it. The amount entered into the Space Before and Space After fields is in addition to any amount entered into these fields for adjoining paragraphs.

Paragraphs and Pagination

There are four check boxes in the Paragraph Formats dialog box (Figure 2.28).

When the Keep with Next ¶ box is checked, the active paragraph will always be placed in the same text box as the paragraph that follows it. This option is very useful for keeping headings and titles with the subject paragraph. If a paragraph with this option checked is the last paragraph in a text box, it is automatically placed in the next text box with the paragraph that follows it. If there is not enough room in the next text box, the text would continue to wrap forward to the next text box. Of course, this will only happen if you have set up links between text boxes so that the text knows where to go. Setting up links between text boxes is discussed in Chapter 4.

The Keep Lines Together command causes a paragraph to move to the next text box if there is not enough room in the current text box for the entire paragraph. Again, you must set up links between text boxes so that the lines know where to go.

The Lock to Baseline Grid command locks a text *baseline,* or the line on which most characters sit, to an invisible, underlying horizontal grid. Locking paragraphs in such a way enables you to align baselines from column to column and from box to box across a page and across spreads.

Drop Caps

The Drop Caps check box in the Paragraph Formats dialog box brings up a dialog box that allows you to create an automatic drop cap and control its attributes.

A drop cap is a large capital letter that is the first letter in a paragraph and extends below the first line. Figure 2.31 shows an example of this.

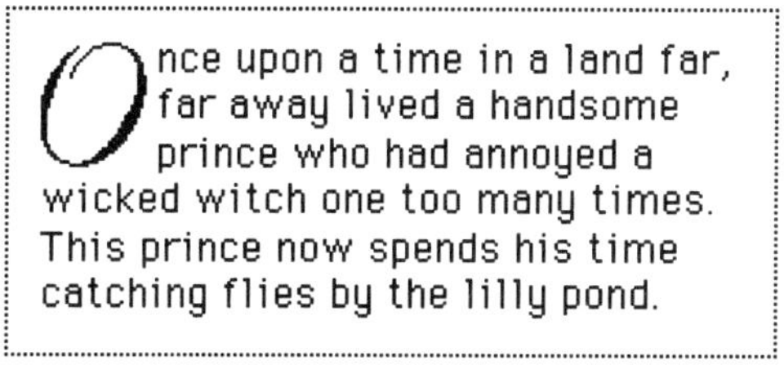

> *O*nce upon a time in a land far, far away lived a handsome prince who had annoyed a wicked witch one too many times. This prince now spends his time catching flies by the lilly pond.

Figure 2.31. A paragraph containing an initial drop cap.

When the Drop Caps option is checked in the Paragraph Formats dialog box, two additional options are presented—Character Count, which controls how many letters are extended, and Line Count, which controls how many lines down the letters are extended. Figure 2.32 shows these options as they would be set for the results shown in Figure 2.31, in which one letter extends three lines down.

64 ▼ *Teach Yourself QuarkXPress 3.1*

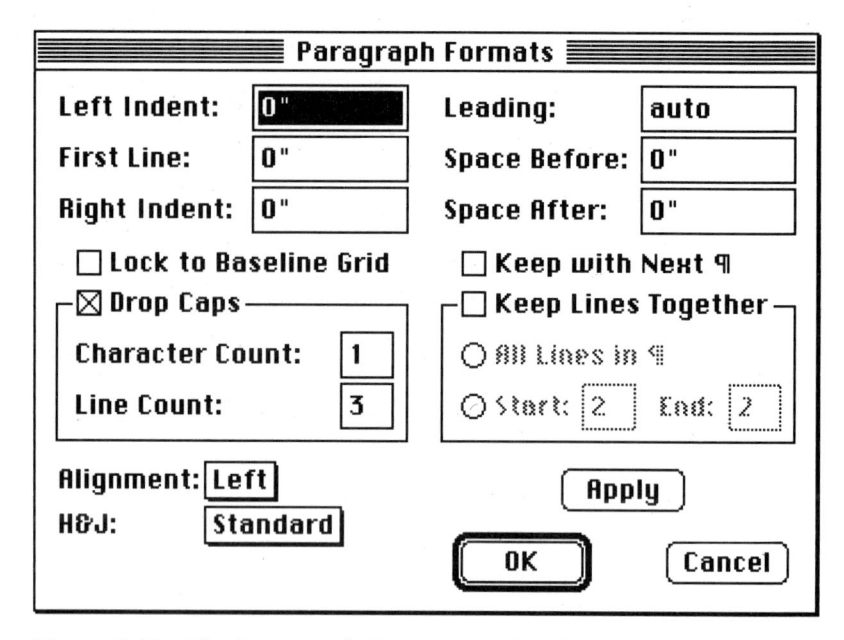

Figure 2.32. The Paragraph Formats Dialog box showing the Drop Caps options for Figure 2.31.

Alignment

In the lower-left corner of the Paragraph Formats dialog box is a pop-down list that allows you to control the alignment of the active paragraph. The four options that appear (left, right, center, and justified) are identical to the alignment options available under the Style menu and are discussed in the Text Attributes section of this chapter.

Tabs

Setting Tabs

QuarkXPress allows you to set a variety of tabs for text. When a tab is set, it applies to the paragraph that contains the insertion point at that time, or to all paragraphs containing highlighted text. Selecting the Tab command from the Style menu places a text ruler above the active text box and brings up the Paragraph Tabs dialog box, as shown in Figure 2.33.

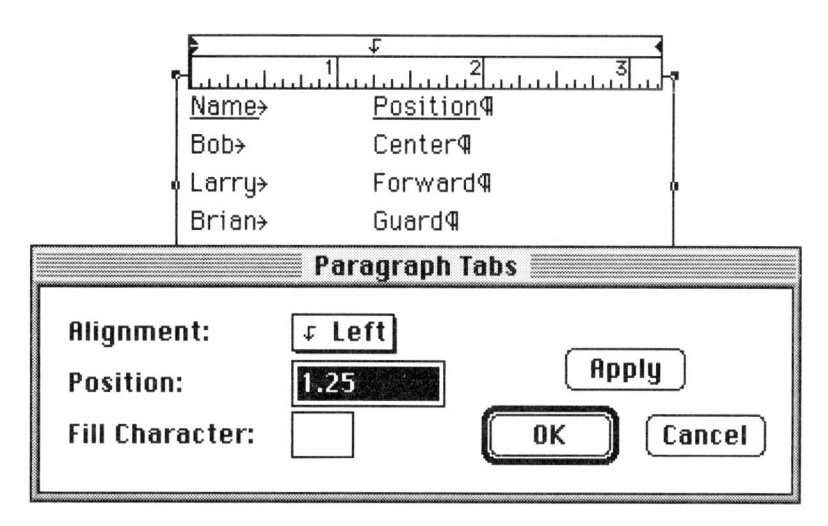

Figure 2.33. Text showing a left tab positioned at one and a half inches along the text ruler.

In this example, the first word on each line has been separated from the second word with a tab, thereby creating two columns. When Show Invisibles is enabled, the small arrow on the text ruler indicates where the tab was entered. You can click on that rule to enter a tab stop in the place where you have positioned your cursor; then, when you return to the text and press the Tab key, your text will align with the tab stop you have set. As you can see from the Position field in the Paragraph Tabs dialog box, the tab stop has been positioned at 1.25 inches.

If you wanted the names and positions to be centered under the headings, you could change the left tab to a center tab—but that would cause only the positions to be centered. To get the names to center under the Name heading as well, you would have to place a tab where you wanted the names to be centered, and place a tab before the names and the heading to make them move to the new tab's position. This is shown in Figure 2.34.

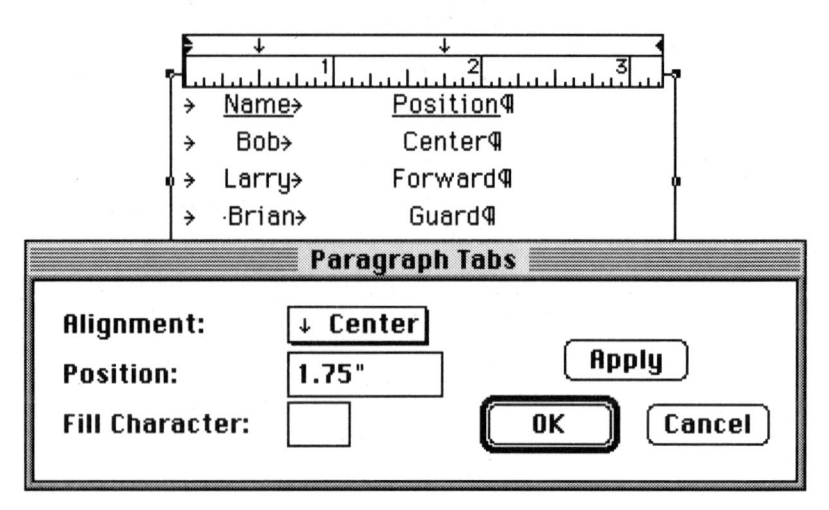

Figure 2.34. Two center tabs have been used to center the two sections under their respective headings.

The type of tab stop is chosen from the Alignment pop-out menu, shown in Figure 2.35.

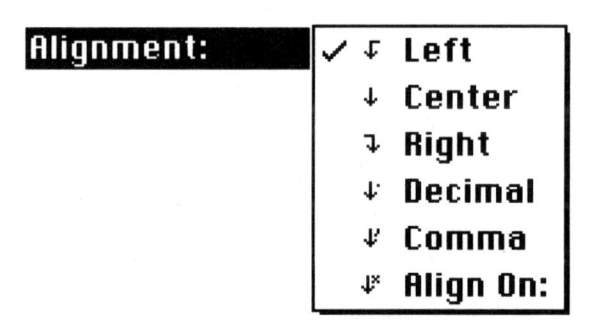

Figure 2.35. The types of tabs available in QuarkXPress.

- Left. The left edge of text entered after a left tab aligns with the position of the tab.
- Center. Text entered after a center tab centers itself on the tab's position.

- Right. The right edge of text entered after a right tab aligns with the position of the tab.
- Decimal. Whether or not it is used as a decimal, any period entered after a decimal tab is centered under the tab position, and the text flows to either side of that point.
- Comma. If there is a comma in the text entered after a comma tab, it is centered under the tab position and the text flows on either side of that comma.
- Align On. When this option is selected, an additional field is included on the Paragraph Tabs dialog box, as shown in Figure 2.35. You can enter a specific character that you wish to align to the tab's position. Just as the comma tab aligns on the comma, text will align on whatever character is entered into this field.

There is another field in the Paragraph Tabs dialog box called the Fill Character field. This field can be used to repeatedly enter a character automatically from the place where the Tab key was pressed to the text at the tab position. One of the most common uses for a fill character is in tables of contents or price lists like the one shown in Figure 2.36.

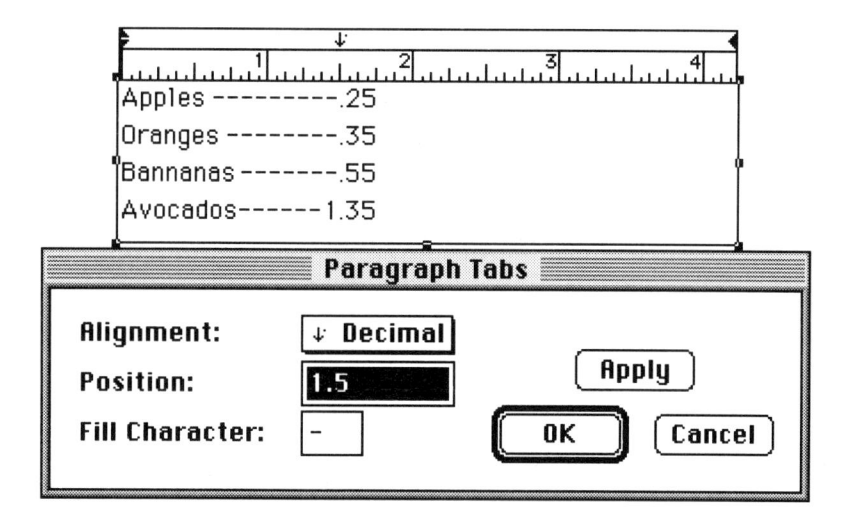

Figure 2.36. Decimal tab with a dash for a fill character.

The price has been separated from the item by a decimal tab, which causes the prices to align with the cents to the right of the tab and the dollars to the left. A dash has been entered into the Fill Character field, causing the space between the item and the price to be filled with dashes. Any character can be used as a fill character.

Clicking on the Apply button will allow you to see the results of your tab choices without having to close the Paragraph Tabs dialog box. Clicking on the OK button applies the settings and closes the dialog box. Clicking on the Cancel button returns the text to how it was before the dialog box was opened.

Moving and Removing Existing Tabs

If you have applied a tab to several paragraphs, you must have all of those paragraphs selected in order to move or remove all existing tabs. If you place a tab in two paragraphs and then move that tab with only one paragraph selected, the tab will be changed only in that paragraph.

To move a tab, select Tabs from the Style menu to place the text ruler over the text box. Then you can click and drag on any tab you wish to move. You must click on the OK button to make that change permanent. To remove a tab, click and drag that tab up and away from the text ruler and release the mouse button.

▼ **NOTE** ▲ If you enter a number into the Position field in the Paragraph Tabs dialog box that corresponds to the location of an existing tab, a second tab will be placed over the first. If you don't want a tab at that position, you will have to remove both tabs individually.

Summary

▼ The Content tool is used to select text and to place the cursor at the desired insertion point.

▼ The Get Text menu item is used to import text. Text can be imported from many word processors and retain its formatting.

▼ Type styles are separated into families called fonts. Within each family can be several styles, such as plain, bold, and italic. In addition to the styles included in a font family, QuarkXPress can apply style attributes such as underline, strike thru, outline, shadow, small caps, superscript, subscript, and superior.

▼ Text can be left aligned, right aligned, centered, or justified (that is, aligned along both edges).

▼ Font height is measured in points. One point is 1/72nd of an inch. The width of some fonts is proportional to the width of the individual letter; these are called proportional fonts. Other fonts apply the same amount of space to every letter, and are called nonproportional.

▼ Space between lines of text is called leading.

▼ Kerning is the space between individual pairs of letters. Tracking is the space between a run of letters. Both can be controlled in QuarkXPress.

▼ The Measurement palette can be used to view and control many text attributes.

▼ Style sheets can be used to record and apply complex sets of text attributes. Style sheets can be imported or appended from other documents, and can be edited individually.

▼ The Formats command allows you to control a paragraph's margins and tabs. It also lets you control the spacing between lines of text in a paragraph.

▼ Drop caps can be automatically created using the Drop Caps command in the Paragraph Formats dialog box.

CHAPTER 3

In This Chapter

- ▼ **Adding Graphics**
    - Image Formats
    - Picture Boxes
    - Importing an Image
    - Manipulating an Image
    - Send to Back/Bring to Front
    - Picture Box Background
    - Frames/Borders
    - Suppressing Picture Boxes
    - Picture Box Measurement Palette
- ▼ **The Picture Style Menu**
    - Picture Style Commands
- ▼ **The Picture Usage Dialog Box**
    - Missing Image Files
    - Modified Image Files
- ▼ **Modifying Picture Box Shapes**
    - The Picture Box Shape Pop-out Menu
    - Reshape Polygon
- ▼ **Runaround Options**
    - None
    - Item
    - Auto Image
    - Manual Image
- ▼ **Summary**

You Will Learn

- ▼ How to create and resize a picture box and import an image into it.

- ▼ How to control a picture box's border, shape, and background.

- ▼ How to use the Style menu to manipulate a graphic image.

- ▼ How to use the Picture Usage dialog box to keep track of and update modified pictures.

- ▼ How to control the way text flows around a picture box.

Adding Graphics

QuarkXPress is not a drawing or painting program. It is possible to do some very simple drawing with the Line tools, but QuarkXPress is intended to help you place and manipulate graphic images, rather than create them.

You can import and manipulate already created images called clip-art, or you can create your own images in some type of graphics program and then pull them into QuarkXPress. There are hundreds of painting and drawing programs on the market, and almost all of them can be used to create an image that can be imported into QuarkXPress.

There are many different graphics formats supported by the Macintosh, all of which can be described as either *bitmapped* or *object-oriented*. Say, for instance, that you wanted to create a square. A bitmapped format would place a bunch of dots in the shape of a square and remember where each of the dots goes. An object-oriented format knows what a square looks like, so it would record that it is a square and its dimensions.

Each format has its own benefits. For example, programs that use a bitmapped format are usually best for retouching and manipulating scanned images, while object-oriented programs are better for the type of precision needed for technical drawings and line art.

Image Formats

The formats that can be imported into QuarkXPress are:

- MacPaint. MacPaint was the first Macintosh paint program, and it is still in use today. It is a bitmapped format that can record only black and white dots. No color information is saved in MacPaint format files. There is a MacPaint II format, which can record color information, but it is not very widely used. Many graphics programs can read and write MacPaint format files, but often you lose much of the image quality.
- PICT. This is an object-oriented format that has a couple of variations. The Macintosh clipboard saves images in PICT

format. Anything copied from a program to the clipboard is pasted as a PICT image.
- TIFF. Tagged Image File Format is a high-quality bitmapped format that is able to record images in great depth. QuarkXPress handles TIFF images very well.
- EPS. Encapsulated PostScript is an object-oriented format that gives you extremely detailed control over the drawing process. PostScript is the most common page description language, and EPS files can be easily resized and retain their quality.

Most Macintosh graphics programs save images in their own formats when you use the Save command. In many of these programs you can use the Save As or Export command to save the image in another format. If the default format is not compatible with QuarkXPress, use Save As or Export to save images in a compatible format.

Picture Boxes

You need to create a picture box to place any graphic image, just as you needed to create a text box before you could place text in a document. In the Tool palette are four picture box tools. These are the Rectangle picture box tool, the Rounded-corner Rectangle picture box tool, the Oval picture box tool, and the Polygon picture box tool.

The first three picture box tools operate in the same manner: you select the tool, place the cursor on the page, and click and drag to create a picture box of the desired size. The Polygon Picture Box tool works a little differently. After selecting the Polygon Picture Box tool, you place the cursor on the page and click and release to place the first point of the polygon. Move the cursor to where you want the next point of the polygon, and click and release to create the first side. Repeat this process for the number of sides desired. To complete the polygon you can either place the cursor over the first point and click the mouse button, or simply double-click the mouse button, which will set the last point and automatically connect it to the first point.

When you have finished drawing a picture box, the Content tool automatically becomes active.

Resizing Picture Boxes

As with text boxes, each picture box has a set of control handles that can be used to resize the box. Using either the Content tool or the Item tool, you can place the cursor over a control handle and click and drag to resize the picture box. The control handles in the corners resize both height and width, while the control handles on the top, bottom, and sides resize only horizontally and vertically.

Importing an Image

Once you have created a picture box you can import a graphic image into it. When a picture box is selected, the Get Text command under the File menu changes to Get Picture. The Content tool must be active for the Get Picture command to be accessible. If the Item tool is selected, Get Picture will be greyed and inaccessible.

When you select the Get Picture command, you are presented with the Get Picture dialog box shown in Figure 3.1, which is similar to the standard Open dialog box.

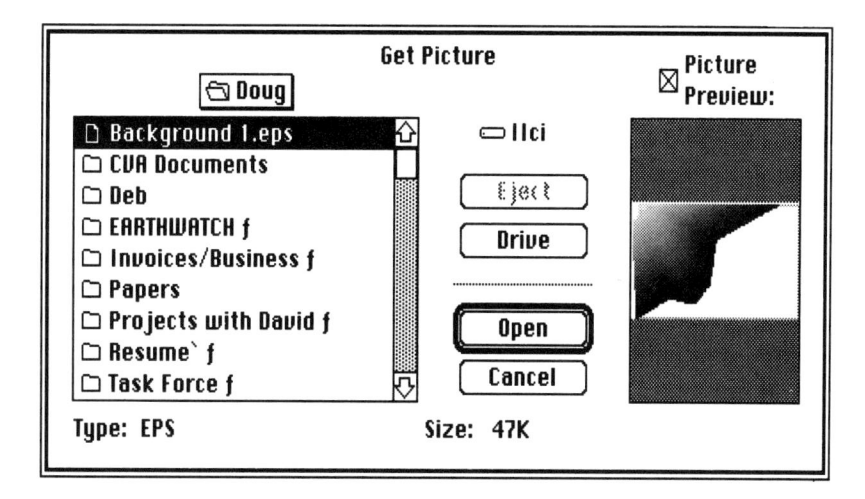

Figure 3.1. The Get Picture dialog box.

Only files that have been saved in a compatible graphic format will appear in the file field along with the names of folders. In Figure 3.1 only one graphic file is available, "Background 1.eps." This file was created in a drawing program and saved as an encapsulated PostScript file. There are other graphics files in this folder but they have been saved in incompatible file formats so their names do not appear.

▼ **NOTE** ▲ Make sure you know the correct name of an image and exactly what disk and folder it is in before you try to import it. That way, if its name doesn't show up in the Get Picture dialog box, you know you haven't lost the picture, but that it is in an incompatible file format.

If the Picture Preview box is checked, you will see a thumbnail view of most images. A *thumbnail* is a small, low-resolution copy of the image. Versions of QuarkXPress before 3.1 couldn't show previews of TIFF images. With Version 3.1, the only ones you won't see a preview of are encapsulated PostScript images that were saved without the optional viewable image portion.

To import an image into the active picture box, you can click on its file name in the file field to select the image, then click on the Open button, or you can simply double-click on its file name in the file field. The image will be placed in the picture box so that its top-left corner is aligned to the top-left corner of the box. If the image is larger than the picture box you will see only part of the image.

If you move the cursor over the picture box, the cursor changes to the hand of the Content tool. Click and drag on the image with this cursor to move the image within the box.

You can click and drag on the control handles of the picture box to resize it according to the size of the image. Resizing a picture box to show more or less of an image is called *cropping*.

A new feature of QuarkXPress 3.1 is that it allows you to see the image as you crop the picture box. In earlier versions, if you enlarged the picture box to show more of the image, the hidden parts of the image remained hidden until you released the mouse button. In QuarkXPress 3.1, if you click and immediately drag a control handle, the hidden portions of the image remain hidden just as before—but if you click on the control handle and hold for half a second before dragging, the hidden parts of the image will be shown as you enlarge the picture box. This makes it easy to enlarge a picture box to the desired size in a single step rather than continually stopping while the image redraws.

If you wish to move the picture box itself, use the Item tool to click and drag on it.

Manipulating an Image

QuarkXPress allows you to manipulate an imported image in a variety of ways. Many of the controls used to manipulate an image are accessed through the Modify command in the Item menu, which brings up the Picture Box Specifications dialog box shown in Figure 3.2.

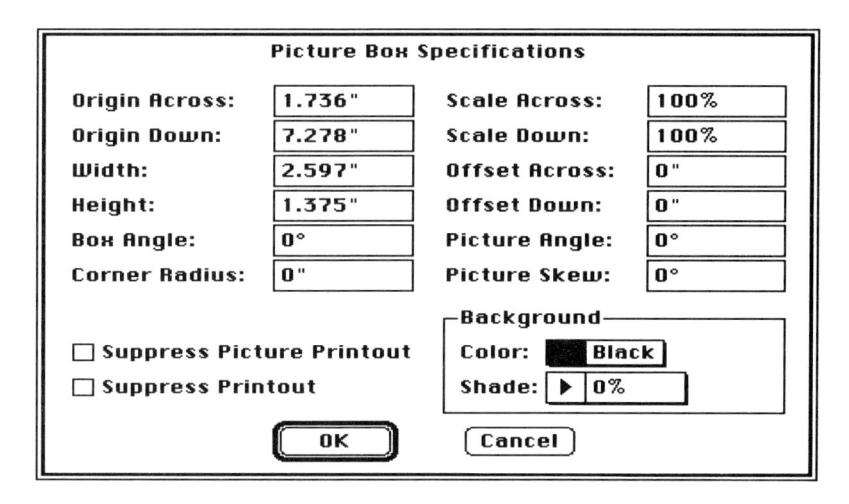

Figure 3.2. The Picture Box Specifications dialog box.

This dialog box controls the following attributes of a picture box and its contents:

- Origin Across controls how far from the 0 point on the ruler the picture box is horizontally.

- Origin Down controls how far from the 0 point on the ruler the picture box is vertically.
- Width controls the width of the picture box.
- Height controls the height of the picture box.
- Box Angle controls the rotation angle of the picture box. When you rotate the picture box, the picture within the box is rotated to the same degree.
- Corner Radius is the difference between a Rectangle picture box and a Rounded Rectangle picture box. A Rectangle picture box has a corner radius of 0", which is a sharp corner, while a Rounded Rectangle picture box has a corner radius of 0.25", which is curved. You can enter into this field any number or fraction between 0 and 2. You cannot specify a corner radius for an Oval or a Polygon picture box.
- Scale Across controls the horizontal magnification of the image. You may enter a percentage between 10% and 1000% into this field.
- Scale Down controls the vertical magnification of the image, and will also receive any percentage between 10% and 1000%.
- Offset Across controls the horizontal distance between the image and the frame of the picture box. Entering a positive number into this field will move the left edge of the image to the right that amount relative to the left edge of the picture box. Entering a negative number into this field will move the left edge of the image to the left that amount relative to the left edge of the picture box.
- Offset Down controls the vertical distance between the image and the frame of the picture box. Entering a positive number into this field will move the top edge of the image down that amount relative to the top of the picture box. Entering a negative number into this field will move the top edge of the image up that amount relative to the top of the picture box.
- Picture Angle allows the image to appear at an angle within the picture box. The amount entered into this field is equal to the amount the picture will be rotated (see Figure 3.3). If the

picture box itself is rotated, the picture will be rotated that amount in addition to the picture box rotation.
- Picture Skew allows the image to be skewed within the picture box. Skewing differs from rotation in that it causes the top of the image to be moved to the right or left as many degrees as indicated, while the bottom remains in the same position. This difference is shown in Figure 3.3.

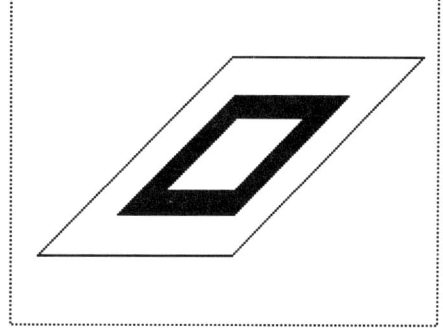

Figure 3.3. The image on the left is rotated 45°; the image on the right is skewed 45°.

Send to Back/Bring to Front

When two items occupy the same space on a page, one has to be in front of the other. In QuarkXPress the item that was created first is the one that is laid down on the page first—thus it is under any items that were created later. For example, if you create a text box, import or enter text into it, then create a picture box and drag it into the text box, the picture box will be in front of the text box. This is shown on the left in Figure 3.4. Under the Item menu are the commands Send to Back and Bring to Front. If you select the picture box and then go to the Item menu, you will see that Bring to Front is greyed, since the picture box is already in front of the text box. Send to Back is available—if you select it, the picture box will be placed behind the text box, as shown in the example on the right in Figure 3.4.

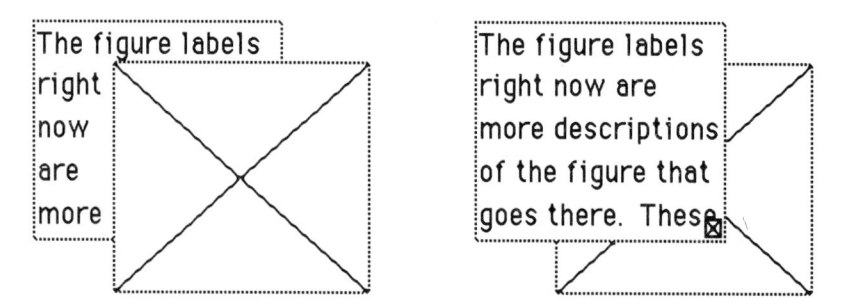

Figure 3.4. The effect that the Send to Back command has on a picture box.

Something new to QuarkXPress 3.1 is the ability to control an item's drawing layer one level at a time. The Send Behind and Bring Forward commands move the selected item just one level. Figure 3.5 shows the previous example with a line added.

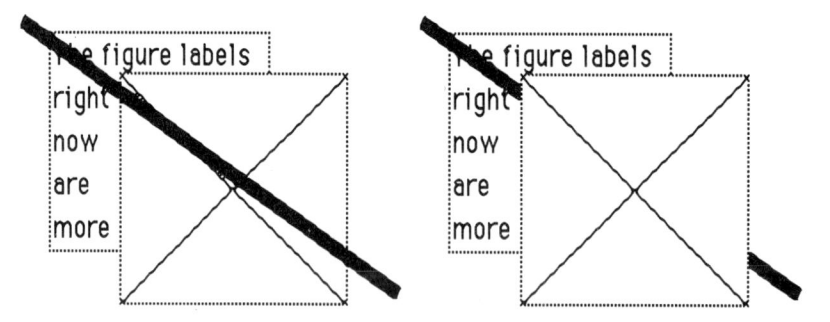

Figure 3.5. The Send Behind command was used on the line in the example on the left.

In the example on the left in Figure 3.5, the line is in front of both the text box and the picture box. When the line is selected and the Send Behind command is applied, the line moves behind the first item, in this case the picture box, as shown in the example on the right. Notice that the line is still in front of the text box. Using the Send Behind command again would send the line behind the text box as well.

Picture Box Background

The bottom-right corner of the Picture Box Specifications dialog box has two pop-out lists that allow you to shade and color the background of a picture box. If you click and hold on the Color pop-out list, you will be presented with a range of colors, as shown in Figure 3.6. While still holding down the mouse button, place the cursor over one of the colors and release. This colors the area in the picture box not covered by the image.

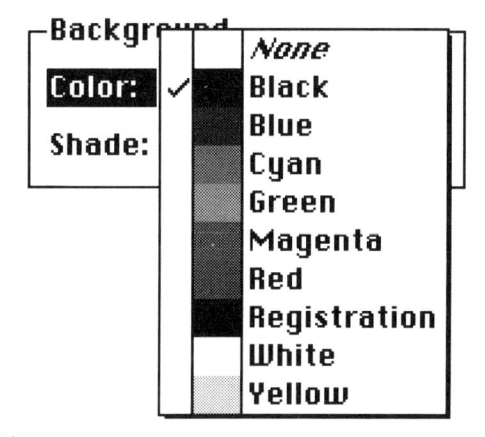

Figure 3.6. Picture Box Background colors.

You also need to give the background color a shade percentage. Clicking and holding on the Shade pop-out menu allows you to choose from the list of shadings from 0% to 100%. If you want a percentage not shown in the list you can double-click on the percentage in the Shade field and enter any value between 0% and 100% in 1/10% increments.

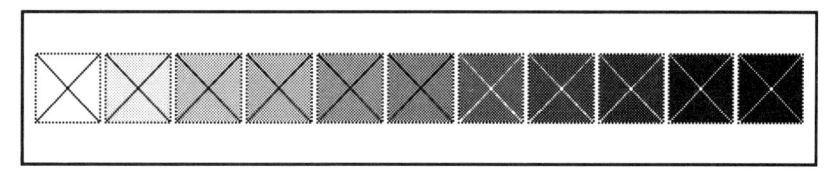

Figure 3.7. Eleven picture boxes showing 0% to 100% shading in 10% increments.

Figure 3.7 shows eleven picture boxes. Each box has had black applied as its background color. The box on the left shows the black background shaded 0%; it appears white. The box on the far right shows the black background shaded 100%, or solid black. The boxes in between are shaded in 10% increments.

If the background color of these boxes were red, the box on the far left would be a very pale red, or pink. As the shade of red increased, from left to right, the boxes would appear progressively darker until the last box, which would be the same shade as the red in the Color pop-out list.

None and White

When you select none or white as background fill, the Shade option is greyed. You cannot apply a percentage of either none or white.

There is a significant difference between none and white. For example, Figure 3.8 shows a text box with a picture box placed on top of it. In the example on the left the picture box is filled with white, which makes it cover the text. In the example on the right, the picture box is filled with none and the text shows through. Also, when you fill a picture box with 0% of a color, you won't see any color, but the picture box will cover anything under it.

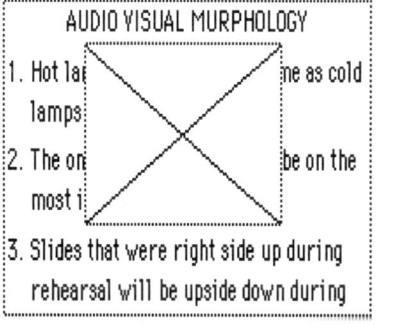

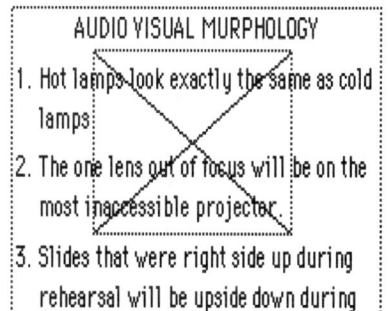

Figure 3.8. The picture box in the left example is filled with white; the one on the right is filled with none.

Another example is shown in Figure 3.9. These two images were created in a drawing program and imported into a picture box in QuarkXPress. The background of that picture box was then set to 40% black. The images are identical, except that the outer section of the image on the left is filled with white and the outer section of the image on the right is filled with none. The background shows through none, but is covered by white.

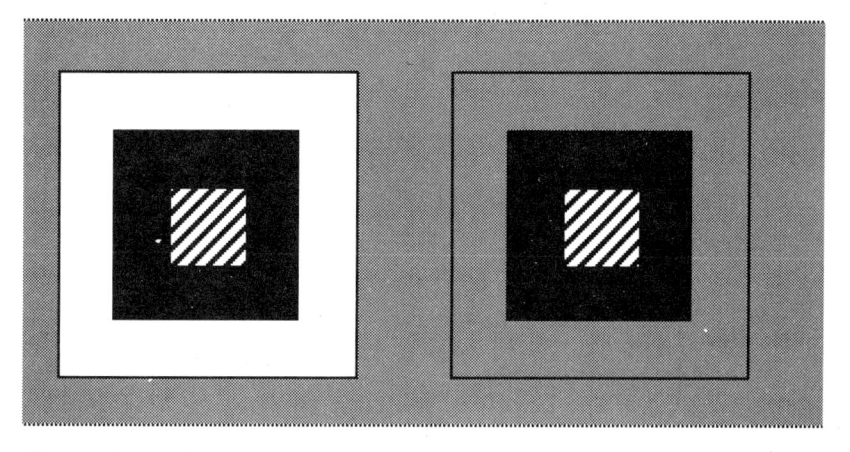

Figure 3.9. The image on the left is filled with white, while the image on the right is filled with none.

You may find that portions of some images that appear to be white are actually not filled, and a background may show through where you don't want it. You may have to open the image in a drawing program and fill those areas with an appropriate color.

Frames/Borders

QuarkXPress allows you to place a frame around a text or picture box. The Frame Specifications dialog box, shown in Figure 3.10, is accessed through the Frames command under the Item menu.

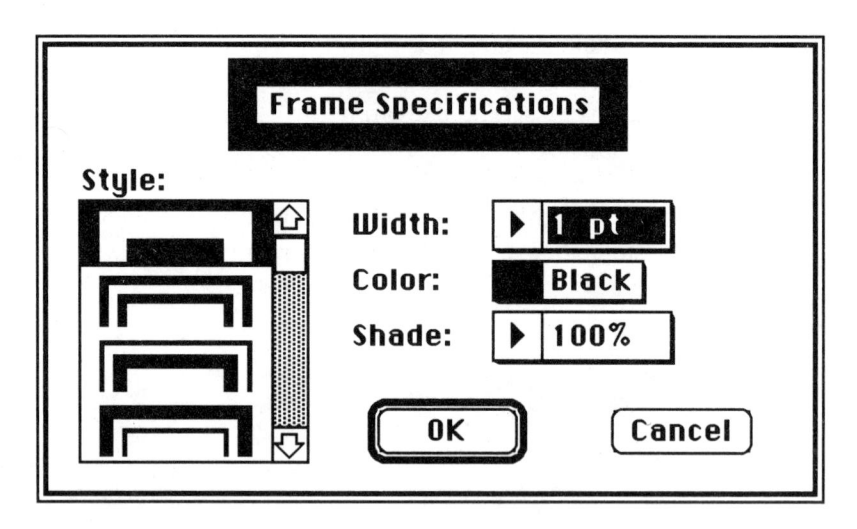

Figure 3.10. The Frame Specifications dialog box.

You can scroll through the Style field on the left of the dialog box to select the style of frame you wish to apply to the active text or picture box. Some examples are shown in Figure 3.11.

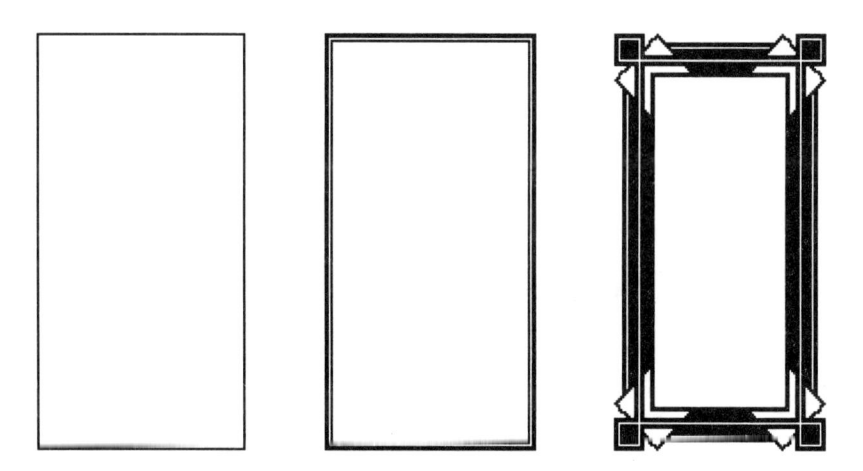

Figure 3.11. Examples of frames.

Frame Width

You use the Width field to indicate how wide you want the frame to be. Width may be entered in points or inches. When you access the Frame Specifications dialog box, the Width field is already selected, so you can simply type a number for this value. If you follow the number with "pt," then the width will be in points. If you follow it with the inches symbol ("), the width will be in inches. If you enter a number that would cause the frame to be larger than the box, QuarkXPress will give you a message indicating this.

Clicking and holding on the Width field accesses a pop-out list with various widths to choose from. The box on the left of Figure 3.12, for example, has a simple one-line frame 1 point wide. The center box has a frame with a thicker outer line and a thinner inner line. The entire frame is 4 points wide. The right box has one of QuarkXPress's "fancy" frames applied to it. The frame is 20 points wide in this example.

Frame Color and Shade

You can also apply a color and shade to a frame using the Color and Shade pop-out lists. As with picture and text boxes, you can select a shade amount from the pop-out list or enter a percentage between 0% and 100% in 1/10% increments.

Frame Inside/Outside

When you apply a frame to a box, the frame starts at the edge and continues either completely inside or completely outside the box. The General Preferences option in the Edit menu allows you to select which one.

If you click and hold on the Framing field under General Preferences, two options pop out—Inside and Outside. Placing the cursor over one of these options and releasing the mouse button selects that option. Any option you select applies to every frame in the entire document. Frame Inside/Outside is discussed in greater detail in Chapter 6.

Suppressing Picture Boxes

There are two check boxes in the lower-left corner of the Picture Box Specifications dialog box. If the Suppress Picture Printout box is checked, the image in the picture box will not print. Any frame or background color applied to the picture box will print, but the image itself will be suppressed. The Suppress Printout check box will suppress printing of the entire picture box.

Picture Box Measurement Palette

A picture box has a Measurement palette just as a text box does. Some of the contents of the palette are different, as they represent the attributes of a picture box rather than a text box. Figure 3.12 shows a typical Measurement palette.

| X: 2" | W: 1.375" | △ 0° | X%: 50% | X+: 0.222" | △ 0° |
| Y: 1.5" | H: 1.7" | ⌐ 0" | Y%: 75% | Y+: 0.139" | ⟋ 0° |

Figure 3.12. A typical Measurement palette for a picture box.

The first three portions of the Measurement palette give information about the picture box itself; the second three, about the image in the picture box. To change any of these values, simply click on them to place the insertion point.

In the first portion of the Measurement palette shown in Figure 3.12, the X value is the picture box's position along the horizontal ruler of your document. The Y value is the picture box's position along the vertical ruler.

The W and H in the second portion give the picture box's width and height.

In the third portion, the angle on top represents the rotation of the picture box; the angle on the bottom represents the corner radius.

The two percentages in the fourth portion of the Measurement palette show the magnification of the image in the picture box. The next two values represent the horizontal and vertical offset of the image within the picture box. In addition to changing these values by placing the cursor, you can click on the arrows to move the image within the picture box.

In the final portion of the Measurement palette, the angle on top represents the rotation of the image within the box. The angle on the bottom indicates the amount of skew applied to the image.

The Picture Style Menu

When a picture box is selected with the Content tool, the Style menu, shown in Figure 3.13, holds commands that allow you to manipulate and modify the image in the picture box in a variety of ways.

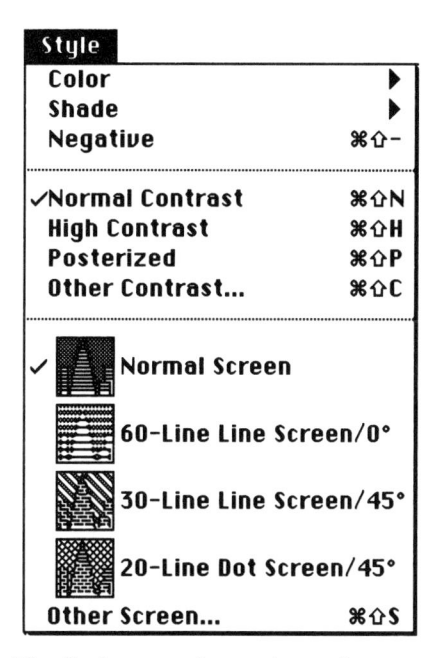

Figure 3.13. The Style menu for a picture box.

Not all of these options will be available for every image. In fact, for some images none of these options will be available. Let's look at what these commands do.

Picture Style Commands

Color

If you have an image that is black and white, you can apply color to the black portions of the image with the Color command. When you select the Color command from the Style menu, a pop-out menu appears listing the available colors—black, blue, cyan, green, magenta, red, registration, white, and yellow. When you select one of these colors the black portions of the image are changed to that color.

The Color command is greyed when a color image is selected. You must use the Contrast commands to manipulate the colors in a color image.

Shade

You can use the values from the Shade pop-out menu to lighten a black-and-white image. For example, if you chose 40% from the Shade menu, the black portions of the selected black-and-white image would be changed to 40% grey.

When a color or greyscale image is selected, the Shade command is greyed. You must use the contrast controls to manipulate the shading of a color or greyscale image.

Negative

When the Negative command is selected, the active image's color and contrast are reversed. For example, in a black-and-white image, the black areas are changed to white and the white areas are changed to black. In a color image, each color is changed to its complementary color. Red is changed to cyan, blue is changed to yellow, and so forth.

Contrast

The second part of the Style menu for picture boxes holds the Contrast commands. Contrast is the relationship between the light and dark areas of an image. Normal contrast is the contrast of the image when you imported it. When this option is checked, QuarkXPress doesn't modify the image's contrast at all. You can use the other three contrast options to modify your picture's contrast.

High contrast makes the areas of the image that are shaded less than 30% print black, and the areas shaded more than 70% print white, as shown in Figure 3.14. This creates a rather stark image that can be very effective in some applications.

Posterizing reduces the range of contrast, but does it in specific levels. A normal eight-bit greyscale image has 256 different shades of grey in it. When you posterize that image it is reduced to black, white, and four distinct levels (20%, 40%, 60%, and 80%).

Figure 3.14. The image on the left has normal contrast applied to it and the middle image, high contrast; the image on the right has been posterized.

The third part of the Style menu for picture boxes, which controls halftone screening, will be discussed in Chapter 5.

The Picture Usage Dialog Box

You can use the Picture Usage command in the Utilities menu to keep track of the pictures you have imported into a document, the type of images they are, and their status. When you select this command you are presented with a dialog box like the one shown in Figure 3.15, in which four images have been imported into a document.

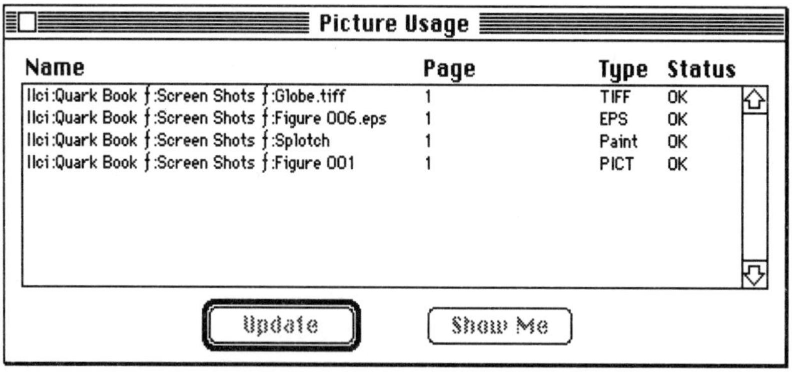

Name	Page	Type	Status
IIci:Quark Book ƒ:Screen Shots ƒ:Globe.tiff	1	TIFF	OK
IIci:Quark Book ƒ:Screen Shots ƒ:Figure 006.eps	1	EPS	OK
IIci:Quark Book ƒ:Screen Shots ƒ:Splotch	1	Paint	OK
IIci:Quark Book ƒ:Screen Shots ƒ:Figure 001	1	PICT	OK

Figure 3.15. The Picture Usage dialog box.

The Name field in Figure 3.15 tells where each image was located, when it was imported, and the file name. For example, the first image, Globe.tiff, was in the hard drive, IIci, in a folder called Screen Shots, which was in a folder called Quark Book. If the original image were moved to another drive, or even another folder, that change would not be noted in the Name section of this dialog box.

The second piece of information we are given is the page on which the image appears in the document. This information is dynamic; if you drag the image to another page of the document, the new page number will be indicated in the Picture Usage dialog box automatically.

In its third column, the Picture Usage dialog box tells you the type of image file. In Figure 3.15, the first image is a TIFF file, the second an EPS file, the third a Paint file, and the last a PICT file.

Paint images don't necessarily come from MacPaint. Many programs can save in the Paint format, and QuarkXPress doesn't really care which program the image came from, as long as it follows Apple's guidelines for that format. Also, there are a couple of variations to the PICT format but QuarkXPress will import all current ones. There are two instances in which it makes a difference what type of PICT an image is:

- If you take an image saved as one type of PICT and resave it as a different type of PICT, you will be told that the image has been modified, and allowed to update it.

- Different options will be available to you under the Style menu, depending on the type of PICT file an image is.

The last piece of information in the Picture Usage dialog box is the status of the image file. It will tell you if the image has been moved or changed since it was imported into the QuarkXPress document; if so, you will be allowed to update the image.

Missing Image Files

QuarkXPress keeps track of all of the images in a document. It checks to see if the original image is in its original location, and if not it will inform you of this in the Picture Usage dialog box.

Not all of the information needed to print a complicated image is stored in a QuarkXPress document. If it were, the document would soon become unmanageably large. When large graphic images are imported into a QuarkXPress document, a low-resolution copy of the picture is used to approximate the final image. When the document is printed, the original image file is called upon for the information needed for printing.

When an original image file has been moved or renamed, the Status portion of the Picture Usage dialog box will say "missing," as shown in Figure 3.16. In this figure the image called "Splotch" is no longer in the Screen Shots folder.

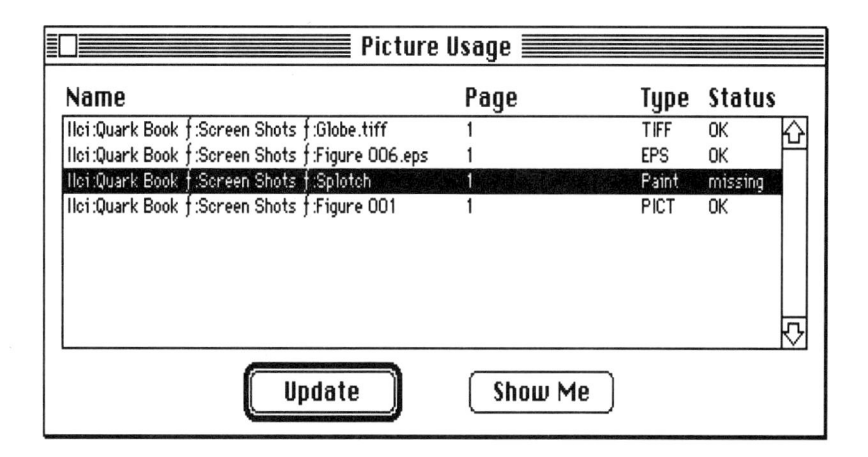

Figure 3.16. Missing files are reported in the Status column.

You can click on the image name in the dialog box to select it and activate the Update button. Clicking on the Update button will bring up a Find dialog box like the one shown in Figure 3.17, which contains the names of all images that are of the same type as the missing file.

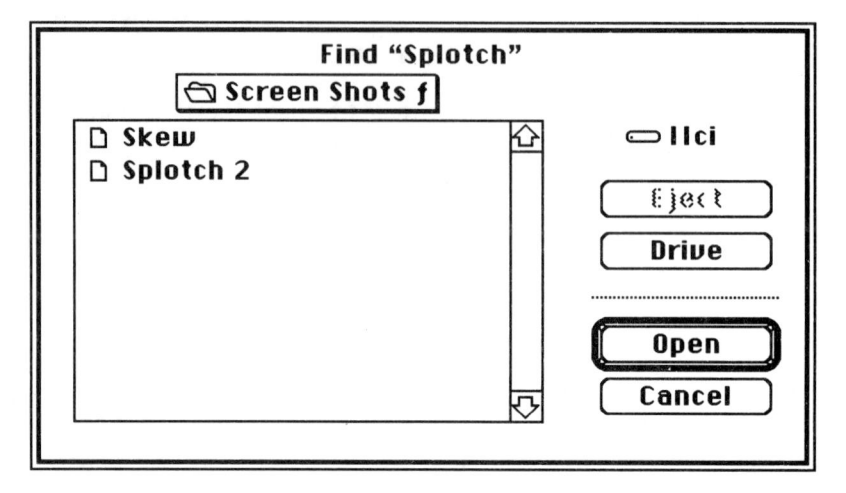

Figure 3.17. The Find dialog box for a missing image.

In this case, the Splotch file was renamed Splotch 2. To update the image you would click on the new name, then click on the Open button. This would automatically import the new image into the picture box where the original Splotch file had been placed.

QuarkXPress doesn't differentiate between files that have been renamed, files that have been renamed and changed, and files that are simply gone. If the file has been removed from the hard drive you can just place a copy back onto the hard drive from your backup source. (You do back up all of your work, don't you?)

Don't just use the Find dialog box to navigate to the backup copy; always copy text or an image from the backup source to your hard drive before working with it, then go back to the Picture Usage dialog box and update to this file.

Modified Image Files

If you open an image that has been imported into QuarkXPress in a drawing program and resave that image, the Picture Usage dialog box will tell you that the image has been modified, as shown in Figure 3.18.

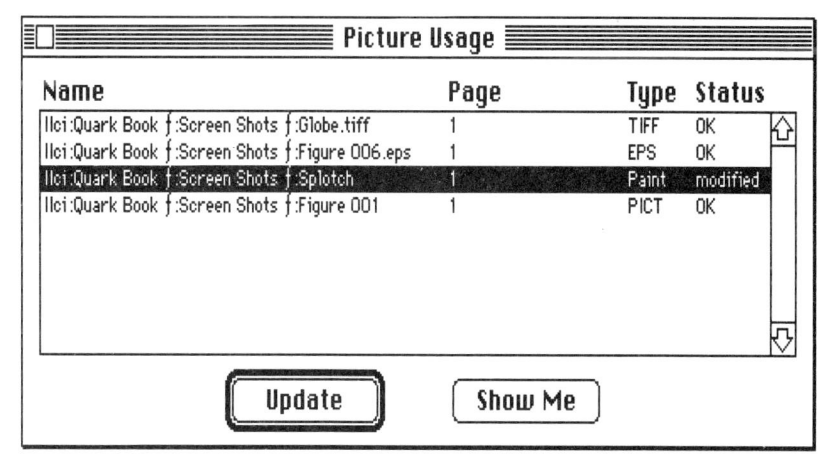

```
================= Picture Usage =================
Name                                      Page    Type    Status
IIci:Quark Book f:Screen Shots f:Globe.tiff    1       TIFF    OK
IIci:Quark Book f:Screen Shots f:Figure 006.eps 1      EPS     OK
IIci:Quark Book f:Screen Shots f:Splotch       1       Paint   modified
IIci:Quark Book f:Screen Shots f:Figure 001    1       PICT    OK

              [ Update ]      [ Show Me ]
```

Figure 3.18. The Picture Usage dialog box showing that the Splotch file has been modified.

In this figure the Status column indicates that the Splotch file has been modified. Selecting this file will activate the Update button, which brings up the dialog box, shown in Figure 3.19, that asks if you really want to update the image. You will be told that a file is modified even if the file was opened and saved with no changes. QuarkXPress notices only that the save time and date have changed.

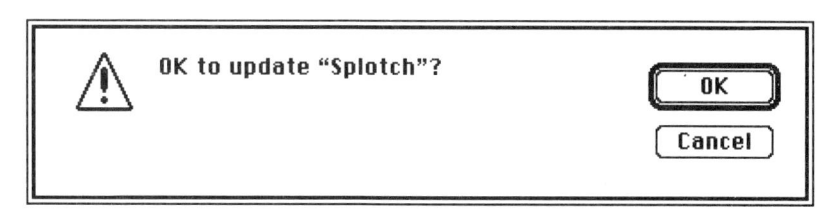

```
   ⚠   OK to update "Splotch"?            [   OK   ]
                                          [ Cancel ]
```

Figure 3.19. The dialog box asking if you really want to update the modified file.

Modifying Picture Box Shapes

It is possible to change the shape of a picture box after it has been created and even after it has had an image placed into it. There are two ways to do this: through the Picture Box Shape pop-out menu, and with the Reshape Polygon command.

The Picture Box Shape Pop-out Menu

Under the Item menu is a pop-out menu called Picture Box Shape, shown in Figure 3.20.

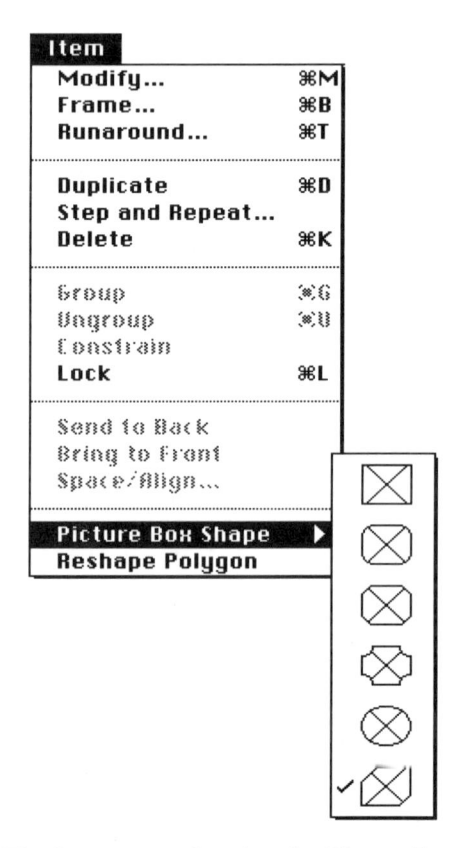

Figure 3.20. The Item menu showing the Picture Box Shape pop-out menu.

The picture box shapes can be used to change the shape of an existing picture box. To do this you select the picture box that you wish to change, then select the desired shape from the menu.

You can use the Reshape Polygon command to adjust all of these shapes except the circle. If you wish to modify a circle you must first change it into a polygon. To do this, select the circle with either the Item or Content tool. Then access the Picture Box Shape pop-out menu from the Item menu and select the last shape, the polygon. This will add control handles to the circle without actually changing its shape. You can then activate the Reshape Polygon command, which is discussed in detail in the next section, and reposition, add, or delete control handles.

An example of this is shown in Figure 3.21. The circle on the left was changed to a polygon and the Reshape Polygon command was selected. This created the second object, a rounded polygon. The cursor was then placed over one of the control handles and that handle was moved, creating a cartoon speech balloon. The final step was to place a text box over the balloon and enter the words.

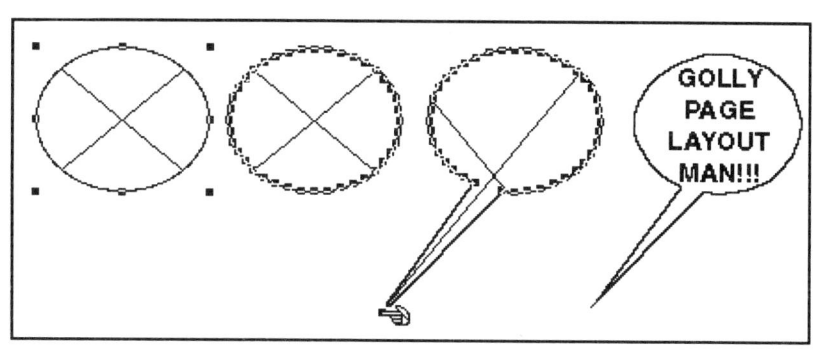

Figure 3.21. Creating a cartoon speech balloon from a round picture box.

Reshape Polygon

When a polygonal picture box is active it has eight control handles that can be used to resize the box horizontally, vertically, or both. Selecting the Reshape Polygon command under the Item menu with a polygonal picture box selected removes the usual control handles and places new ones on each corner of the polygon, as shown in Figure 3.22. These control handles work in the usual way. Use the cursor to click and drag on them to reposition the corners of the polygon.

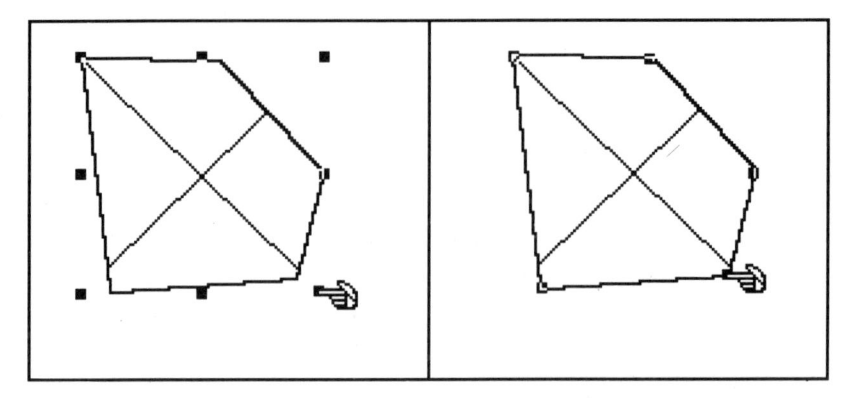

Figure 3.22. The picture box on the left displays the usual control handles. The one on the right shows where the control handles are located when the Reshape Polygon command is checked.

If you place the cursor over a line segment of a polygonal picture box while the Reshape Polygon command is checked, the cursor changes to the line segment cursor, as shown in Figure 3.23. You can click and drag on a line segment with this cursor, causing the polygon to re-form.

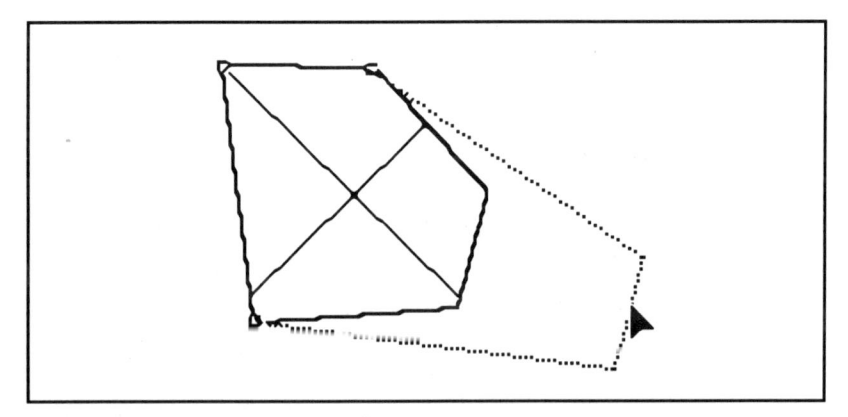

Figure 3.23. The line segment cursor being used to change the shape of a polygonal picture box.

Chapter Three ▼

The Reshape Polygon command will remain selected until y__ choose it again from the Item menu to deselect it.

Adding a Handle to a Polygon

It is also possible to add corners to the polygon when the Reshape Polygon command is checked. If you hold down the Command key when the cursor is over a line segment of a polygon, the cursor changes to the handle creation cursor, shown in Figure 3.24.

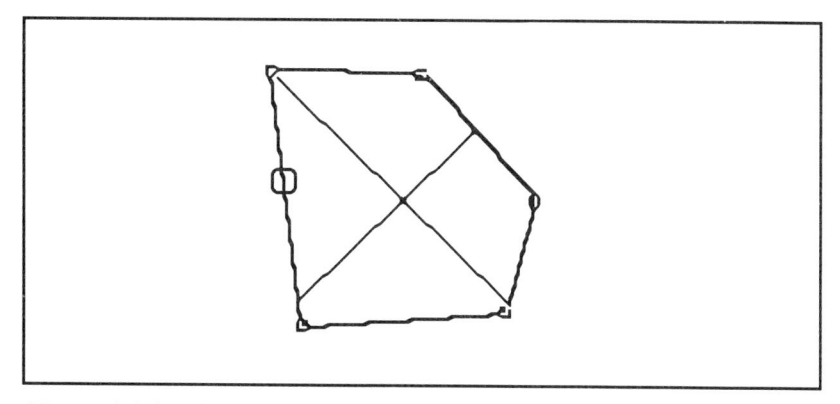

Figure 3.24. The handle creation cursor.

Clicking on a line segment with this cursor adds a control handle to the polygon at that point. When you release the Command key and place the cursor over this new control handle, the cursor changes to the pointing finger cursor, allowing you to move the new control handle.

Deleting a Handle from a Polygon

Holding down the Command key and placing the cursor over a control handle when the Reshape Polygon command is checked causes the cursor to change into the handle deletion cursor. Clicking on an existing control handle with the handle deletion cursor removes that handle. A single line then connects the two adjacent handles.

Runaround Options

Often you will want to wrap text around an image; for this you can use the Runaround option in the Item menu. When you select this option you are presented with the Runaround Specifications dialog box, shown in Figure 3.25.

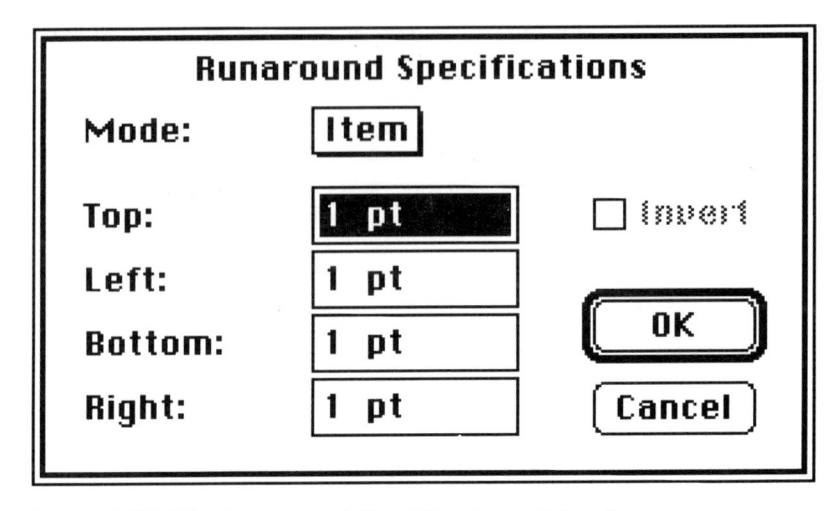

Figure 3.25. The Runaround Specifications dialog box.

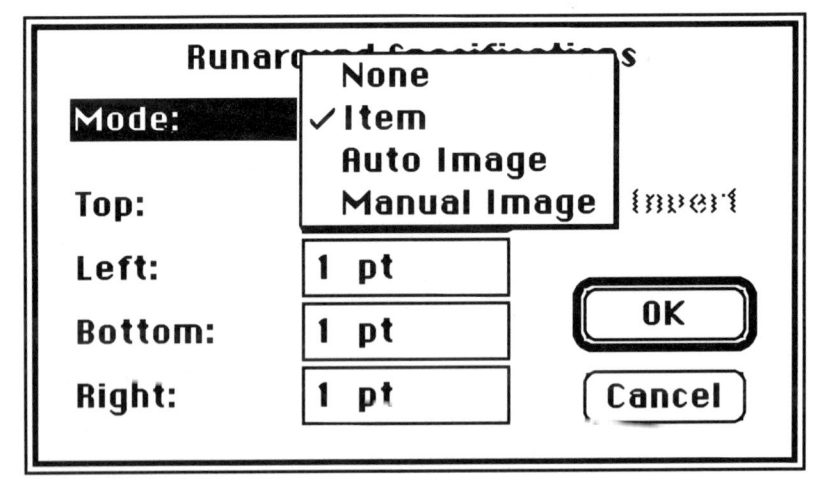

Figure 3.26. The Mode pop-out menu.

The pop-out list on the top labeled Mode, shown in Figure 3.26, allows you to change the runaround options. When a text box is selected, only Item and None are available. Item is the default; it flows text around the item selected in your document. None flows text behind the active item. For a picture box, all four options are available. You will most often apply a runaround option to a picture box that is on top of a text box.

None

The first runaround option is None. When this option is applied to a picture box the path of the text is not changed at all. It will appear as if the picture were placed over the text. When None is selected as the runaround option, there is no need to specify a text outset because the text isn't affected by the picture box over it.

Figure 3.27 shows two examples of a text box over which a picture box has been placed, using the None option.

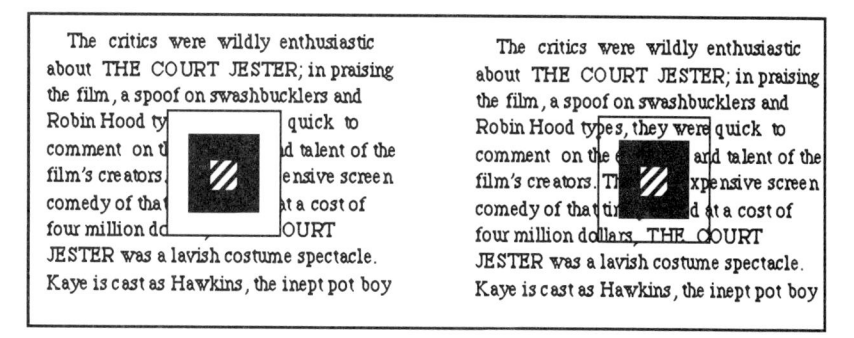

Figure 3.27. Two examples of a text box over which a picture box has been placed using the None option.

The text flows uninterrupted behind both images. The difference between them lies in the treatment of the image's background. Remember that you control the fill of a picture box using the Modify command in the Item menu. The fill behind the black-framed image in the picture box on the left was filled with white, which occludes the text where it runs behind the object. The fill behind the graphic image on the right is filled with none, so the text shows through the image.

Figure 3.28 shows what happens when the background of the picture box is filled with something other than none and white.

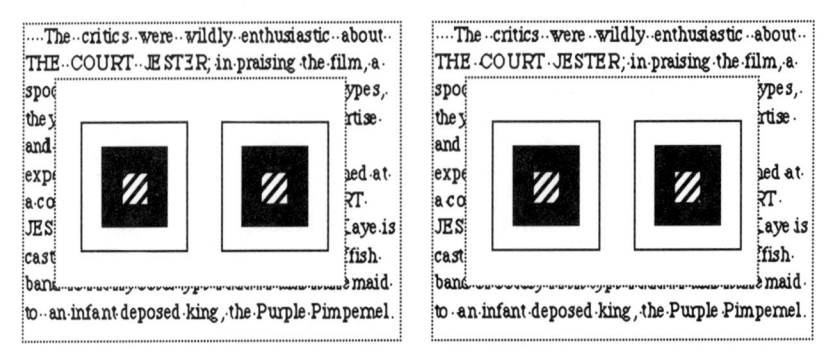

Figure 3.28. The picture box over the text has been filled with 40% black in the example on the left, and 0% black in the example on the right.

In the example on the left of Figure 3.28, the picture box is filled with 40% black. This fill covers the text behind the entire area of the picture box. In the example on the right, the background is filled with 0% black, which has the same effect as filling it with white. Even though the shade is 0%, the text cannot show through.

Item

Item runaround causes the text to continue along a line until it hits the edge of a picture box, where it will begin to wrap to following lines. If the active item is a text box or a Rectangle picture box, the Top, Left, Bottom, and Right fields become active when you choose Item. These four fields are used to set the text outset, which determines how close text comes to the image before it is affected by the runaround. Thus, the amounts entered into these fields determine how close to the edge of the box the text comes before it wraps to the next line. Figure 3.29 shows a Rectangle picture box with Item runaround and 1 point text outset applied.

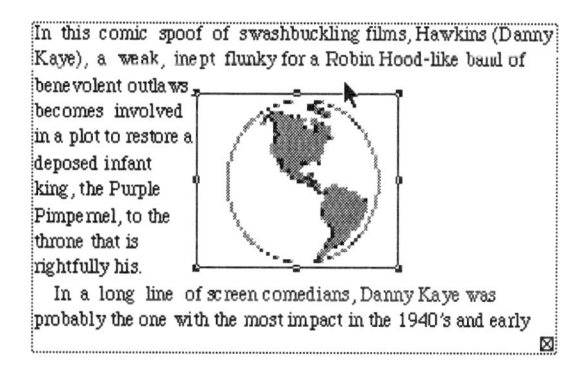

Figure 3.29. Item runaround has been applied to this picture box.

Notice that the text isn't 1 point from the edge of the picture box on many lines. This is because of the text alignment. Remember that when text is left aligned, if there is not enough space at the end of a line for a word, that word is wrapped to the next line, leaving a space at the end of the line and causing the right edge of the text to appear ragged. This also happens when runaround is used. If a word won't fit on the line or comes closer than the text outset distance, it is wrapped to the next line, leaving a space.

With right alignment, the text will be placed evenly along the side of the picture box and the extra space will appear along the left edge of the text, as shown on the left in Figure 3.30. If the text is justified, it will align smoothly along both the edge of the text box and the edge of the picture box, as shown on the right in Figure 3.30.

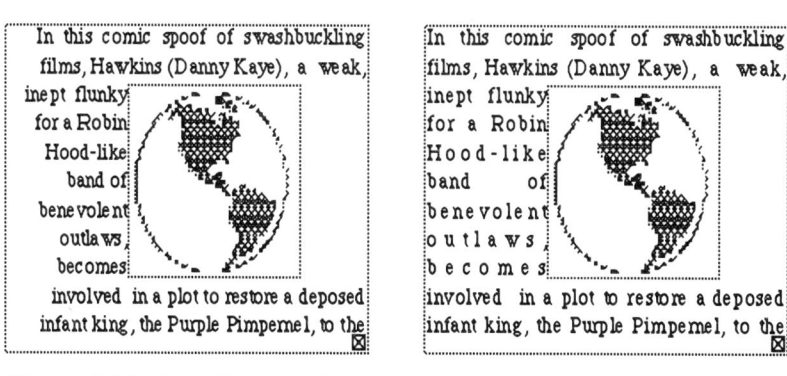

Figure 3.30. Text that is right aligned and justified, respectively, with a 1 point text outset.

The text doesn't continue on the far side of the picture box even though there is enough room for it. This is just the way that QuarkXPress handles runaround. If you want the text to wrap on both sides of an image, you must place the text in more than one column.

Auto Image

When Auto Image is selected as the runaround option, QuarkXPress creates a border around the edge of the image within the picture box rather than around the picture box itself. When Auto Image is chosen, only one Text Outset field is active; the amount entered into this field determines the amount that the image's border is offset. Figure 3.31 shows three text boxes with picture boxes over them. In all three examples, Auto Item runaround has been applied to the picture box so that the text wraps around the globe that has been imported into it.

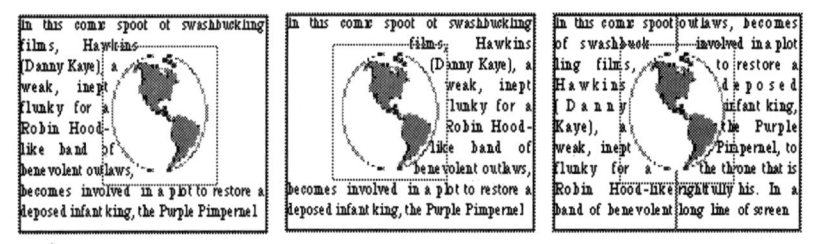

Figure 3.31. These examples illustrate the effect of Auto Item runaround.

In the first example, the image is offset slightly to the right of the text box, causing the text to wrap around the left side of the image. In the middle example, the image is offset slightly to the left, causing the text to wrap around the right side of the image. In the third example, the text has been placed in two columns, allowing it to wrap around both sides of the image.

Manual Image

The last of the runaround options is Manual Image. This option works much the same as Auto Image, except that you can manipulate the border, which is placed around the image by entering a number into the Text Offset field into the Runaround Specifications dialog box.

Occasionally, particularly for some irregularly shaped objects, the border will come closer to some portions of the image than you wish. With Manual Image selected, you can click and drag the border's control handles to place it closer or further from the image. Figure 3.32 shows an enlarged portion of an image to which Manual Image has been applied. In the example on the left, the border overlaps the bumper of the car, allowing text to touch the image. In the example on the right, the border's control handles have been dragged away from the image, causing the text to wrap further away from it.

Figure 3.32. The border around the image on the right has been dragged further from the image, causing the text to wrap properly.

You can add a control handle to a Manual Image border by holding down the Control key and clicking on a segment of the border. To remove the handle, place the cursor over it, hold down the Control key, and click once. The two control handles on either side of the removed handle will be connected with an unbroken segment.

When Manual Image is selected, the Invert option becomes available. With it you can flow text *within* a picture shape. To do this, you must make sure that the text box is behind the picture box containing the runaround polygon, and, to restrict the flow of text to within the runaround polygon, that the text box and the picture box are the same size.

Summary

- ▼ QuarkXPress can import images that have been saved in MacPaint, PICT, TIFF, and EPS formats. A thumbnail view of a graphic image can be viewed before the image is imported.

- ▼ You must create a picture box for any image you wish to import. You can create a picture box that is rectangular, round/oval, or free-form polygon. A picture box can be resized at any time.

- ▼ The picture box Specifications dialog box can be used to manipulate a picture box's origin across, origin down, width, height, angle, and corner radius, as well as the image's scale across, scale down, offset across, offset down, angle, and skew.

- ▼ The object created most recently appears over objects created before it.

- ▼ The background of a picture box can be controlled using the Picture Box Specifications dialog box. The background can be none, or a color shaded between 0% and 100%.

- ▼ The Frame Specifications dialog box can be used to select and apply a frame or border to a picture box. You also have control over that frame's width, color, and shade.

- ▼ The picture box Measurement palette can be used to control a picture box's dimensions, corner radius, and position on the page.

- ▼ The Picture Style menu can be used to control many attributes of a graphic image, including its color and shade, whether it is negative or positive, and the picture contrast.

- ▼ The Picture Usage dialog box allows you to update any pictures that have been modified since they were placed into the document. It will also notify you of any missing images. You can preview a thumbnail of the modified image before updating it.

- ▼ A picture box's shape can be changed after creation using the Picture Box Shape pop-out menu under the Item menu. A shape can be selected from those presented, or the current shape can be modified.

- ▼ The Runaround option under the Item menu can be used to control how text flows around a picture box or around the image within it.

CHAPTER 4

In This Chapter

- ▼ **Moving Around a Document**
    - The Scroll Bars
    - The Go To Command
- ▼ **Flowing Text**
    - Linking
    - Adding/Deleting Text in Linked Boxes
    - Breaking Links
- ▼ **Master Pages**
- ▼ **Automatic Text Chain**
    - Automatic Page Insertion
    - Automatic Linking
- ▼ **Inserting and Arranging Pages**
    - Sections and Automatic Page Numbers
- ▼ **The Document Layout Palette**
    - Creating Master Pages with the Document Layout Palette
    - Adding Pages with the Document Layout Palette
    - Deleting Pages with the Document Layout Palette
    - Moving Pages with the Document Layout Palette
- ▼ **Automatic Page Numbering**
- ▼ **Jump Commands**
- ▼ **Grouping**
- ▼ **Locking**
- ▼ **Summary**

You Will Learn

▼ How to link text boxes so that text can flow through several boxes.

▼ How to create and use Master pages and automatically insert them into a text chain.

▼ How to designate groups of pages as sections with their own page numbering scheme.

▼ How to rearrange pages within a document.

▼ How to use the Document Layout palette to add, delete, and move pages.

▼ How to use the Automatic Page Numbering commands.

▼ How to combine several items into a group, and how to lock items in place.

Moving Around in a Document

The Scroll Bars

You can click on the arrows at the top and bottom of the vertical scroll bars to scroll forward or backward within a document. If you click on either the up or down scroll bar arrow, the document will move in that direction one width of the control handle, which is the white square in the right-hand scroll bar. If you click on the scroll bar above or below the control handle, the document will scroll in that direction one screen length. Clicking on the control handle and dragging it up or down moves you within the document.

If you hold down the Option key while dragging on the scroll bar control handle, you can view a *live scroll;* that is, you will see your document scrolling as you drag the control handle.

The Go To Command

Under the Page menu is the Go To command. When this command is selected, a dialog box with one field is presented. You enter the number of the page that you wish to move to in that section and click on the OK button.

If you have split your document into several sections you will be taken to the first instance of the page number entered, unless you also enter the prefix. (Prefixes will be discussed in greater detail later in this chapter.) If you wish to go to a specific section and page, enter the prefix and the number. This command is not case-sensitive; that is, you can get to page B by entering "b" in the Go To field.

Placing a plus sign (+) before the page number in the Go To field will take you that number of pages into the document, even if you have split the document into several separately numbered sections. For example, "+17" would take you to the seventeenth page of the document, even if you have designated it as, say, the first page in the fourth section.

Flowing Text

In order to place text on a page you must have a text box to contain it. When you have more text than can fit into one text box, QuarkXPress allows you to create another text box and tell the text to continue into that box. This continuation is called *flowing*. If the text won't fit into two boxes you can flow it into three, four, or as many as you wish.

The Linking and Unlinking tools, the last two tools on the Tool palette, are used to connect text boxes. The Linking tool looks like three chain links; the Unlinking tool looks like three links with the middle one broken.

Linking

To link two text boxes, select the Linking tool and click on the box in which you want the text to begin. That box will become highlighted with the moving, marquee border. You can then click on the box that you want the excess text to flow into. These two boxes can be directly next to each other on a page, or they can be separated by as many pages as you have memory for on your Macintosh.

Text doesn't have to flow in sequential order within the document, either; you can have it start in a box on page 99 and continue in a box on page 2. To do this you would use the Linking tool to select the box on page 99, then, without changing tools, you would go to page 2 and click on the box on that page.

If you have used the Linking tool to connect two boxes but later discover that you want the text to flow into a third box, you can add that connection at any time. To have text flow into more boxes you would use the Linking tool to select the last box in the chain, then click on the box that you wish to add to the chain. This process can be repeated as many times as needed.

Because the text can flow to any page, whether previous or following, you must remember that the order in which you click on the boxes is more important than the order in which the boxes appear within the document. Say, for instance, that you created a text box and imported text into it, then created a second text box for the excess text to flow into. If the second text box is selected with the

Linking tool before the first, the text will flow from the second box to the first even though it was originally imported into the first box.

You can tell which text boxes are linked by clicking on either the Linking or the Unlinking tool, then clicking on one of the boxes. When one of the linked boxes is selected with either tool, arrows appear showing the linking relationships between the text boxes in that chain, as shown in Figure 4.1. You can tell in which direction the text is flowing by the direction of the arrow. Its feathered end starts in the bottom-right corner of the "from" box, and takes its pointed end to the top-left corner of the "to" box.

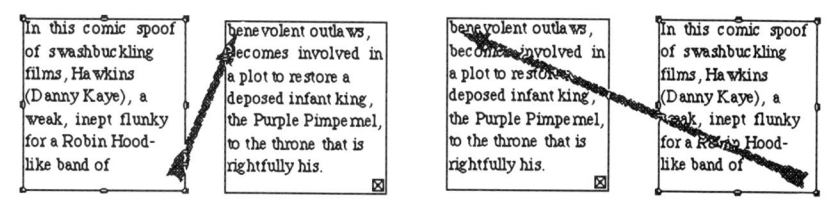

Figure 4.1. Text flows from the first box into the second, and from the fourth box to the third.

Adding/Deleting Text in Linked Boxes

If you add or delete text in a box that is part of a set of linked text boxes, the text will reflow throughout all of the text boxes in the linked set. If you add text to a set of linked boxes, you should check the last box in the set to make sure all of the text fits. If it doesn't, a square with an x in it will appear in the bottom-right corner of the last box; this is called the *text overflow indicator.*

When you use the Select All command from the Edit menu, all of the text in the linked set of boxes will be selected. Any changes made to the selected text (such as changing the font size, or bolding text) will apply to all of the text in the chain.

▼ **NOTE** ▲ Remember that if you press any key when text is selected, the selected text will be replaced with that keystroke.

Even if all of the text has been removed from a set of linked text boxes, the links themselves remain. If you wish to enter or import text into a set of empty linked boxes, no matter which box you click on with the Content tool, you will only be able to place the cursor into the first text box in the chain. That won't necessarily be the box on the earliest page; it will be the box that you selected first with the Linking tool.

Breaking Links

To break the link between two boxes, select the Unlink tool and click on the feathers of the arrow between the two boxes. Sometimes part of the feathers is inside the box and part is outside. You must click the Unlinking tool on the part of the feathers inside the text box for the unlinking to take effect. When you click on the feathers, the arrow disappears and the text no longer flows beyond that text box. If the text boxes that you unlink are part of a set of text boxes, text will not flow beyond the place where the link was broken. The link between subsequent boxes will remain, however, and if you import new text into the box following the one where the link was broken, the overflow will still go into the next.

Master Pages

Master pages are templates that can be used when new pages are created. They contain the same types of objects as normal pages—text boxes, picture boxes, and lines. Items placed on a Master page are called *Master items*, and can include letterheads, logos, footers, background patterns, pre-set layout patterns of text, and picture boxes—almost anything that you want to place on more than one page should probably be put on a Master page.

Anything that exists on a Master page will exist on a page created based on that Master page.

Automatic Text Chain

If you import text into a set of linked text boxes and there is more text than fits in the available space, you can tell QuarkXPress to automatically create new pages to hold the overflow. You must have a Master page with a text box, and Automatic Linking must be turned on. First we'll talk about how to enable Automatic Page Insertion, and then we'll see how to turn on a Master page's Automatic Linking.

Automatic Page Insertion

Automatic Page Insertion is turned on and off and its options selected through the General Preferences dialog box, accessed through the Preferences pop-out menu under the Edit menu.

In Figure 4.2, the Auto Page Insertion pop-out menu has been "popped out" from the General Preferences dialog box, showing its options.

```
Auto Page Insertion:  Off
                      End of Story
                     ✓End of Section
                      End of Document
```

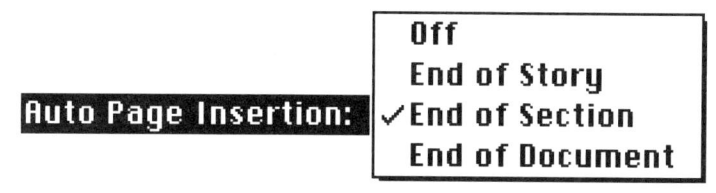

Figure 4.2. The Auto Page Insertion options.

When Auto Page Insertion is turned off, no pages will be inserted if an imported story is too long. The default selection is End of Section. When a story is too long to fit in the linked text boxes, enough additional pages will be inserted at the end of the section to hold the overflow. The new pages will be based on the same Master page as the last page in the section. When End of Story is selected, pages will be inserted after the page that holds the last text box in the current chain, and the new pages will be based on that page's Master page format.

When End of Document is selected, the new pages will be inserted at the end of the document, and will be based on the Master page of the last page in the document.

In all three instances, the Master page on which the new pages are based must have a text box, and Automatic Linking must be applied to it.

Automatic Linking

The top-left corner of all Master pages contains the Link/Unlink icon. This icon is the connection to the document for linking text to that Master page. When the icon is the broken chain, that Master page can't be used with Automatic Page Insertion.

To enable Automatic Linking, the Master page first must have a text box. It doesn't matter whether the text box was created manually or by selecting Automatic Text Box when the document was created. Once there is a text box, you use the Linking tool to click on the Linking icon in the top-left corner of the Master page, then on the text box on that Master page.

There can be more than one text box on the Master page, and they can be linked to one another. But you must use the Linking tool to link the Automatic Linking icon to the first box in that Master page's chain.

Inserting and Arranging Pages

You may insert pages using the Insert command from the Page menu. This brings up the Insert Pages dialog box shown in Figure 4.3.

The Insert field in the Insert Pages dialog box is where you enter the number of pages you wish to add to the document. There are three buttons you can use to indicate where you wish these new pages to be inserted: before the current page, after the current page, or at the end of the document.

You will be able to access the Link to Current Text Chain box only if these conditions are met:

1. A text box is active on the current page.
2. The page(s) being inserted contain a text box—either from a Master page that contains a text box, or because Automatic Text Box was selected when the document was created.

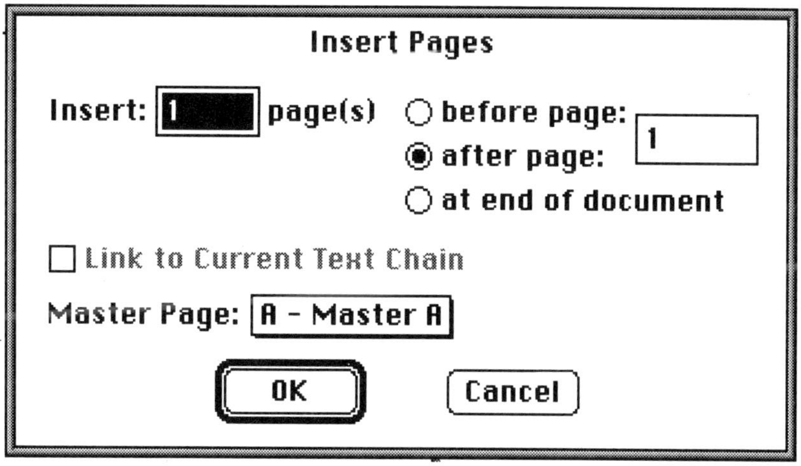

Figure 4.3. The Insert Pages dialog box.

If these conditions are met then the text box(es) on the inserted page(s) will be linked to the active text box on the current page.

If you have created several master pages, the Master Page pop-out menu on the Insert Pages dialog box allows you to select which of these will be copied to create the new page(s). Click on the OK button to add the desired number of pages.

All pages are given an automatic page number. If pages are inserted into the document, the automatic page numbers will change on all following pages. The following sections explain how to control these page numbers.

Sections and Automatic Page Numbers

Next to the current viewing percentage, in the bottom-left corner of the Document window, is the Page Number field. This field shows the number of the current page. Sometimes you will be able to see parts of more than one page in the document window; the page number coincides with the page that occupies the very top of the document window.

If you use the Insert command under the Page menu to add pages to a document, they will be numbered consecutively, from the first page to the last, using Arabic numerals. QuarkXPress gives you control over this numbering scheme through the Section command under the Page menu. When this option is selected, the Section dialog box is presented, as shown in Figure 4.4.

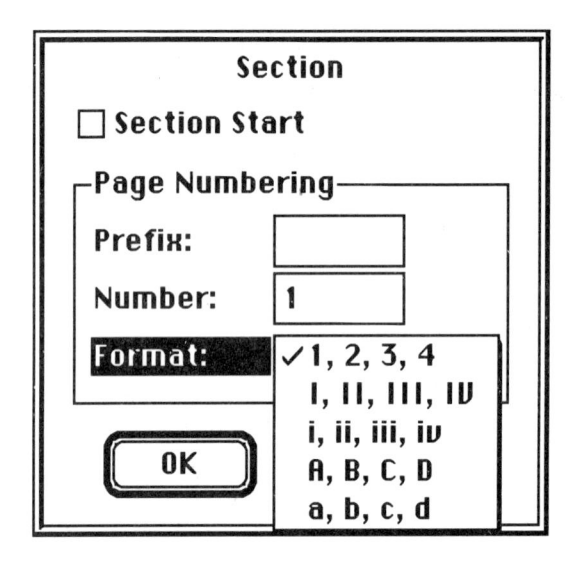

Figure 4.4. The Section dialog box allows you to start a new section and control the automatic page numbering in that section.

Controlling Sections and Page Numbers

The Section dialog box allows you to split up the current document into several parts, or sections, each with its own page numbering scheme. For example, if you were creating a document with a long table of contents, several chapters, an appendix, and a glossary, you could make each one a section.

To do this, you would go to the page that you wished to make the first page in a section and select the Section option from the Page menu to bring up the Section dialog box. Checking the Section Start box would make that page the first page in the new section, and its page number would be whatever you entered into the Number field.

The Prefix field will accept up to four characters to be placed before each page number in a given section. For example, if you went to the first page of the third chapter in our imaginary document, checked the Section Start box, entered "1" into the Number field and "3-" into the Prefix field, then the first page in that section would be number "3-1," the second page "3-2," the third "3-3," and so on.

The Format pop-out menu allows you to choose whether the page number will appear in Arabic numerals, uppercase or lowercase Roman numerals, or uppercase or lowercase letters. For example, if you had selected lowercase Roman numerals in the previous example, the first page would be "3-i," the second "3-ii," the seventy-fourth "3-lxxiv," and so on.

You must always enter the page number into the Number field in Arabic numerals. If you want the page number to appear in another format, select that format from the Format pop-out menu—don't enter that format into the Number field.

Merging Adjacent Sections

It is very easy to merge two sections. They must, however, be next to each other in the document. First, make sure that the page number in the bottom-left corner of the document window indicates that you are viewing the first page of the second of the two sections you wish to merge. Then select the Section option from the Page menu to access the Section dialog box, and uncheck the Section Start box. The page Prefix, Number, and Format fields become greyed, and all pages from the current page to the first page of the next section become part of the previous section.

The Document Layout Palette

Selecting Show Document Layout from the View menu brings out a Document Layout palette like the one shown in Figure 4.5, which shows the layout for a document that has four pages.

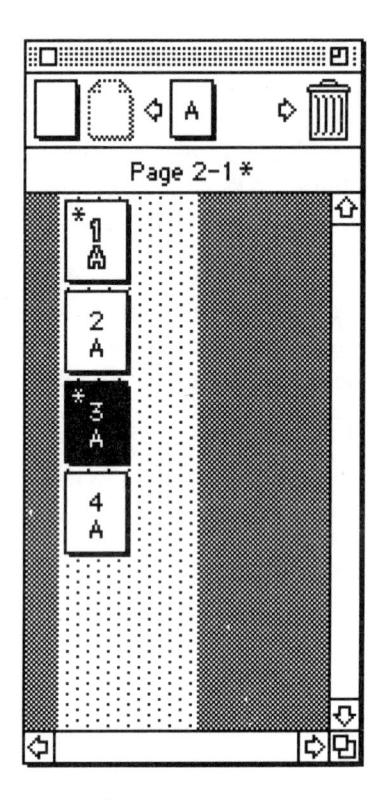

Figure 4.5. A Document Layout palette.

The pages in Figure 4.5 are consecutively numbered even though the document has been split up into two sections. The third page in the document—called the *absolute* third page—is the first page in the second section, which is prefixed with "2-."

The absolute third page has been selected and its page number (with prefix) is listed above the page thumbnails. In this case the third page is numbered "2-1," and there is an asterisk next to it, indicating that it is the first page in a section.

The "A" under the absolute page number on the thumbnail tells you on which Master page that page was based when it was created. If there is no letter under the absolute page number, then it was created based on a blank page.

You can use the Document Layout palette to move to a specific page by double-clicking on that page's thumbnail. When a page is selected in the Document Layout palette, you can click on its section/page number (below the thumbnails) to access the Section dialog box.

Creating Master Pages with the Document Layout Palette

You can create new Master pages from the Document Layout palette. At the top of the Document Layout palette there is already one Master page, called Master A.

If you double-click on the Master page thumbnail in the Document Layout palette, that Master page will be displayed in the document window. Or you can access a Master page by selecting its name from the Display pop-out menu under the Page menu.

To create a new Master page, select either blank-page thumbnail from the top of the Document Layout palette. Drag the page you have selected to the right of the Master A thumbnail, and drop it to the area between the scroll arrows. Release the mouse button when the cursor changes to look like a cross with arrows. A new Master page is created, and double-clicking on its icon will display it in the document window so you can work with it. You can create up to 127 master pages for a document.

If you click on a Master page's thumbnail, its name is preselected to appear in the space below it. To name a new master page, simply click once on its icon to highlight the field where Master page names are displayed, and enter the name you desire. You can enter up to sixty-three characters, and can also click on a Master page name to place the insertion point and edit the name.

Adding Pages with the Document Layout Palette

The Document Layout palette can be used to add, delete, and move pages. Along the top of the Document Layout palette are a trash can and several thumbnails indicating the types of pages that can be created. The first thumbnail, on the left, is a blank page. The page containing the capital "A" is Master Page A.

You can add a new page, based on either the blank page or Master Page A, to your document by clicking and dragging one of these thumbnail pages to the dotted document area below. The new page will be inserted into the document in the position where you release the mouse button.

If you drag the new page so that the outline overlaps an existing page, the cursor changes into a small, down arrow, indicating that the new page will be inserted below that page. If you drag the image until the cursor highlights an existing page, that page will be replaced with the new page when you release the mouse button; you will lose all information that was on the original page when it is replaced.

Deleting Pages with the Document Layout Palette

To delete a page in the Document Layout palette, simply click on that page and drag it into the trash can at the top of the palette. That page will be deleted from the document and the page numbers of the following pages will change to reflect their new positions.

Moving Pages with the Document Layout Palette

You can click and drag on a page thumbnail to change that page's location within the document. When you release the mouse button, that page, and all following pages, will be renumbered to reflect the changes. If you move a page from one section to another, the moved page's number will change to contain the prefix of the new section. For example, in Figure 4.4, there are two pages in section 1 and two pages in section 2. If you were to place the first page in section 2 between the first and second pages of section 1, then section 1 would have three pages numbered "1-1," "1-2," and "1-3." Section 2 would have one page numbered "2-1."

All of this is much easier than it sounds. Basically, reordering the thumbnails in the Document Layout palette reorders the pages in the document the same way.

Automatic Page Numbering

There is an automatic page number command that retrieves the current page number. Holding down the Command key and pressing "3" when the cursor is in a text box causes the current page number to be automatically placed in that box. This is particularly useful on a Master page. You can create a text box in a corner (or wherever you wish the page number to appear) and enter the Current Page Number command (Command-3) into that box. Every page created based on that Master page will automatically show its current page number.

The text box containing the Current Page Number command doesn't have to be linked to anything or overlap anything. It simply has to be on the page.

Jump Commands

Anyone who has ever read a newspaper or magazine is familiar with the term "Continued on page...." This is called a *jump line,* because it indicates where the end of the article will "jump" to. To jump in Quark, you must link text boxes that are not adjacent. You could finish your document and manually find the jump pages and enter them for each story, but QuarkXPress offers you a better way. You can enter jump lines with automatic page-numbering commands to keep track of where a story started and where it continues. Figure 4.6 shows a text box that is the second of three linked text boxes.

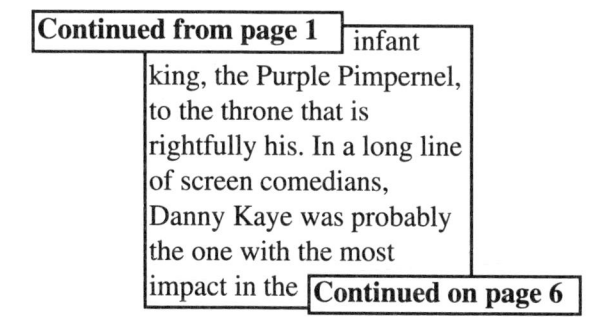

```
┌─────────────────────────┐
│ Continued from page 1   │ infant
├─────────────────────────┤
│ king, the Purple Pimpernel, │
│ to the throne that is       │
│ rightfully his. In a long line │
│ of screen comedians,        │
│ Danny Kaye was probably     │
│ the one with the most       │
│ impact in the │ Continued on page 6 │
└───────────────┴─────────────────────┘
```

Figure 4.6. The second text box in a jumped article.

Text was imported into the first box and automatically flowed into the other two. Overlapping the linked text box are two smaller text boxes: one in the top-left corner, and one in the bottom-right corner. Neither of these smaller text boxes is linked to anything. To make jump lines, create text boxes such as these on your page.

Into the top text box, enter the text "Continued from page"; then hold down the Command key while pressing "2." The number of the page that your text is continued from will automatically appear. Command-2 is the Previous Box Page Number command. When a text box that contains this command overlaps a linked text box, it searches out the previous link and retrieves its page number. If the text box that this text flows from is moved to another page, that change will automatically be reflected by the Previous Box Page Number command in the jump-line text box.

You can use a similar procedure for the jump line at the bottom of your page. Enter the text "Continued from page," then hold down the Command key and press "4." Command-4 is the Next Box Page Number command, and retrieves the page number of the next text box in the linked set.

The text boxes containing the Previous Box Page Number and Next Box Page Number are not linked to anything. They must simply overlap a text box that is part of a linked set.

Grouping

Figure 4.6 contains three separate text boxes. The two text boxes containing the jump lines must overlap the linked box. If you need to move the main text box you must also move the two jump line text boxes to retain their effect. One way to do this is to select all three boxes each time you move them. Another way is to combine them into a group.

To group several items you must first select them. There are two ways to select several items. One is to select an item with the Item tool, then hold down the Shift key while selecting more items.

Another way is to click and hold the Item tool on an unoccupied area of the screen—that is, outside of any text boxes—and drag a rectangle over several objects. All objects within this rectangle will become selected.

Once you have several items selected, you can invoke the Group command from the Item menu to combine them into one group. Selecting any item in a group selects the entire group. You can group any combination of text boxes, picture boxes, and lines.

When a text box is part of a group, it cannot be individually selected with the Item tool, but the text within it can be edited with the Content tool. Grouping also has no effect on how text flows through linked text boxes.

Selecting the Ungroup command from the Item menu separates the currently highlighted group.

Locking

If you are sure that you have a linked text box in its final location, you can use the Lock command from the Item menu to lock it on the page, preventing accidental adjustment.

When an item is selected and the Lock command is used, that item can no longer be moved or resized by the Item tool. When you click on a locked item, the cursor changes into a padlock icon. A locked item's location and attributes can still be manipulated using the Measurement palette or the Modify dialog box from the Item menu.

Summary

▼ The Linking tool is used to cause text to flow from one text box to another.

▼ The Unlinking tool is used to break the link and stop text from flowing between two linked text boxes.

▼ Master pages are used as templates to create new pages. Any object (text box, picture box, line, etc.) on a Master page will be reproduced on a page based on that Master page. These objects are called Master objects.

▼ When Automatic Linking is enabled, QuarkXPress can be directed to insert new pages to contain imported text that overflows the text box it is imported into.

▼ Text flows from box to box in the order that the boxes were linked.

▼ The Insert Page command is used to place a new page between two existing pages.

▼ A document can be broken into sections using the Section command. Page numbers within a section can be independent from surrounding sections, can start at any number, and can use any one of several numbering formats.

▼ Adjacent sections can be merged by disabling the Start Section check box in the Section dialog box.

▼ Holding down the Command key while pressing "3" when the text insertion point is in a text box will place the current page number in that text box.

▼ The Group command under the Item menu can be used to combined several selected objects into one object. Text in a text box that is part of a group can be edited normally. The Ungroup command from the Item menu can be used to separate objects that have been grouped.

▼ The Lock command from the Item menu can be used to prohibit an object from being repositioned or removed from a page.

CHAPTER 5

In This Chapter

▼ **The Printing Process**

▼ **The Traditional Printing Press**
   Single-Color Printing
   Printing in More Than One Color
   Process Versus Spot Printing

▼ **Halftone Screens**
   Manipulating an Image's Halftone Screen
   Examples of Halftone Screens

▼ **Manipulating Colors**
   Registration
   Adding a New Color to the Palette
   Editing a Color
   Duplicating a Color
   Deleting a Color
   Using Colors from Another Document
   Edit Trapping

▼ **The Separation Process**

▼ **An Example**

▼ **Summary**

You Will Learn

▼ Documents created in QuarkXPress can be printed on a number of different output devices.

▼ Documents can be printed in one color, full color, or any combination of colors.

▼ Each document has its own editable Color palette.

▼ Separating colors for printing can be done automatically by QuarkXPress.

The Printing Process

After you have created a document in QuarkXPress, you will probably want to print it (a printed page is much easier to carry than your computer). Documents created in QuarkXPress can be printed in black and white, partial color, or full color. You can output positive or negative images onto paper or film, controlling the size, number of copies, and virtually all aspects of the output process.

There are three basic steps involved in printing large quantities of a document. First, you will print it out, perhaps several times, on a dot-matrix or personal laser printer, until you feel certain you have caught all the errors, and your pages are exactly as you want them. You will do the majority of your printing at this stage. Even documents that will eventually be printed on a high-resolution device and then on a traditional press are usually proofed on a laser printer.

A *laser printer* places static electricity on the paper in the shape of the letters and images of the document, then spits a mist of a fine black powder, called *toner,* at the paper. The toner and the electricity are oppositely charged, so the toner is attracted to the paper, sticking in the shape of the document. The paper is then passed over a hot roller and the toner is baked onto the page.

The next step is to send your document to a service bureau, which will output it (make a hard copy) on a high-resolution *imagesetter,* or *typesetter,* which uses a chemical reaction to turn the paper black where the type and images should be. Imagesetters can produce much clearer, sharper type than laser printers can.

Both laser printers and imagesetters can put only black ink on a page. If you wish to print an image that contains shades of grey, these printers must use a technique called *halftone screening,* which is addressed later in this chapter.

Finally, your document will go to a traditional printer, who will make a plate of each page. *Plates* are thin sheets of metal that carry the printing image, and whose surface is treated so that only the image is ink-receptive. Your sales representative should be able to help you choose the ink and paper to use based on the type of document you are creating, the quantity you need, and the amount of money you wish to spend. The printer will then transfer your document to paper, fold or bind it, and perhaps even *drop-ship* it—that is, send many copies to the same address.

It is wise to invest some time "shopping" for a good printer and service bureau. The more helpful the people at these locations are, the easier your job and the better the final result will be. Sometimes one location can handle both your imagesetting and offset printing needs. If you can't find one location that does both, or are not happy with one aspect of a company, feel free to use another company. It's your nickel.

There is much more to printing than could ever fit into one chapter of an introductory book, but by the end of this chapter you should have a good idea what questions to ask your contact at the printer or service bureau to get the desired results.

The Traditional Printing Press

Laser printers and imagesetters are fine for one or two copies of a document, but when you need many copies the best answer is a traditional printing press.

The following sections should make you familiar with what you need to know to get your document from your computer screen to paper using a traditional printer. First we'll talk about single-color printing, then multiple and full-color printing.

Single-Color Printing

Single-color printing means that only one color ink will be pressed onto the paper. Single-color printing is most often done with black ink, but any color can be used.

Traditional printing presses use plates that contain raised images of your document; ink is spread onto those raised images and then transferred to paper. The quality of the final document depends on the quality of the plate, and the quality of the plate depends on the quality of the print used to make the plate. So an imagesetter should be used to create a high-resolution print for the plate to be made from.

There are several types of output you can get from an imagesetter. Before you start, ask your contact at the printer what is preferred. Your printer may want paper or film, positive or negative, with the emulsion up or down. You don't need to know what these options mean, but if you are aware of them you can give the service bureau the correct instructions for your printer's needs.

Printing in More Than One Color

The only difference between a one-color print job and a multicolor print job is that you must make a plate for each color that will be printed on the offset press. This is called *color separation.*

Let's start with something easy. Consider a document that has text in the middle and a border around the edge. The text is to be printed black and the border, red. When the document was created, the default color of black was used for the text. When the border was created, the text box was selected, Frame was chosen from the Item menu, and the frame style, size, and color (100% red) were indicated.

In this instance you would need two plates—one for black ink and one for red. QuarkXPress can be told to make the color separations for you, so that you don't have to create two separate documents. Near the bottom of the Print option in the File menu is the Make Separations check box. When it is checked, the Plate pop-out menu can be selected. When the default setting, All Plates, is selected, QuarkXPress will print all of the plates necessary to print the current document, which in this case would be just the black and red ones. (Of course this is a misnomer; QuarkXPress is not printing plates, but prints that will be used to create the plates for the press.) You can choose to print just one of these plates by choosing the color of the desired plate.

Process Versus Spot Printing

The Process Separation check box can be accessed under Colors in the Edit menu; it is part of the Edit Color dialog box that appears when you double-click on one of the colors in the Colors for Document box. It lets you specify whether the color you are adding to the color palette should be treated as a spot color or a process color.

Every *spot color* is printed on its own page. If, for instance, you were printing the page with black text and a red frame that we used in the earlier example, clicking on the Print button would cause two pages to be printed—one with the black elements of the document, and one with the red elements. Two plates are made for the press, and paper is run through the press twice—once pressing the plate with black ink onto the paper, then again, after the black ink dries, pressing the plate with red ink onto the paper. The final result is a document with black text and a red border.

It is theoretically possible to add as many spot colors as you wish to a document. When separations are printed, each color will print as its own page; a plate must be made from each of these pages, and the paper must run through the press that many times. As the number of colors to be used in a document rises to a certain level, spot colors may become impractical. When this happens it becomes easier to use process colors.

Anyone who painted as a child has mixed two colors together and created a new color (whether on purpose or accidentally, on the floor). Most people know that if you mix yellow and blue paint you get green, that red and yellow makes orange, and so forth. This is the same concept that is used when printing with *process colors,* which are four base colors—cyan, magenta, yellow, and black—that can be mixed together in varying proportions to create thousands of colors with a minimum of photography, platemaking, and press work. Documents created in this way are said to have been created with the *CMYK method,* also known as *four-color printing.*

In the four-color process the paper is either passed through one press four times, applying one of the process colors each time, or through a special press that presses the four plates in one pass. For example, green is made by combining cyan and yellow. Thus, if you wanted to print green text using process colors, the text would be printed twice—once with the cyan plate and once with the yellow plate.

A color—say, for instance, green—can be defined as either a process color or a spot color for a particular document. If it is defined as a spot color, a plate is made to hold the green ink. If it is defined as a process color, QuarkXPress separates the green into its cyan and yellow components. This is described in the next sections, along with other ways to control a QuarkXPress document's color palette.

Halftone Screens

Most daily newspapers print in black ink, using thousands of tiny dots. These dots appear when continuous-tone art is photographed through a screen and then reproduced lithographically. This is halftone screening in action. Halftoning alternates black and white in varying ratios to simulate levels of grey. Darker areas have more black and less white; as images lighten, the ratio of white to black increases.

A halftone screen can be made using any one of a number of different patterns at varying resolutions. The resolution of a halftone screen is measured in *lines per inch* (lpi). The lpi ratio in QuarkXPress can range from 15 to 400, and you can select from patterns containing dots, lines, squares, or ellipses. The lpi ratio determines how many rows of the pattern can alternate between black and white within an inch. The higher the lpi ratio, the finer the pattern appears and the better it simulates grey.

For best results, the lpi ratio must be optimized for the resolution of the output device that will be used. A laser printer that has a resolution of 300 dots per inch (dpi) prints best with an lpi ratio of 40 to 60, while an imagesetter with a resolution of 1,275 dpi or more can reproduce 150 lpi very nicely. Using an lpi ratio that is too high for your printer will cause images to appear too dark and they will lose detail. Using too few lpi makes the pattern more visible, often obscuring the image.

If you will be outputting your final pages on an imagesetter, don't trust your laser printer to accurately represent shades. Because it prints at a lower resolution, a laser printer will represent shades much darker than an imagesetter will. Your printer or service bureau personnel should be able to provide you with a sheet showing sample shadings as they will appear on their equipment. Use these samples, rather than your laser output, as a guide.

Manipulating an Image's Halftone Screen

When you have a picture box that contains a greyscale image and the Content tool is selected, you will be able to access the Style menu, which will contain the halftone screen controls. The default setting for an image is Normal Screen. The normal screen is determined by the Page Setup dialog box under the File menu. What this dialog box shows depends on the printer driver you are using. Most Page Setup dialog boxes have a Halftone Screen field, into which you can enter a value to be used as the normal lpi ratio. If your driver doesn't have a Halftone Screen field, your printer may or may not support variable halftone screens. To find out, check your owner's manual, or phone the company that made your printer.

In addition to the normal halftone screen setting, you can use QuarkXPress's Style menu to specify a particular halftone screen for individual picture boxes. Selecting the picture box with the Content tool will allow you to apply one of the three pre-set halftone screen options: 60 lpi using a line pattern rotated zero degrees, 30 lpi using a line pattern rotated 45 degrees, or 20 lpi using a dot pattern rotated 45 degrees.

The Other Screen option brings up the Picture Screening Specifications dialog box, as shown in Figure 5.1.

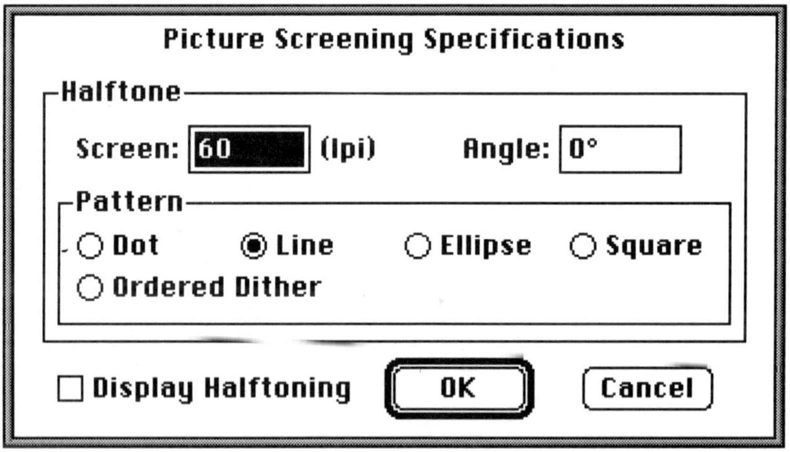

Figure 5.1. The Picture Screening Specifications dialog box.

Through this dialog box you can indicate exactly how many lpi you want, the angle of the pattern, and the type of pattern. Check the Display Halftoning button to show the chosen halftone screen on the computer monitor.

The Ordered Dither option creates a pattern that has been specially designed for low-resolution laser printers and quite often gives the best results. *Dithering* is the creation of an additional color or shade of grey by altering the values of the dots that make up all on-screen images and type. The drawback to dithering is that it causes QuarkXPress to redraw the screen more slowly. Dithering should not be used when printing to a high-resolution device such as an imagesetter.

If you will be using a service bureau to output on an imagesetter, consult with the bureau's personnel so that you can fine-tune the graphics in your document for their equipment.

Examples of Halftone Screens

For Figure 5.2, a bar was created that blended smoothly from black at the top to white at the bottom; it was then imported into five different picture boxes. In each picture box the bar was screened using different lpi ratios and patterns. The image has been enlarged 400% so that the pattern is more visible.

Figure 5.2. This bar has been reproduced in different halftone screens.

The first bar in Figure 5.2 was screened at 150 lpi. The second used a 60 lpi line pattern angled at 45 degrees. The third is also a line pattern at 45 degrees, but in this example it appears at a ratio of 20 lpi. This makes the lines thicker and the pattern much more obvious. The fourth bar is made with a square pattern at 150 lpi. The Ordered Dither option has been applied to the fifth bar.

Manipulating Colors

In QuarkXPress you can apply color to text, picture and text box backgrounds, box frames, lines, and the black portions of a black and white image in a picture box. Every document contains a color palette from which you can choose the colors you can apply to these items. You can access a document's color palette by selecting the Color command from the Style menu or from the Modify dialog box.

The default set of colors for a document includes the four standard process colors (cyan, magenta, yellow, and black), white, red, green, blue, and registration. The Color command under the Edit menu brings up the dialog box shown in Figure 5.3. You control a document's color palette through this dialog box.

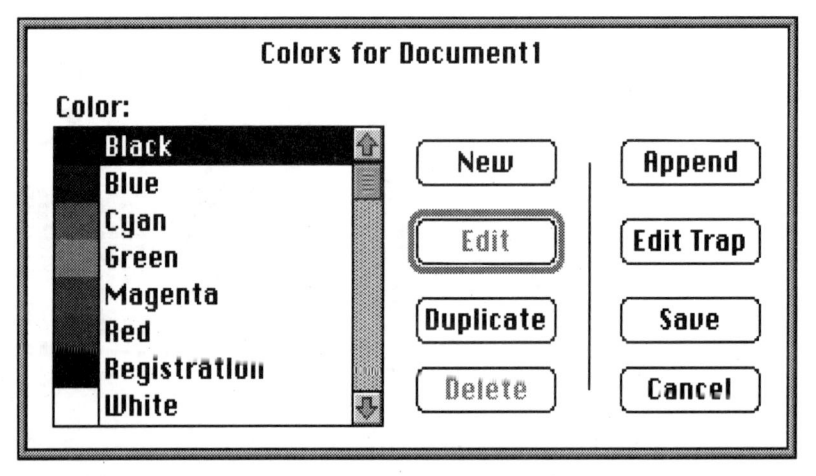

Figure 5.3. The Colors for Document dialog box.

Registration

The colors in the Colors for Document dialog box are self-explanatory except for registration. First, let's backtrack to the check box in the Print dialog box, which allows you to place registration marks on each individual plate. *Registration marks* are circles with crosses through them that appear at the top and on the side of the page outside the document area. They are used to position the plates on the press so that colors align properly. When the Registration Marks option is checked, you may select whether you want your registration marks to appear in the center of your margins, or off-centered.

The registration color is used primarily for registration marks, although any object that has this color applied to it will appear on every plate when the color separations are made.

Adding a New Color to the Palette

The New button allows you to create a color and add it to the document's color palette. Clicking on this button brings up the Edit Color dialog box shown in Figure 5.4. The first field in this dialog box is the Name field, into which you can enter the name of a new color.

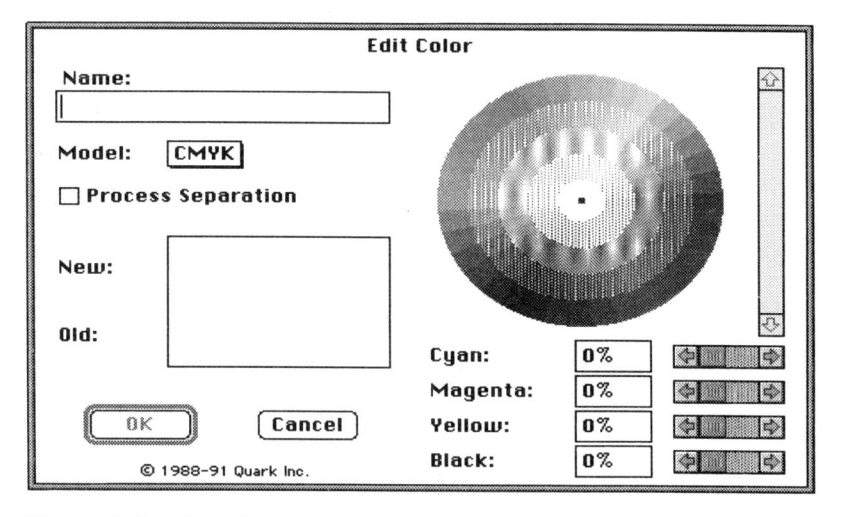

Figure 5.4. The Edit Color dialog box.

Below the name field is a pop-out menu that allows you to pick the color model that will be used to create the new color. The color models supported by QuarkXPress 3.1 are HSB, RGB, CMYK, Pantone, Trumatch, and Focoltone. The fields in the bottom-right corner of the Edit Color dialog box change to reflect the appropriate components for the selected color model. For example, the Pantone color model is selected in Figure 5.5.

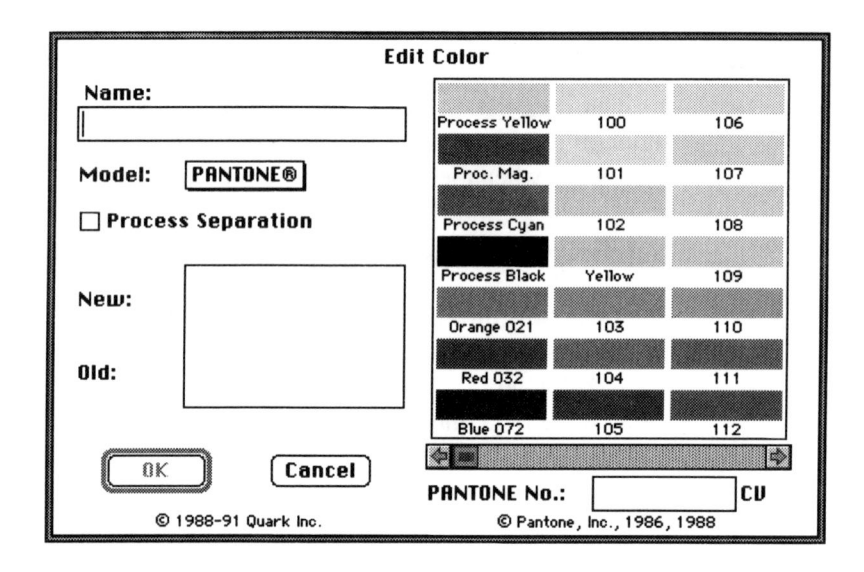

Figure 5.5. The Edit Color dialog box with the Pantone color model selected.

HSB stands for Hue, Saturation, and Brightness. This model gives you three fields into which you can enter a number between 0 and 100 indicating the hue and a percentage for both the saturation (depth) of that color and its brightness.

RGB stands for Red, Green, and Blue, which can be combined in various ratios to create most other colors. This model gives you three fields into which you can enter a percentage for each of these colors. For example, 100% of all three makes white, red and green make magenta, red and blue make cyan, blue and green makes yellow.

Both HSB and RGB are discussed in greater detail in Chapter 6.

CMYK represents the standard process colors. You can enter a percentage for each into the appropriate field, or use the scroll bar next to each field to set the level.

Pantone, Trumatch, and Focoltone are standards used by many printers to describe specific colors. When you say "purple," you probably think of a different shade of purple than another person would. If you say "Pantone 246," that person can look in a book of Pantone color samples to see exactly what you mean. The same is true for specific colors in the Trumatch and Focoltone systems.

When you choose one of these color models, the Edit Color dialog box displays color samples from that model in the large field on the right. You can enter the appropriate number/name in the field below the samples to select that color, or, if you have a color monitor, you can scroll through the field to scan the colors and click on one to select it.

Editing a Color

The Edit button allows you to change the parameters of a color. The four process colors and white cannot be edited; for these the Edit button remains dimmed.

Selecting an editable color and clicking on the Edit button brings up the Edit Colors dialog box. You can change the color model for that color, choose whether or not it is a process color, and use the color component fields to alter the color.

The square in the left middle of the Edit Color dialog box will show the original color below a sample of the changes you make to it, allowing you to see the changes as you make them. Clicking on the Cancel button will leave the color unchanged; clicking on the OK button will replace the color with its edited version in the color palette. You must click on the Save button in the Color Palette dialog box to make the change permanent.

Duplicating a Color

Use the Duplicate button in the Color Palette dialog box to make a copy of an existing color. When you duplicate a color, the Edit Color dialog box is automatically opened, allowing you to make changes to the new color. When you have finished editing this new color you must use the Save button in the Color Palette dialog box to add this color to the palette permanently.

Deleting a Color

Selecting a color and clicking on the Delete key will remove that color from the color palette. You must click on the Save button in the Color Palette dialog box to make the change permanent.

Using Colors from Another Document

The Append button is used to import colors from another QuarkXPress document into the current document. Clicking on the Append button brings up the standard Open dialog box, from which you can select the document whose colors you wish to append to the current document. Selecting a QuarkXPress document and clicking on the Open button automatically imports that document's color palette. Colors that occur in both documents will not be duplicated.

Edit Trapping

When one color is printed over another, the first is usually removed, or cut out, where the overlaying color will appear. This process is called *trapping*. If you don't want the background color to be trapped, you can indicate this in the Trap Specifications dialog box. To access this dialog box, select the color that you wish to edit from the Color Palette dialog box, and click on the Edit Trap button.

Figure 5.6 shows the Trap Specifications dialog box for yellow as the object color.

To change how the black background will be trapped when yellow is the object color, select black from the list on the left. Automatic is the default, which causes black to be removed wherever it occurs under yellow. Clicking on the Overprint button will make black print unchanged. The yellow will *overprint,* or print on top of, the black. When Overprint is chosen as the trapping method, the background color will often bleed through the object color, so usually it is not a good idea. Automatic trapping is almost always the best choice.

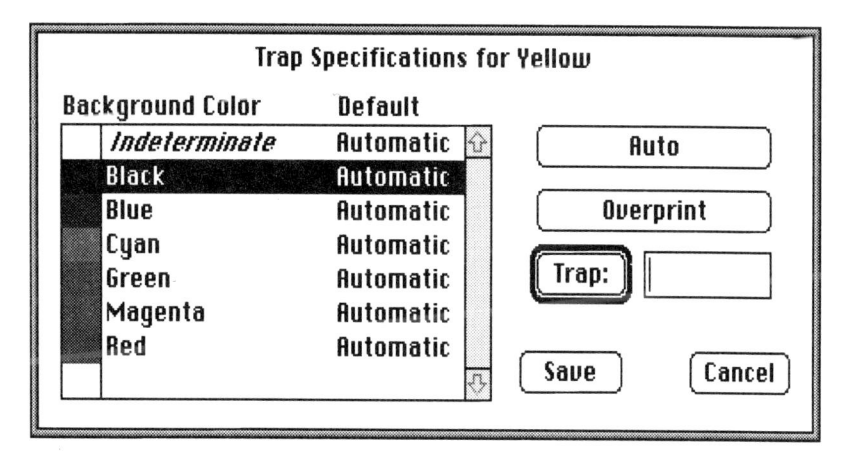

Figure 5.6. The Trap Specifications dialog box for yellow.

You can choose between Auto and Overprint for any combination of object color and background color in a document's color palette.

The Separation Process

When color separations are made for a document, QuarkXPress looks at that document to determine what colors from its color palette have been used. If there has only been one color used, QuarkXPress must check to see if that color has been defined in the Process Separation box in the Edit Color dialog box. If the Process Separation box has not been checked, QuarkXPress prints only one plate, the one for that color.

If the Process Separation box has been checked for the color, QuarkXPress calculates which of the four process colors must be used to create that color and prints plates for the necessary process colors. For example, if the color is green, QuarkXPress knows that cyan and yellow must be mixed, and will check the green in the document to see how much cyan and how much yellow must be mixed to create that shade of green. Two plates are then printed—one with the appropriate level of cyan, and one with the appropriate level of yellow.

You will not see the colors on their plates; you will see black or shades of black created with halftone screen patterns. The darker the black on the plate, the more color will appear on the paper.

For example, to print a square that is 100% green, the cyan and yellow plates will each contain a 100% black square. To print a square that is 50% green, the cyan and yellow plates will each contain a 50% black (grey) square.

When more than one color has been used on a document, QuarkXPress checks each color to see if its Process Separation box has been enabled. QuarkXPress will create a spot color plate representing each color for which this box has not been checked. For colors whose Process Separation box has been checked, QuarkXPress will separate that color into its CMYK components and place them on the appropriate CMYK plate.

A document that only contains process colors will generate only the four process color plates. Documents with process colors and spot colors will generate the four process color plates plus one plate for each spot color. The paper must go through the press once for each plate that is generated.

An Example

Figure 5.7. Imagine that the border is black, the background is red, and the word "SALE" is yellow.

Figure 5.7 is a text box with a black frame applied; the Modify dialog box has been used to fill the background with red, defined as a spot color. The text of the word "SALE" has been made yellow using the Color command under the Style menu. This document was then printed with the Make Separations check box in the Print dialog box selected.

When this document is printed for separations, three plates are created—the spot color plate for red and the process color plates for black and yellow. Figure 5.8 shows how the black plate appears, Figure 5.9 shows the yellow plate, and Figure 5.10, the red.

Figure 5.8. The black plate would contain the frame since it is the black part of the image.

The paper must be pressed by each plate to create the final output. Since all three colors were used at a shade of 100%, the image appears on all three plates at 100% black. Even though yellow is much lighter than red or black, the yellow plate prints 100% black, indicating that the yellow will be printed at full intensity.

SALE

Figure 5.9. The yellow plate would contain the word "SALE."

SALE

Figure 5.10. The red plate would contain the background. The area that matches the part of the yellow plate that overlaps has been cut out, or trapped.

In Figure 5.10, the red plate, holes have been cut for the yellow ink that will make the word "SALE." This is automatic trapping. If Overprint had been specified for yellow objects on a red background, the red plate would have been solid red. In that case the red ink would probably show through the yellow ink, creating some sort of blend that is not desirable.

Summary

▼ Low resolution printers such as dot matrix and laser printers are often used to make copies for proofreading.

▼ Laser printers and imagesetters can print only in black and white; greys are simulated by alternating patterns of black and white in halftone screens.

▼ Halftone screens can be made with a variety of patterns printed at different angles and at white to black ratios ranging from 15 to 400 lpi.

▼ The lpi ratio of images in a document should be optimized for the output device that will be used; high-resolution devices can reproduce a higher lpi ratio than can low-resolution devices.

▼ The Style menu is used to manipulate an image's halftone screen. The Page Setup dialog box is used to define the default, or normal, lpi ratio.

▼ The best results for color printing are obtained on an offset press.

▼ To print more than one color on a document requires that the paper is pressed by more than one plate.

▼ A color that is created by one plate is a spot color. A color that is created by combining the colors from more than one plate is called a process color. A color is defined as either a spot or process color in the Edit Color dialog box.

▼ The Edit Color dialog box is used to add new colors to and edit the existing colors of a document's color palette.

▼ Full color documents are created by combining cyan, magenta, yellow, and black.

▼ A document must be separated into its component colors so that a plate can be made for all of them. QuarkXPress does this separation automatically when the Make Separations box in the Print dialog box is checked.

▼ You can print all plates or select an individual plate to print in the Print dialog box.

▼ The Edit Trapping dialog box is used to dictate whether a background color will be trapped or the object color will be overprinted.

CHAPTER 6

In This Chapter

▼ **Preferences**
    Application Preferences
    General Preferences
    Tool Preferences
    Typographic Preferences

▼ **Summary**

You Will Learn

▼ How to customize most default settings using the four Preferences dialog boxes: Application, General, Tool, and Typographic.

▼ How to set overall program parameters using Application Preferences. Changes made to these parameters are saved and used every time you open QuarkXPress.

▼ How to set General Preferences, which apply only to the current document.

▼ How to manipulate the way your Tool palette works through the Tool Preferences dialog box. These settings can be saved as defaults, or can apply only to the current document.

▼ How to set text attributes using the Typographic Preferences dialog box.

Preferences

Defaults are pre-set parameters, or settings. When you start a new document, the margin markers, for example, are a certain color; when you create a text box and start typing, a certain font is already selected. These preferences are stored in a file called "XPress Preferences," located in the same folder as the QuarkXPress application file.

It is possible to change many of these default settings using the Preferences commands under the Edit menu. Placing the cursor over the Preferences command causes a pop-out menu to appear showing the four groups of preferences that can be affected: Application, General, Tool, and Typographic. Selecting one of these groups brings up the dialog box containing the items that can be set for that group. Let's talk about these groups in the order they appear.

Application Preferences

The Application Preferences dialog box, shown in Figure 6.1, contains the overall program parameters that can be set. Changes made to these parameters are saved and used every time you open QuarkXPress.

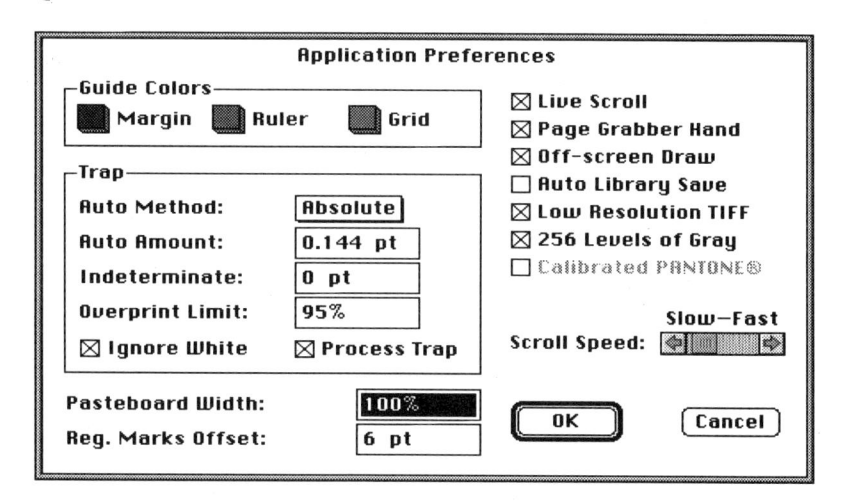

Figure 6.1. The Application Preferences dialog box.

Guide Colors

There are three squares of color in this section that allow you to choose a color for the Margin Guides, Ruler Guides, and Baseline Grid lines. Clicking on one of the colored squares brings up the standard Macintosh Color Picker dialog box, shown in Figure 6.2. You use the Color Picker to select the desired color.

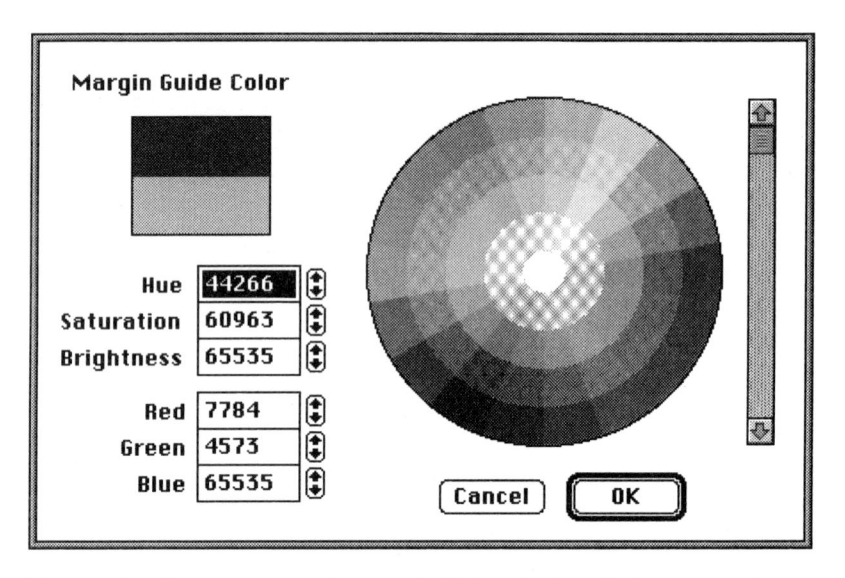

Figure 6.2. The standard Macintosh Color Picker dialog box as it appears when setting the Margin Guide color.

There are two modes used to describe a color in this dialog box. One mode uses Hue, Saturation, and Brightness (HSB); the other uses varying combinations and levels of Red, Green, and Blue (RGB). Colors can also be picked by clicking on the color wheel and dragging the scroll bar next to it to select a color.

The color wheel contains the range of colors at various brightnesses. When you click on a section of the color wheel, that color is selected and shown in the top half of the Margin Guide Color field in the top left corner of the dialog box. The lower half of this field contains the color currently used for the margin guides.

The scroll bar to the right of the color wheel allows you to adjust the brightness range of the color wheel. Dragging the control handle down decreases the overall brightness of the colors on the wheel. Dragging the control handle up increases the brightness.

The second way to choose a color is to enter values into the Hue, Saturation, and Brightness fields in the lower-left corner of the dialog box.

Hue is the color itself; *saturation* is the intensity of that color. Brightness is the range between black and the maximum for that particular saturation. Zero brightness is always black.

The numbers entered into these fields must range between zero and 65,535. In the Hue field, zero is red, and as the numbers increase the color changes counterclockwise until you are back to red at 65,535. For example, 22,150 is the middle of the green section, and 43,852 is the middle of the blue section.

Saturation ranges from zero, which is no color at all, to 65,535, which is the selected hue at its maximum intensity. Brightness ranges from zero, which is black, to 65,535 which is the maximum brightness for the current hue and saturation.

- Hue equals tint or color.
- Zero saturation and maximum brightness equal white.
- Maximum saturation and maximum brightness equal the richest shade of the current hue.
- Zero brightness always equals black.

To use the Color Picker to create a shade of a particular color, you can adjust the HSB mix until you get the shade that you want. You can do this either by entering specific numbers between 0 and 65,535 into the three fields, or by using the up and down arrow keys next to the fields to scroll through the range of values.

It is easiest to start with the saturation and brightness levels set to maximum, choose a hue, then adjust the saturation and brightness to fine-tune the color.

Another way to select a color is to enter values into the Red, Green, and Blue fields. Every color on a computer (or any video) screen is created with a combination of red, green, and blue. Each *pixel,* or dot, on the screen is actually a group of three dots: a red dot, a green dot, and a blue dot. If a pixel is supposed to appear green, then only the green dot is turned on, and so on. These dots can range from bright to dim. If the red dot is bright you get a full red; if it is dim you get a pinkish.

To make colors other than these three, varying combinations of the three dots are turned on at varying brightnesses. For example, red and green make yellow, red and blue make magenta, green and blue make cyan.

The Red, Green, and Blue fields in the Color Picker dialog box allow you to define a color by entering numbers into them. Unfortunately, the numbers you enter aren't simple percentages of each color. You must enter a number between 0 and 65,535; zero, of course, equals none, and 65,535 equals 100% of that color.

Trap

The next section in the Application Preferences dialog box contains fields for controlling how QuarkXPress traps color when printing with spot or process colors. Trapping is the slight overlap in a color-separated image that prevents gaps from appearing along the edges due to misalignment during printing. Trapping colors for separation is as much an art as a science, and deciding how to set these parameters should be discussed with the printer or service bureau you will use. The kind of paper, inks, and printing method you will be using, as well as the file types included in the document, affect how the trapping should be handled.

Pasteboard Width

The pasteboard is the nonprinting area on each side of a page, on which you can place and manipulate objects for use in your document. The default setting is 100%, which creates an area on each side of the page that is the same width as the page. Figure 6.3 shows a QuarkXPress window with a standard letter-size page. The area marked by dotted lines extends 8.5 inches on either side of the page. This is the pasteboard. If the Pasteboard Width were set at 50%, this area would extend only 4.25 inches on either side. You cannot move or create any objects outside of this area.

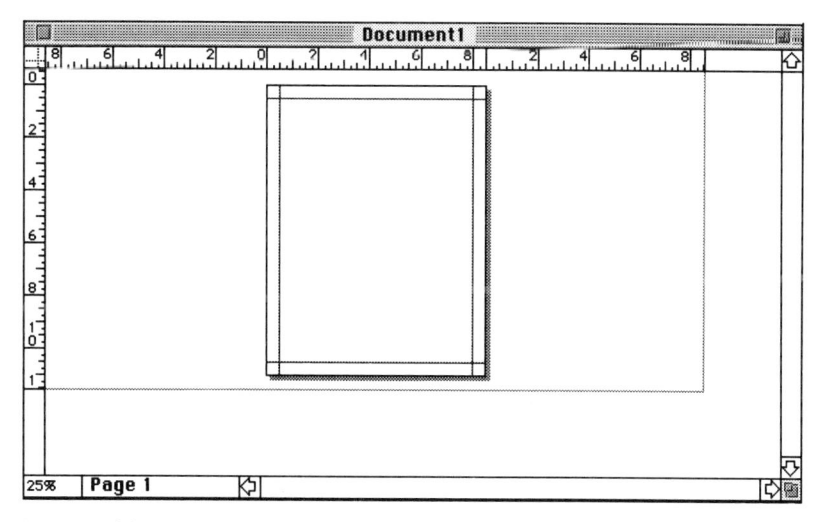

Figure 6.3. This window contains a standard letter-sized page and a pasteboard that is as wide as the page.

Registration Marks Offset

This field allows you to indicate how far from the edge of the page you want the registration marks to be printed. A registration mark, you will recall, is a reference symbol that looks like a circle with a cross through it, and is used by printers to align overlaying plates of camera-ready pages. The default setting is 6 points. Some printers can't print this close to the edge of the page, so this amount may need to be increased.

Live Scroll

When this option is not checked and you drag the control handle in a document scroll bar, the document window doesn't change until you release the mouse button. When this option is checked, the document window updates as you drag the control handle. While the literature states that the view updates "instantly," the reality is that the update speed depends on the speed of your computer, the bit depth resolution of your monitor and card, and the complexity of the images in the document window.

Page Grabber Hand

When this option is checked, holding down the Option key changes the cursor into the Page Grabber Hand pointer. Clicking and dragging with this cursor scrolls the page. The page is redrawn as you drag whether or not the Live Scroll option is checked.

Off-screen Draw

When you scroll a document, the portions that were off screen must be drawn. Normally when the screen is redrawn it is done line by line. When Off-screen Draw is checked, the new parts of the image are redrawn in memory then placed on the screen all at once.

Auto Library Save

This option automatically saves any entries you add to the QuarkXPress library.

Low Resolution TIFF

The image on the left in Figure 6.4 was imported with the Low Resolution TIFF option checked. The image on the right was imported at the higher resolution.

Figure 6.4. The image in the left box was imported with the Low Resolution TIFF option checked.

When this option is checked, the preview image for imported TIFF files is shown at 36 dpi. When this option is not checked, the preview image will be displayed at 72 dpi. The lower resolution is preferable when you wish to keep the size of the document down, but higher resolution previews give a more accurate on-screen presentation of the image. This option will not affect any images already imported.

256 Levels of Grey

When this option is checked, imported greyscale pictures will be displayed with 256 levels of grey (8 bit greyscale) if the monitor is capable of that level. Figure 6.5 shows an image that graduates from black at the top to white at the bottom, with 256 levels of grey in between. It was imported into the box on the left with the 256 Levels of Grey option not checked, and imported into the right box with this option checked. Notice the banding in the image on the left.

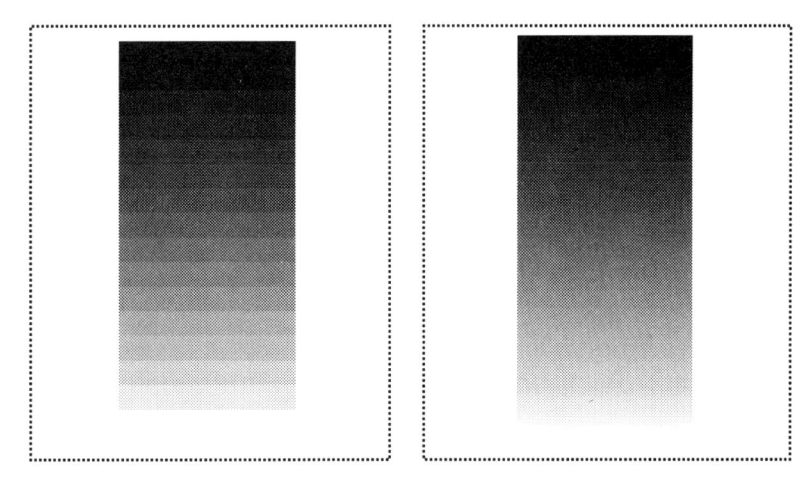

Figure 6.5. For the image on the left, the 256 Levels of Grey option was not checked.

Scroll Speed

The Scroll Speed affects the speed at which the document window scrolls when you click and hold on the arrows at the ends of the scroll bars. When it is set to slow, the windows start scrolling slowly, then pick up speed as you hold the mouse button down. When the speed is set to fast, the window scrolls quickly as soon as you click on an arrow.

General Preferences

Selecting General Preferences from the Preferences pop-out menu under the Edit menu brings up the General Preferences dialog box for the current document (see Figure 6.6). Settings and changes you make in this dialog box apply only to that document.

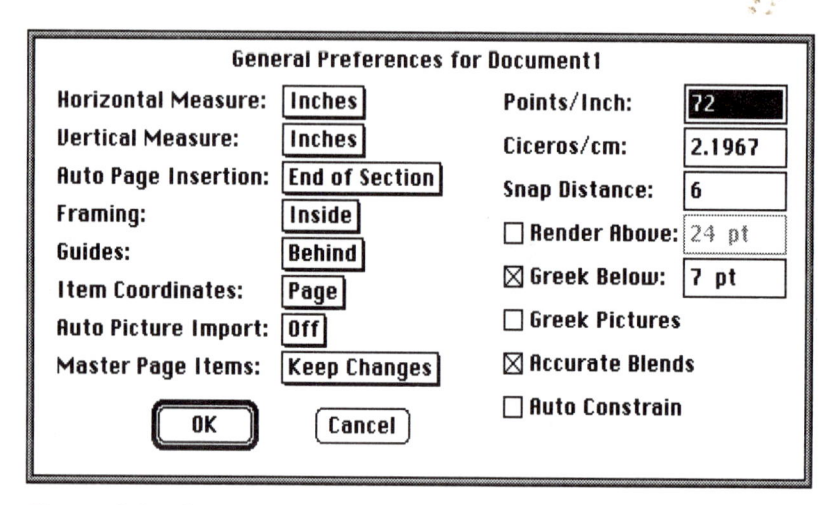

Figure 6.6. The General Preferences dialog box.

Auto Page Insertion

When you import more text into a text box than it can contain, you can tell QuarkXPress to add enough additional pages to your document to contain the entire text. Auto Page Insertion controls where these pages will be placed. This command is discussed in greater detail in Chapter 4.

Horizontal/Vertical Measure

The first two items in the General Preferences dialog box allow you to specify what type of measure will be displayed on the rulers. When the rulers are displayed, the Horizontal Measure is displayed along the top of the document window and the Vertical Measure is displayed along the left side of the document window. Figure 6.7 shows the pop-out menu containing the types of measures available for both the Horizontal and Vertical measures. The option with the check-mark next to it is the currently selected measure.

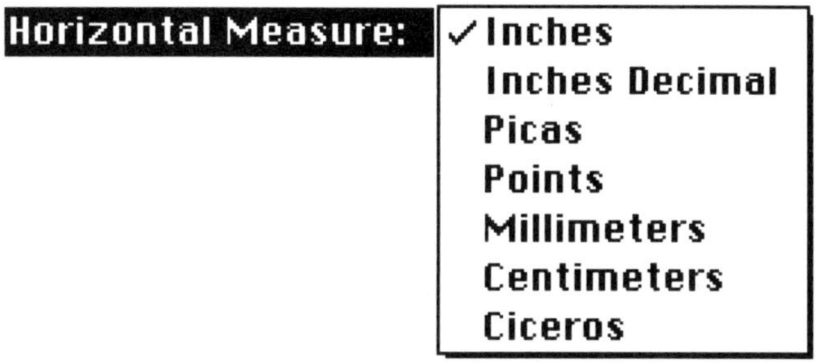

Figure 6.7. The Horizontal Measure option.

Framing

When you use the Frame command under the Item menu to place a border around a text or picture box, that frame is placed either inside or outside the box's guide. Figure 6.8 shows two text boxes. Each of them is 2 inches square and has a frame that is 20 points wide. The box on the left had the frame placed inside, while the box on the right had it placed outside. Changing this setting will not affect the frame of boxes already created.

If you create a box at the edge of your document and wish to place a frame around it, framing should be set to Outside so that the frame doesn't bleed off the edge of the page.

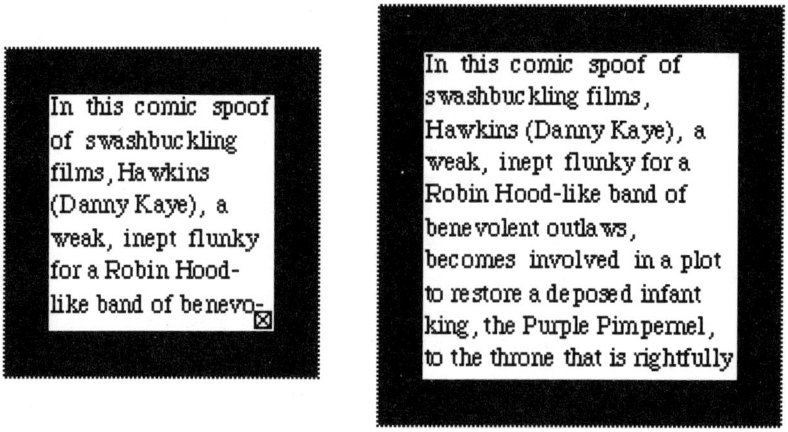

Figure 6.8. The frame on the left was created inside the text box; the frame on the right was created outside.

Guides

When you specify margins for a document you've created, QuarkXPress places guides on the page to indicate the location of the margins. Ruler guides can be placed on the document by clicking and dragging from either the horizontal or vertical rulers.

The Guide command in the General Preferences dialog box allows you to specify whether you want the guides to appear behind or on top of the other items in the document.

Item Coordinates

When working with multipage spreads (also called facing pages), you can indicate whether you want the horizontal ruler to run continuously or restart for each page of a spread.

Selecting Page for the Item Coordinates will cause the horizontal ruler to restart at zero at the beginning of each page in a spread. When you select Spread, the ruler will start at zero at the left edge of the first page and run continuously.

Auto Picture Import

Remember that when you import a picture into QuarkXPress, the picture itself is not placed into the document. QuarkXPress places a preview of the image into the document and remembers where the original is located. If the original is moved or modified, QuarkXPress has three options, as shown in Figure 6.9.

Figure 6.9. Auto Update options for importing pictures.

The default setting of Auto Picture Update is off; you will not know whether a picture has been moved or modified unless you either access the Picture Usage command under the Utilities menu, or attempt to print the document. When you attempt to print a document with missing or modified images, you will be notified and asked if you wish to update them.

When Auto Picture Update is on, QuarkXPress automatically updates all modified images when the document is opened. Pictures that have been moved or are missing will not be updated. "On (verify)" will cause QuarkXPress to notify you when you open a document that has missing or modified files. You will be able to go directly to the Picture Usage dialog box and update the files.

Be sure to save your document when you change the Auto Picture Update setting, or that change will be forgotten.

Master Page Items

Suppose you had a Master page that contained a text box and you inserted into your document a page based on that Master page. The inserted page would contain a text box (a Master item). Now suppose you created a new Master page that contained only a picture box, and applied this new Master page to the existing page. If Delete Changes had been selected for the Master Page Items preference, then the text box would be removed and the picture box from the new Master page would be inserted.

When a new Master page is applied to an existing page, all items that came from the original Master page, and their contents, are removed. If an object has been modified, setting the Master Page Items preference to Keep Changes will cause that object to remain. If an object has not been modified, it will be removed even when Keep Changes has been chosen.

Points/Inch

Normally, 72 points equal an inch. You can modify that value, in .01 point increments up to 73 points per inch, by entering your selection in the Points/Inch field. The value you choose will be used for all point and pica measurements and for point-to-inch conversions.

Ciceros/cm

You can also specify a value between 2 and 3 for use as the Cicero-to-centimeter value. A Cicero is a French typesetting measure approximately equal to 4.552 millimeters.

Snap Distance

When Snap to Guides (under the View menu) is enabled, objects that are moved near a margin or ruler guide automatically align themselves with that guide. The Snap Distance is how close the object must come to the guide before it "snaps" into place.

If you are having trouble getting objects to snap, you may wish to increase this value; if things snap when you don't want them to, you can either decrease this value or turn off Snap to Guides.

Render Above

Sometimes fonts at larger sizes can suffer a severe case of the "jaggies." QuarkXPress can *render,* or smooth, fonts on screen for you. You can turn font rendering on or off by checking the box next to the Render Above option in the General Preferences dialog box. When this option is enabled you can tell QuarkXPress above what font size to render. Rendering can slow down your screen redraw, so you may want to turn on this option only for your final page proofs. There are other programs that render fonts, such as Adobe Type Manager, and if you are running one of these you probably will not need QuarkXPress's rendering also.

Greek Below

In QuarkXPress, *greeking* uses grey bars in place of text to speed up the screen redraw so the document displays faster, since even if text is too small to be readable the calculations are done to draw it correctly on the screen. Text that appears as a grey bar on the screen will print normally.

In the Greek Below box, you can enter the point size below which you want QuarkXPress to substitute greeking for text. Magnifying the screen will allow you to see the greyed text.

The first line of text in Figure 6.10 is 12 point, and the second line of text is 6 point. Since the Greek Below value is set to 7 points, the bottom line appears as a grey bar.

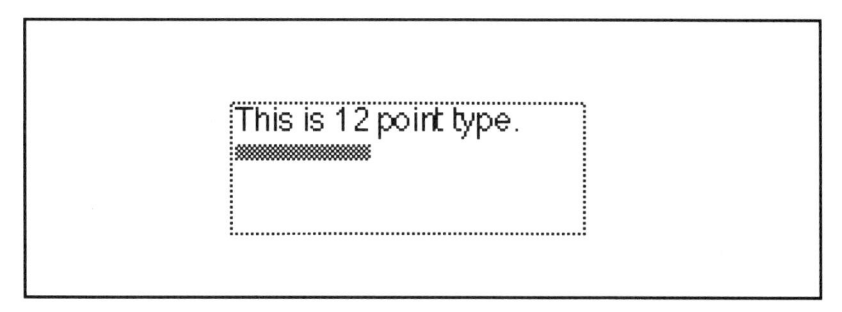

Figure 6.10. The bottom line is greeked.

Greek Pictures

Checking this option will cause QuarkXPress to place a grey pattern in all inactive picture boxes. When a picture box is made active, its picture is displayed. Greeking pictures can significantly speed up scrolling and screen redraw, and does not affect the way in which images print.

Accurate Blends

When this option is checked, QuarkXPress will use a dithered pattern (see Chapter 5) to more accurately represent color blends. When this option is unchecked, color or grey bands are used to approximate a blend.

Auto Constrain

Constraining items prevents them from being enlarged or moved beyond the sides of the box that contains them. Turning on Auto Constrain in the General Preferences dialog box automatically constrains items by the box into which they are pasted or within which they are created.

Figure 6.11 illustrates this. On the left, the box containing the globe was pasted into the grey box with Auto Constrain off. The globe box was then dragged to the right until half of it was outside the grey box. On the right in the same figure, the globe box was pasted into the grey box with Auto Constrain turned on. In this instance, when the globe box was dragged to the right it was stopped by the edge of the grey box, and could not be dragged further.

Auto Constrain affects boxes and lines, whether they are pasted into or created in a box.

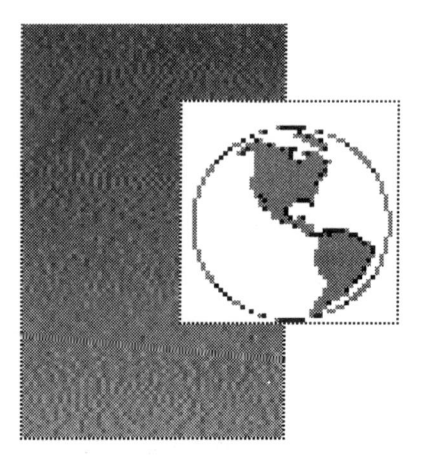

Figure 6.11. The globe box on the right was pasted in with Auto Constrain turned on.

Tool Preferences

Each tool in the Tool palette has a range of attributes that can be changed. You can use the Tool Preferences dialog box to set and record the attributes you use most often so that they become the default settings. Changes made in the Tool Preferences dialog box when a document is active apply only to that document. If you make changes to the Tool Preferences dialog box with no document open, the changes are saved as the defaults for all documents created from that point on.

The Tool Preferences dialog box can be accessed either through the Preferences pop-out menu under the Edit menu or by double clicking on a tool in the Tool palette. To change a tool's attributes, select that tool from the left side of the Tool Preferences dialog box. The attribute buttons and fields appropriate for that tool then become active.

Zoom Tool

The attributes that can be modified for the Zoom tool are the three View Scale settings, as shown in Figure 6.12.

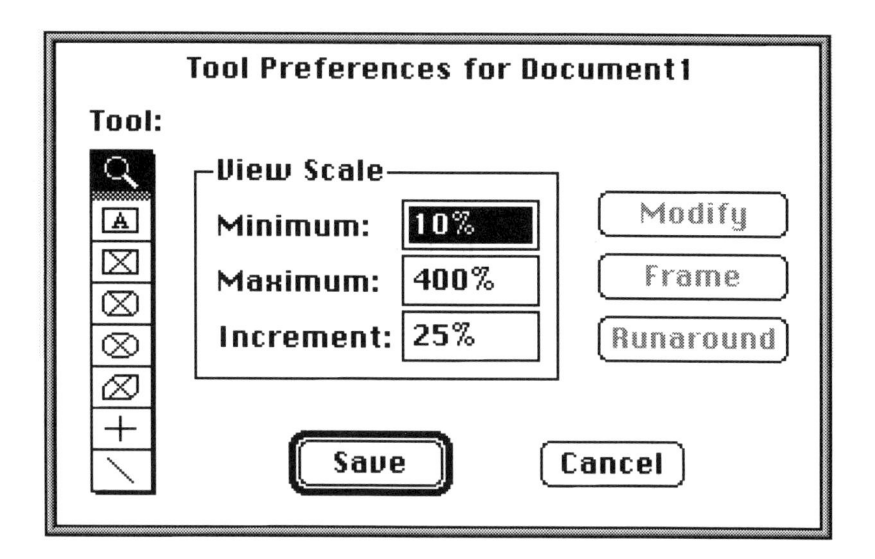

Figure 6.12. The Tool Preferences dialog box with the Zoom tool attributes available.

The Minimum field contains the smallest percentage at which the document can be viewed; 10% is both the default value and the smallest allowed. The Maximum field contains the largest percentage at which the document can be viewed; 400% is both the default value and the largest allowed. When the Zoom tool is used to increase or decrease the document view, that view will be changed by the value placed in the Increment field; the default value is 25%.

Text Tool

When the Text tool is selected (see Figure 6.13), the Modify, Frame, and Runaround buttons become active. Clicking on one of these buttons brings up its dialog box, allowing you to set attributes that will be applied when a text box is created. If you continually find yourself accessing the Modify, Frame, or Runaround dialog boxes to make changes, you may wish to make those changes once and save them as defaults.

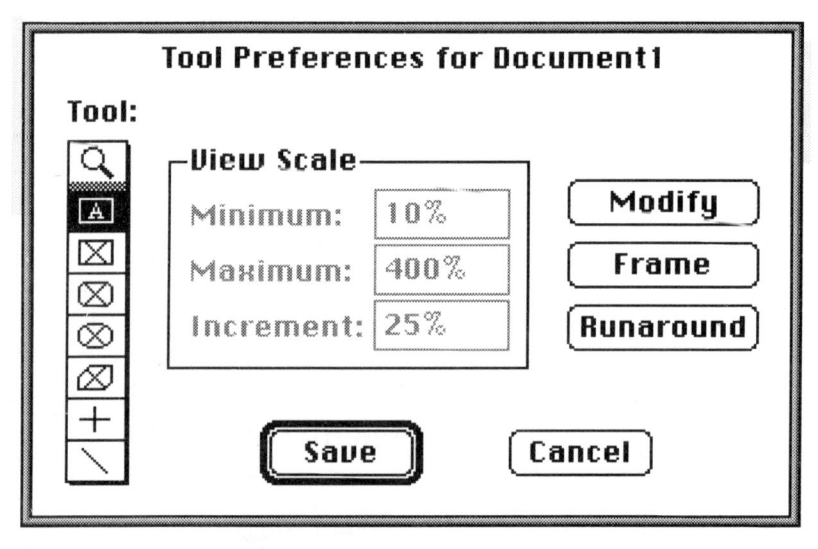

Figure 6.13. The Tool Preferences dialog box with the Text tool selected.

Clicking on the Modify button brings up the Modify dialog box, as shown in Figure 6.14. Notice that the Origin, Width, Height, and

Box Angle fields are greyed. You cannot set defaults for these attributes. For the remaining attributes you can indicate choices and values that will be applied when the Text tool is used to create a text box. For more on these attributes, see the sections in chapters 2 and 3 that describe the Modify dialog box.

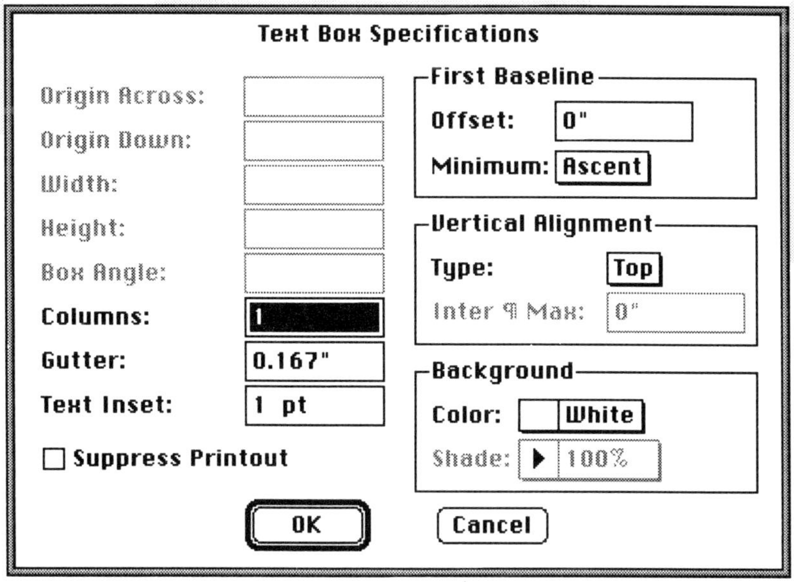

Figure 6.14. The Modify dialog box as it appears for setting Text tool default attributes.

Clicking on the Frame button brings up the standard Frame dialog box, as discussed in Chapter 3. After choosing a frame style and entering a point size, click on the OK button and every new text box will be created with that style and size frame. It is possible to modify the frame after a text box has been created without affecting previously created text boxes.

Clicking on the Runaround button brings up the standard Runaround dialog box (discussed in Chapter 3), which allows you to dictate how the runaround will be handled for text boxes created in the future.

Picture Box Tool

Clicking on any of the Picture Box tools allows you to set default attributes for that tool. Again, the Modify, Frame, and Runaround buttons are active, and clicking on them brings up the appropriate dialog box. The Modify dialog box has the Origin Across, Origin Down, Width, Height, and Box Angle greyed since you cannot set defaults for these attributes. The remaining attributes can be modified and will be applied to picture boxes created after the modification. These attributes are discussed in chapters 2 and 3.

Line Tool

You can select either of the Line tools and use the Modify button to bring up the Line Style dialog box to set a default line style, width, and shade to be used when creating lines.

Typographic Preferences

The Typographic Preferences dialog box, shown in Figure 6.15, allows you to set the default parameters for many text attributes. To set defaults that apply to a single document, make changes while the document is open. Changes made when no document is open are used as defaults for documents created from that point on.

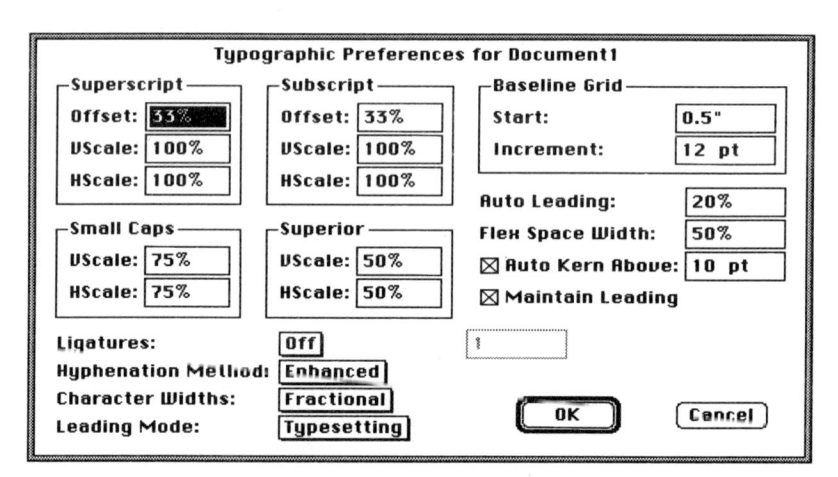

Figure 6.15. The Typographic Preferences dialog box.

Superscript/Subscript

Superscript and subscript can be applied either through the Type Style pop-out menu under the Style menu, or through the Character Attributes dialog box. Both of these styles have three fields:

- Offset controls the percentage of the current font size that the letter will be placed above or below the baseline. The default value is 33%, which would raise 12 point type 4 points above the baseline for Superscript and lower it 4 points below the baseline for Subscript.
- VScale controls the vertical scale, or height, of the superscripted or subscripted text. The scale can be a percentage, from 0% to 100%, of the current font height in .1% increments.
- HScale controls the horizontal scale, or width, of the superscripted or subscripted text. The scale can be a percentage, from 0% to 100%, of the current font width in .1% increments.

Small Caps

Small Caps turns the selected text into all capital letters that are a percentage of the normal capital size for the current font size. The value entered into the VScale field controls the height, and the value entered into the HScale field controls the width. The default values for both of these fields is 75%.

Superior

Superior type reduces text by the percentages entered in the VScale and HScale fields, and aligns the top of the text with the top of the capitals in the surrounding text. Figure 6.16 demonstrates the difference between superscript and superior. Superscript raises the bottom of the affected text a certain distance from the baseline. Superior aligns the top of the affected text to the height of the surrounding capital letters.

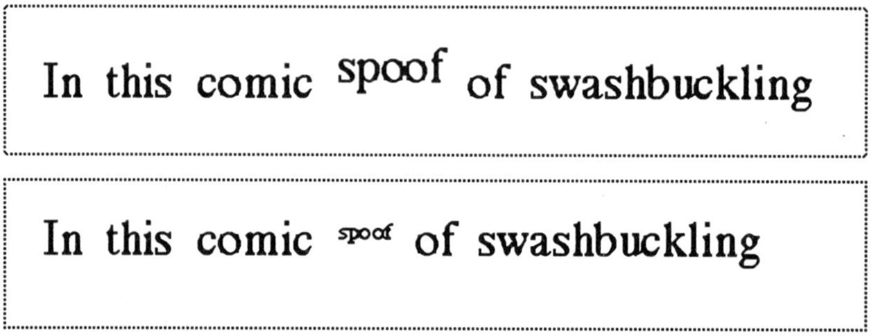

> In this comic ˢᵖᵒᵒᶠ of swashbuckling

> In this comic ˢᵖᵒᵒᶠ of swashbuckling

Figure 6.16. The word "spoof" in the top text box has been Superscripted. In the bottom text box it has had the superior type style applied to it.

Baseline Grid

The Baseline Grid is a set of guides that help you to align text across a page. It can be viewed and hidden using Show/Hide Baseline Grid under the View menu. When it is shown, the Baseline Grid begins the distance from the top of the page entered into the Start field in the Typographic Preferences dialog box. The value entered into the Increment field indicates the distance between subsequent grid lines.

Auto Leading

When you use Auto Leading (in the Leading field of the Leading dialog box, in the Leading field of the Paragraph Format dialog box, or in the Measurement palette), the amount is taken from the Auto Leading field in this dialog box. You can enter either a percentage from 1% to 100%, or an incremental value from -63 to +63 points. When you enter a percentage, the Auto Leading amount is that percentage more than the largest character on each line of a paragraph. When you enter an incremental value, that amount is added to or deleted from the size of the largest character on each line of a paragraph, and the result is used as the leading value.

When you change the amount in the Auto Leading field and click on the OK button, the leading is automatically changed in every paragraph that used auto for its leading amount.

Flex Space Width

Normally, spaces entered with your Spacebar are set to a certain width according to the size font you are using. A *flex space* is a space that you can control the width of. When a *nonbreaking flex space* is placed between two words, those two words will always appear on the same line of text. A nonbreaking flex space is created by holding down the Option and Command keys while pressing the Spacebar.

A *breaking flex space* is created by holding down the Option key while pressing the Spacebar.

The Flex Width field contains the percentage of the width of a normal space for the current font that will be used for the flex space. You can use the default setting of 50%, or any amount between 0% and 400%. To use the flex space as an em space, enter 200%.

Auto Kern Above

Kerning, or the spacing between individual letter pairs, is not very critical at smaller font sizes; as larger type is used, however, the differences in letter-pair spacing becomes more obvious. You can manually adjust individual letter-pair spacing, but most Macintosh fonts have some kerning information built in. Checking the box next to Auto Kern Above allows QuarkXPress to access this built-in kerning, and applies it to fonts larger than the size specified in the Auto Kern Above field. For more information on kerning see Chapter 2.

Maintain Leading

Leading, you will recall, is the space between the baselines of text. If an obstruction comes between the baselines of two lines of text, the leading value is no longer relevant for the lower line, which usually appears too close to the obstruction, as shown on the left of Figure 6.17. Checking the Maintain Leading box allows the line below the obstruction to retain its leading amount, as shown on the right of Figure 6.17. The leading space is applied from the baseline of the text to the bottom of the obstruction.

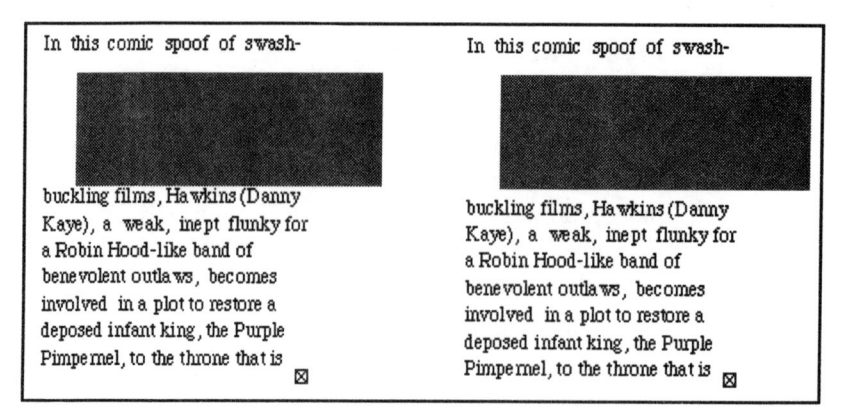

> In this comic spoof of swash-buckling films, Hawkins (Danny Kaye), a weak, inept flunky for a Robin Hood-like band of benevolent outlaws, becomes involved in a plot to restore a deposed infant king, the Purple Pimpernel, to the throne that is
>
> In this comic spoof of swash-buckling films, Hawkins (Danny Kaye), a weak, inept flunky for a Robin Hood-like band of benevolent outlaws, becomes involved in a plot to restore a deposed infant king, the Purple Pimpernel, to the throne that is

Figure 6.17. The text on the left comes very close to the obstruction because the Maintain Leading option is not enabled.

Ligatures

When the ligature feature is turned on and you are using a font that contains them, ligatures will be replaced for the individual letters. A ligature is a character consisting of two or more letters combined into one or joined by a tie. Figure 6.18 shows two common ligatures and the letter pairs from which they were created. With ligatures on, typing "f" and "i," or "f" and "l" automatically produces the ligatures shown. When ligature is turned off, you must access the ligatures using the appropriate modifier keys for that font.

fi fl

fi fl

Figure 6.18. On the top are individual letters; on the bottom are ligatures.

Hyphenation Method

Two methods of hyphenation can be specified in QuarkXPress Version 3.1: standard and enhanced. Enhanced hyphenation allows for better control over the hyphenation within a document. The Standard option should be used when opening a document created in QuarkXPress 3.0, as it will use the normal hyphenation for Version 3.0, avoiding text reflow.

The hyphenation rules are contained within the program, eliminating the XPress Hyphenation file that existed with Version 3.0.

Character Widths

Character Widths has two settings, fractional and integral. Fractional is the default setting, and is best used with a LaserWriter or other PostScript printer. If you will be using a dot matrix printer (also called an impact printer) such as the ImageWriter, then Integral Character Widths will give better results.

Be sure to set the Character Widths option before you begin laying out the document. Changing this setting for an existing document may cause significant text reflow when the character widths change throughout the document.

Leading Mode

There are two leading modes, typesetting mode and word processing mode. The default mode, typesetting, measures leading from the baseline of one line of text to the baseline of the line of text above it. Word processing mode measures from the top of the line of text to the top of the text on the line below.

Summary

▼ The Application Preferences dialog box allows you to set the defaults for many overall program parameters. These include Guide Colors, Trapping parameters, Pasteboard Width, Registration Marks Offset, Live Scroll, Page Grabber hand, Off-screen Draw, Auto Library Save, Low Resolution TIFF, 256 Levels of Grey, and Scroll Speed.

▼ The General Preferences dialog box is used to set parameters for the current document, including the Horizontal and Vertical Measure, Auto Page Insertion, Framing Preferences, the layer of the Margin and Ruler Guides, Item Coordinates, Auto Picture Import, Master Page Items, Points per Inch, Ciceros per Centimeter, Snap Distance, Font Rendering and Greeking, Picture Greeking, Accurate Blends, and Auto Constrain.

▼ The Tool Preferences dialog box is used to set the default parameters for each tool in the Tool palette. The Zoom tool parameters of the smallest and largest percentages the document can be viewed at, and the increment to be enlarged or reduced when using the Zoom tool can be entered here.

▼ Default Text tool parameters for font, style, and size are set in the Tools Preferences dialog box.

▼ Default background color, frame style, and runaround parameters can be chosen from the Tool Preferences dialog box for both text and picture boxes.

▼ The default line style, color, and width can be set also.

▼ The Typographic Preferences dialog box can be used to set text defaults such as Superscript and Subscript amounts, Small Caps sizes, Superior percentages, Baseline Grid measurements, Auto Leading amount, Flex Space Width, Auto Kern Above size.

CHAPTER 7

In This Chapter

▼ **Additional Utilities and Commands**

▼ **File Menu Extras**
   Save Text
   Save Page as EPS

▼ **Edit Menu Extras**
   Subscribe To
   Subscriber Options
   Find/Change
   H&Js

▼ **Item Menu Extras**
   Duplicate/Step and Repeat
   Delete
   Constrain
   Space/Align

▼ **Page Menu Extras**
   Master Guides

▼ **View Menu Extras**
   The Style Sheets Palette
   The Colors Palette
   The Trap Information Palette

▼ **Utilities Menu Extras**
   Check Spelling
   Auxiliary Dictionary
   Edit Auxiliary
   Suggested Hyphenation
   Hyphenation Exceptions
   Library
   Summary

You Will Learn

▼ How to create an EPS picture file from a page in the active QuarkXPress document, and import it into a document that can support EPS figures.

▼ How to search for a word or phrase using the Find/Change command, and change it universally or only in certain instances.

▼ How to customize hyphenation and justification.

▼ How to make one copy or more of an object or group of objects using the Duplicate/Step and Repeat commands.

▼ How to constrain one object or several within the boundaries of a larger object.

▼ How to align items horizontally or vertically.

▼ How to create and edit an auxiliary dictionary to spell-check words you use often that are not contained in the standard QuarkXPress dictionary.

▼ How to create and use a library for easier access to objects that you use often.

Additional Utilities and Commands

There are utilities and commands that have not yet been discussed. These fit under several categories and help you in many aspects of designing and laying out a document. This chapter will discuss these extras as they are grouped under the menus.

File Menu Extras

The Save Text and Save Page as EPS functions under the File menu help you to move QuarkXPress information for use in other programs.

Save Text

The Save Text function is greyed until you select a text box with the Content tool. When it is active, accessing it brings up the Save Text dialog box, as shown in Figure 7.1.

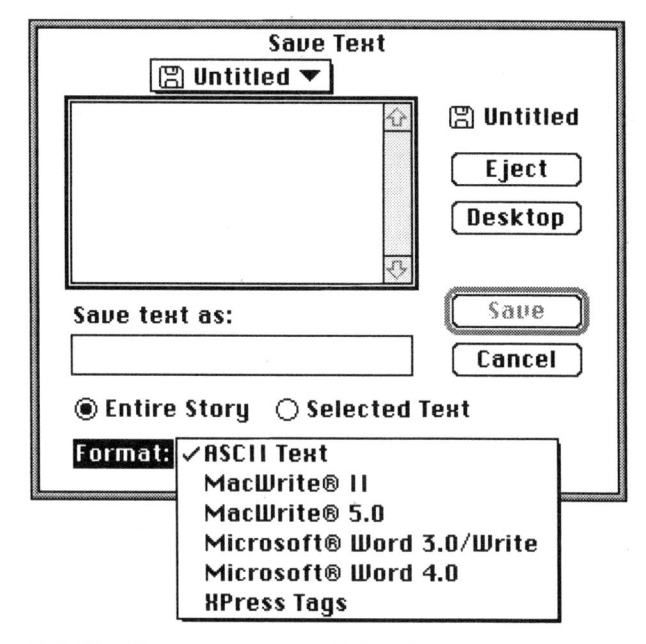

Figure 7.1. The Save Text export dialog box.

This dialog box has many of the same elements as the standard Save dialog box, with a few additions. You use its top part to select the drive and folder to which you wish to save the text, and to enter a name for the text.

The bottom part of the dialog box contains the Format pop-out list, which displays the available filters. The import/export filters that are available are those that reside in the same folder as the QuarkXPress application file. You select the desired format from the list.

Above the Format menu are two check boxes, labeled Entire Story and Selected Text. The Selected Text check box will be greyed unless you have highlighted text in the active text box. If you have, the highlighted text will be placed only in the exported file. Selecting Entire Story will export all of the text in the active text box, including any overflow. It doesn't matter whether the overflow text is hidden or displayed in linked text boxes, it will all be included in the exported file.

You will be able to open the exported text file in the program for which you selected a filter. The file will include any text formatting attributes that are supported by the specified program; bolded text will appear bolded, and so on. Text formatting attributes that are not supported by the specified program will be ignored. For example, most word processors don't support automatic drop caps, so that attribute probably will not appear in the exported text.

In addition to the filters that support a specific word processing program, there is a filter for ASCII text. The ASCII format is a very simple, fairly universal file format that can be opened by most word processors. It doesn't carry any formatting information, just the bare text, but its universality makes it quite useful.

Save Page as EPS

You can create an EPS picture file from a page in the active QuarkXPress document and import it into a document that can import EPS figures.

EPS, you will recall, stands for Encapsulated PostScript. PostScript is a page description language that is used by most laser printers and many high-resolution output devices. An Encapsulated PostScript file contains the information a PostScript printer needs to print an image, and some additional information that can be used to help programs handle the EPS file.

Accessing the Save Page as EPS function under the File menu brings up the Save Page as EPS dialog box, as shown in Figure 7.2. The top part of this dialog box is similar to the standard Save dialog box, and allows you to enter a name for the file and select a drive and folder to which to save the page.

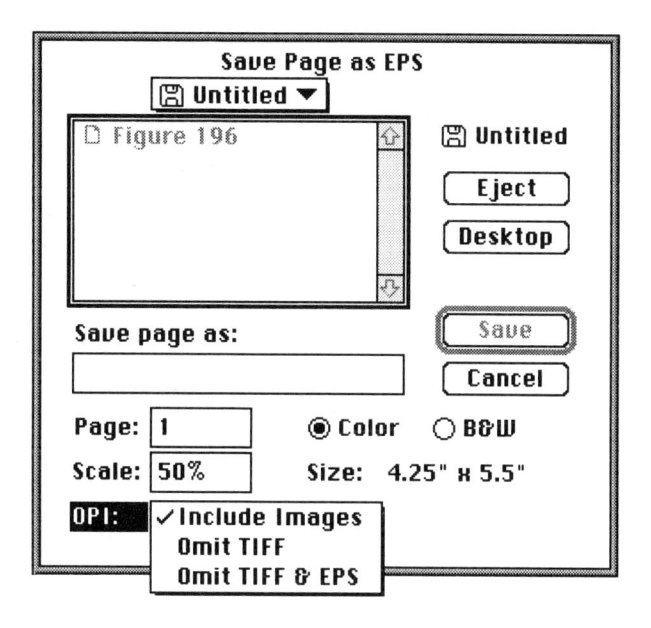

Figure 7.2. The Save Page as EPS dialog box.

The bottom part of the dialog box contains fields and check boxes into which you can indicate attributes for the exported file. You enter a number into the Page field to indicate the page that you wish to save from the current document, and the Color and B&W boxes indicate whether it should be saved in color or black and white. A percentage must be entered into the Scale field to indicate the percentage of the original size to scale the exported file. The dimensions of the exported file, based on the percentage entered into the Scale field, are indicated in the section labeled Size.

The last item is the OPI pop-out list at the bottom of the dialog box. This list has three options that let you choose whether to include process pictures or not. Remember that when pictures are imported as TIFF or EPS files, the image you see on screen is a low-resolution approximation of the actual image; the original file is used only to print the image. When outputting a page as an EPS file, you can include images with the EPS file, omit just TIFF images, or omit both TIFF and EPS images.

Clicking on the Save button makes an EPS copy of the page that includes all text and formatting, all PICT and MPNT images included on the page, and TIFF and/or EPS images as indicated in the OPI field.

This file can be imported into documents created by graphics programs, other page layout programs, some word processors, and more. It cannot, however, be opened or edited in PostScript drawing programs such as Illustrator or FreeHand.

Edit Menu Extras

The first two commands under the Edit menu deal with the Apple System 7's new Publish and Subscribe feature; the third is the Find/Change command; and the last is the H&J, or Hyphenation and Justification, command.

> ▼ **NOTE** ▲ To find out if the programs you use support Publish and Subscribe, check with the software companies that market them.

Subscribe To

If a graphic image or text file is changed after it is imported into QuarkXPress using the Get Text or Get Picture command, the changes are ignored by the QuarkXPress document. The Picture Usage function alerts you when a graphic image has been changed, but you must manually update the picture.

Some programs under Apple's Macintosh System 7 can create documents called Publishers, which are copies of the original document that can be automatically updated. If a program supports the Publish feature, it can create a copy of a document called an edition, and will not be visible in the Get Text or Get Picture dialog boxes. The Subscribe To command in QuarkXPress is used to access editions, and will be greyed unless a text or picture box has been selected with the Content tool.

Figure 7.3 shows the Subscribe To dialog box.

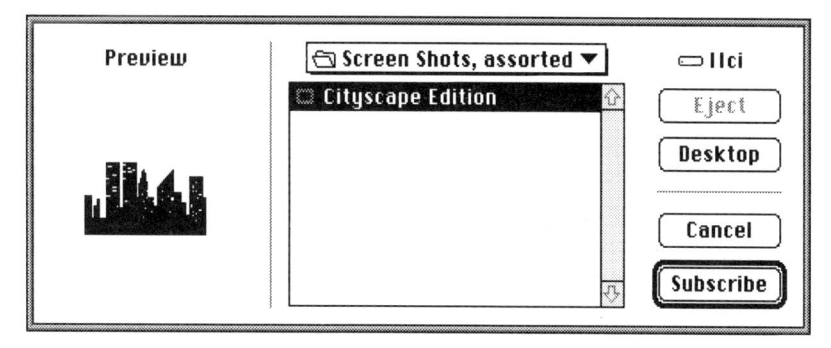

Figure 7.3. The Subscribe To dialog box.

This dialog box is basically the same as the standard Open dialog box except for three things: The Open button has been replaced by a Subscribe button, only the names of editions will appear in the File field, and a preview of the highlighted edition will be shown in the left part of the dialog box.

Clicking on the Subscribe button will bring that file into the currently selected box, just as the Get Text or Get Picture commands would. The difference is that when the edition is opened and changed in the program in which it was created, you can have it automatically updated in the QuarkXPress document.

Subscriber Options

You control how QuarkXPress handles editions through the Subscriber Options dialog box, shown in Figure 7.4, whose top part has a pop-out list that is used to indicate for which edition you wish to set the parameters.

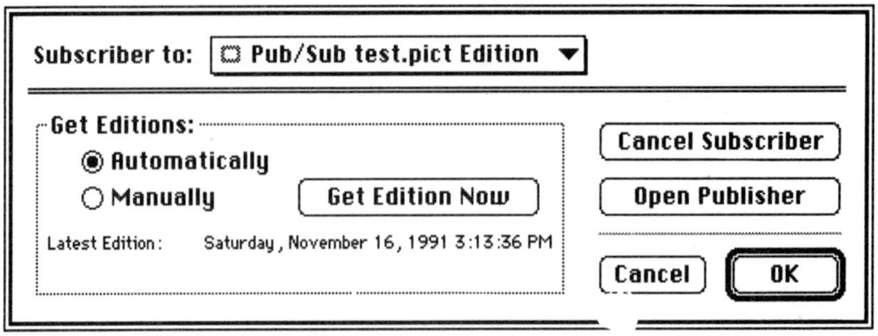

Figure 7.4. The Subscriber Options dialog box.

The Get Editions section contains two check boxes that are used to indicate whether you want editions to be automatically updated when they are changed in their originating program, or to be changed manually using the Get Edition Now button. When the Automatically check box is enabled, the edition will be updated as soon as it is saved in its originating program. If Manually is checked, the edition will be updated only when you click on the Get Edition Now button.

Below these check boxes is listed the time and date of the latest edition and, if Manually is checked, the last edition received.

Clicking on the Cancel Subscriber button removes the link to the edition. Clicking on the Open Publisher button launches the program in which the edition was created. For more on Publish and Subscribe, refer to the Macintosh reference manual that comes with System 7.

Find/Change

You can search for a word or phrase in a QuarkXPress document using the Find/Change command under the Edit menu. Accessing this command brings up the Find/Change dialog box. This dialog box can be expanded to search on text attributes as well as on the text itself, but let's talk about the initial dialog box first.

There are two sides to the Find/Change dialog box: Find What on the left, and Change To on the right. You enter the word or phrase you wish to find in the text box on the Find What side. You can type the text into this field or use the clipboard to paste it in.

The Find Next button in the bottom-left corner of the dialog box becomes active when something is entered into the Find What field; clicking on it starts the search.

Once text has been found, the three buttons next to the Find Next button become active. The Change, Then Find button will change the found text to the contents of the Change To text field, and then find the next instance of the contents of the Find What field. The Change button simply changes the found text to match the contents of the Change To field. The last button, Change All, automatically searches through the entire story or document (depending on the status of the Document check box) to change every instance of the desired text.

Document

Above the Find Next button is a check box labeled Document. Unless this box is checked, the Find command searches only in the current story; check this box to search the entire document.

Figure 7.5 shows a text box and the Find/Change dialog box. The word "the" has been entered into the Find What text field, and the Find Next button has been clicked, which highlights the word "the" in the text box. This is how QuarkXPress indicates the found text. Clicking on the Find Next button again will find the next instance of the desired text.

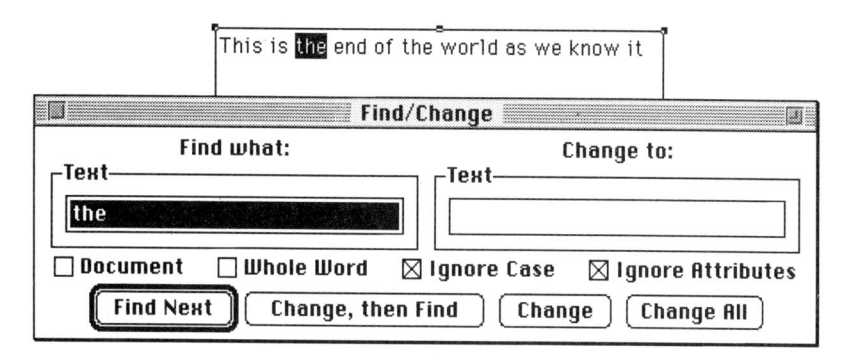

Figure 7.5. The Find/Change dialog box.

If no text is active you will hear a beep indicating that nothing was found. If a story or document has been selected, QuarkXPress will search it from the location of the text insertion point to the end. If the text insertion point is not at the beginning of the story or document, only text after the insertion point will be searched.

Whole Word

Next to the Document check box is a check box labeled Whole Word. When this option is enabled, QuarkXPress will find the contents of the Text field only when they appear as a whole word. If it is not enabled, QuarkXPress will find the contents of the text field even if they appear as only part of a word in the document.

In Figure 7.5, for instance, "the" is entered into the text field and the Whole Word box is not checked. This means that every instance of the three letters "the" will be found, whether they stand alone as a whole word, or are part of another word, such as "theory" or "other."

Ignore Case

When the Ignore Case check box is enabled, it doesn't matter whether you enter lowercase letters or capitals into the text field. When Ignore Case is not checked, the text will be found only if it matches the case of the text field's contents.

Ignore Attributes

When the Ignore Attributes check box is not checked, the Find/Change dialog box expands to show the full range of font, size, and style attributes that can be applied to text, as shown in Figure 7.6.

When the Font check box is enabled, you select a font from the pop-out list and the word in the Find What text field will be found only if it appears in that font. If the Size check box is enabled, the word will be found only if it occurs at the size listed in the Size field. If the Style check box is enabled, it will be found only if it displays the indicated style attributes.

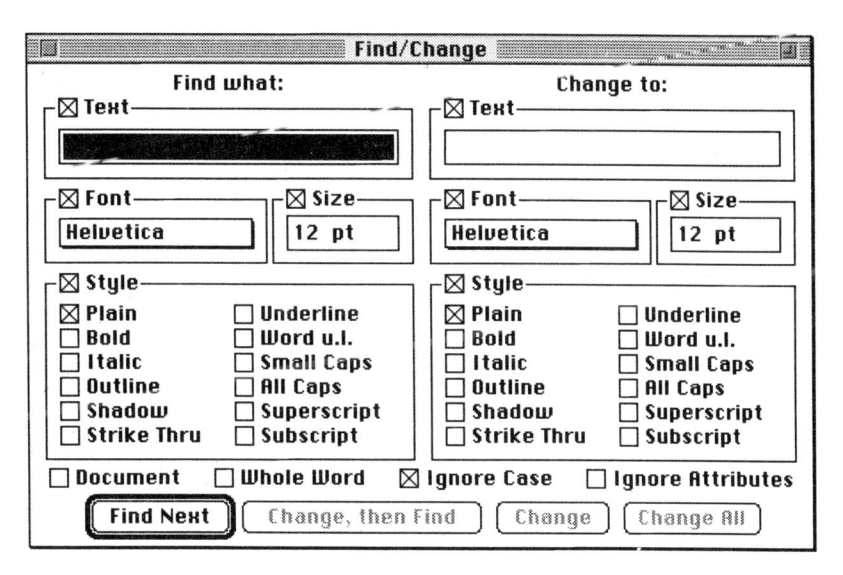

Figure 7.6. The full Find/Change dialog box.

Attributes can be changed individually or in any combination. For example, you could find all instances of the word "crumpet" that appear in 12 point Helvetica Bold, and change the bold to underline. To do this, you would enable the Find What text field and enter the word "crumpet," enable the Font section and choose Helvetica from the pop-out list, enable the Size field and enter 12 pt, and enable the Style section and click in the Bold check box. On the Change To side of the dialog box, you wouldn't have to enable the Text, Font, or Size sections. You only have to enable the Change To Style section and make the desired change, which in this case is to enable the Underline check box. You can then use the Change button to change only the currently found instance; the Change, Then Find button to change the current instance and find the next; or the Change All button to change all instances.

The status of the Whole Word and Document check boxes is still valid when Ignore Attributes is disabled. Once the text that matches the current choices has been found, the Change, Then Find; Change; and Change All buttons can be used to change the matching text to that indicated on the Change To side of the dialog box.

Finding Special Characters

Special Characters are characters like the paragraph mark, tabs, jump line commands, and so on. You can use the Find/Change command to find these characters also. The following table shows what you must type to Find/Change special characters.

To Find	Enter	Shows
Tab	Command-Tab	\t
New Paragraph	Command-Return	\p
New Line	Command-Shift-Return	\n
New Column	Command-Enter	\c
New Box	Command-Shift-Enter	\b
Previous Box Page #	Command-2	\2
Current Page #	Command-3	\3
Next Box Page #	Command-4	\4
Wild Card	Command-?	\?

H&Js

The H&Js command under the Edit menu controls how words are hyphenated, and how line justification is handled. Selecting the H&Js command presents you with the dialog box shown in Figure 7.7.

Clicking on the New button allows you to create new H&J specifications that can be used in the current document. The Duplicate button creates a copy of the currently selected H&J specifications, so that you can test changes without losing the original settings. The Delete button removes the currently selected H&J specifications from the list. The Append button brings up a standard Open dialog box, from which you can navigate to another QuarkXPress document and append its H&J specifications to the current document. The Cancel button closes this dialog box and returns you to the document without making any changes.

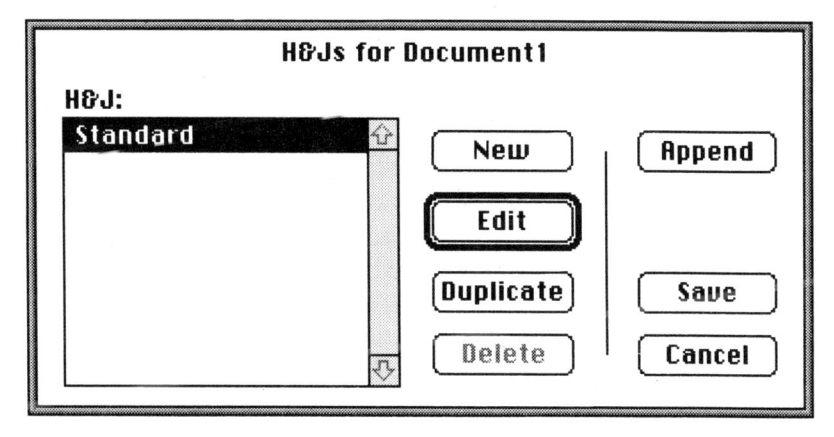

Figure 7.7. The Hyphenation and Justification selection dialog box.

The Edit button brings up the dialog box, shown in Figure 7.8, that allows you to edit the H&J characteristics. After you have made changes to these characteristics, click on the Save button to record them for future use.

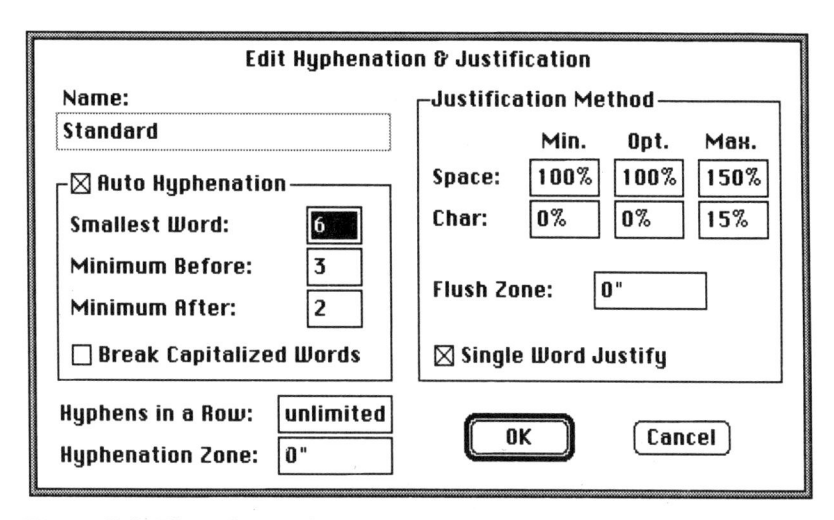

Figure 7.8. The Edit Hyphenation and Justification dialog box.

The left side of the Edit Hyphenation & Justification dialog box holds the hyphenation controls. The justification controls are on the right side.

Hyphenation Characteristics

If you are creating new H&J specifications, you enter a name for the new method into the Name field. If you are editing an existing method, its name will appear in this field. Below the Name field is a check box labeled Auto Hyphenation. When this box is checked, words will automatically be hyphenated according to the characteristics specified. When this box is not checked, no words will be automatically hyphenated..

Words containing fewer than the number of characters in the Smallest Word field will not be hyphenated; instead, they will be wrapped to the next line. The number in the Minimum Before field indicates the earliest point in any word at which hyphenation can occur. No word will be hyphenated at a point that will leave fewer characters after the hyphenation than the amount in the Minimum After field.

Checking the Break Capitalized Words box will allow words that start with a capital letter to be hyphenated. If this box is not checked, capitalized words will be wrapped.

Before a word is automatically hyphenated, QuarkXPress checks the Hyphenation Exceptions list to see if exceptions are dictated for the current word.

The Hyphens in a Row field controls how many consecutive words can be hyphenated. The default is "unlimited," but you can enter any whole number. The Hyphenation Zone is the distance from the right edge of the text box that, in conjunction with the other controls, is used to determine whether a word will be hyphenated or wrapped to the next line. If the first portion of a hyphenated word would be shorter than the Hyphenation Zone, that word is wrapped rather than broken. In Figure 7.9, the same text box is shown with two different Hyphenation Zone settings.

The first has the Hyphenation Zone set at the default of zero inches. Since there is no zone, all words will be broken that conform to the other hyphenation rules. In the second box, the Hyphenation Zone is set to one inch. Notice that the word "benevolent" has been wrapped to the third line rather than hyphenated. This is because when it is hyphenated, the first part ("benev-") is less than one inch long.

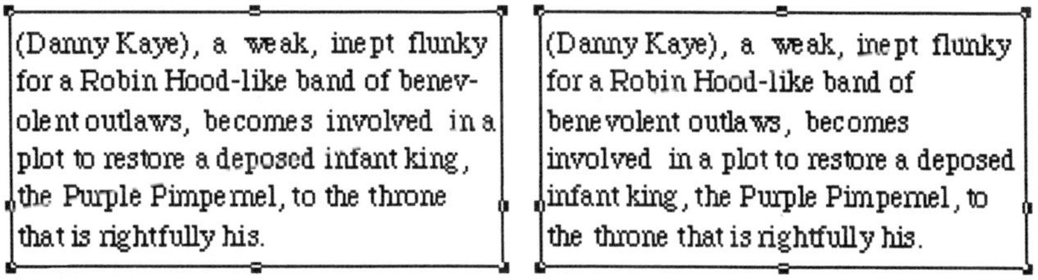

> (Danny Kaye), a weak, inept flunky for a Robin Hood-like band of benevolent outlaws, becomes involved in a plot to restore a deposed infant king, the Purple Pimpernel, to the throne that is rightfully his.

> (Danny Kaye), a weak, inept flunky for a Robin Hood-like band of benevolent outlaws, becomes involved in a plot to restore a deposed infant king, the Purple Pimpernel, to the throne that is rightfully his.

Figure 7.9. The text box on the left has the Hyphenation Zone set to 0", while the box on the right has it set to 1".

Justification Characteristics

When text is justified, space is added between words and between letters within words to make each line the same length. The Justification Method controls determine how much space is added and where. There are three fields for both the Space and the Character adjustments. The field labeled "Min" holds the minimum percent of space that may be applied; the field labeled "Opt" holds the optimal amount of space, and must contain a figure between the minimum and maximum amounts; and the field labeled "Max" holds the maximum amount of space that may be inserted.

The Space fields control the percentage change that will be applied to spaces created with the Spacebar key. The amounts in the Character fields apply to the spaces between individual letters in words (kerning).

The Flush Zone is an area that extends from the right margin to the edge of the text box. The distance it extends from the right margin is determined by the measurement entered into the Flush Zone field. The text must enter the Flush Zone before it will justify. The Flush Zone most obviously affects the last line in a justified paragraph; even if that line barely reaches the Flush Zone, it will be justified, which may make it appear that there is too much space between its letters and words.

Figure 7.10 shows two text boxes, each with a half-inch Flush Zone.

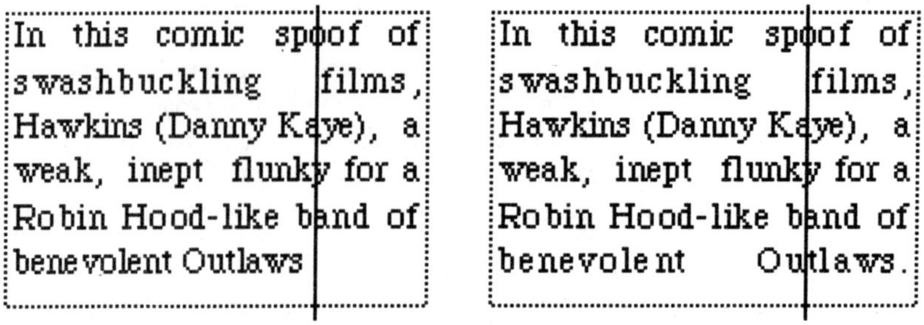

```
In this comic spoof of          In this comic spoof of
swashbuckling    films,         swashbuckling    films,
Hawkins (Danny Kaye), a         Hawkins (Danny Kaye), a
weak, inept flunky for a        weak, inept flunky for a
Robin Hood-like band of         Robin Hood-like band of
benevolent Outlaws              benevolent       Outlaws.
```

Figure 7.10. The last line of text in the box on the left doesn't extend into the Flush Zone, while the last line in the box on the right does.

In the example on the left in Figure 7.10, the last line doesn't extend into the Flush Zone, so it is not justified. In the example on the right, a period has been added to the end of the last line. This makes the line long enough to extend into the Flush Zone, so the line is justified.

The last item in the H&Js dialog box is the Single Word Justify check box. When this box is checked, even single words, such as may be found in the last line of a paragraph, will be justified if they extend into the Flush Zone. When this box is not checked, lines containing a single word will not be justified.

Item Menu Extras

Duplicate/Step and Repeat

The Duplicate and the Step and Repeat commands under the Item menu work together to allow you to make copies of objects. Accessing the Duplicate command makes at least one copy of the currently selected object. If more than one object is selected, all selected objects are duplicated. How many copies are made and where those copies are placed are controlled by the values entered into the Step and Repeat dialog box, as shown in Figure 7.11.

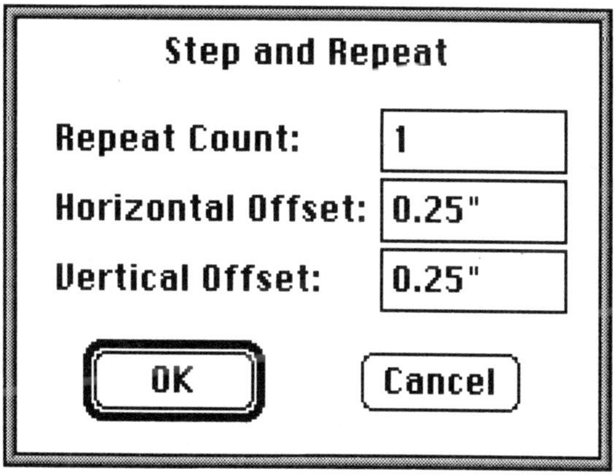

Figure 7.11. The Step and Repeat dialog box.

The first field, labeled Repeat Count, controls the number of copies of the currently selected object(s). The default value is one, but you can enter any whole number between one and ninety-nine. The values in the Horizontal and Vertical offset fields control where the duplicates will be placed relative to the original(s).

If the Repeat Count and the offsets would cause the duplicates to be placed off the page, the alert "You can't make that many duplicates using this number" will be displayed, and you must change one or more of the values.

Delete

The Delete command under the Item menu will delete the currently selected object. If more than one object is selected when this command is accessed, you will be alerted: "This will delete several items and cannot be undone. OK to continue?" Clicking on the Cancel button aborts the Delete command. Clicking on the OK button deletes all of the currently selected objects. The Undo command from the Edit menu cannot be accessed to reverse a multiple-object delete. Pressing the backspace key when objects are selected is the same as activating the Delete command.

Constrain

When objects are grouped, the individual objects cannot be selected, moved, or resized with the Item tool. They can be selected and resized with the Content tool, and resized and moved by editing the values in the Measurement palette.

For the Constrain function to be applied, one or more objects (text, an image, or a line) must be completely within the boundaries of a text or picture box, they must be in front of that box, and they must be grouped with that box.

If these three conditions are not met, the Constrain function remains greyed and cannot be accessed. If these conditions are met, the Constrain function can be applied to that group, making it impossible to move objects beyond the borders of the box that contains them.

It is also impossible to resize the objects so that any part of them extends beyond the outer box. Figure 7.12 shows three boxes that have been grouped and constrained. The larger box is behind the other two and contains them. If you resize one of the inner boxes with the Content tool, you will be able to drag it only to the edge of the outer box. If you enter an amount into the Measurement palette that would cause the inner box to extend or move beyond the boundaries of the outer box, an alert will inform you that "the item must remain totally within its constraining box."

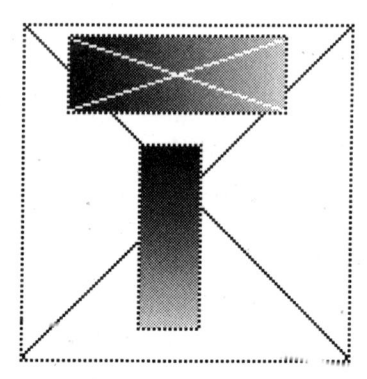

Figure 7.12. These three boxes have been grouped, and the Constrain command has been applied to them.

When a Constrained group is selected, the Constrain command changes to Unconstrain under the Item menu. Selecting this command allows the boxes to be treated as a normal group.

Space/Align

The Space/Align function can align several items or space them evenly along a certain path. This function stays greyed until you select more than one item with the Item tool. When you have selected two or more items, you can access the Space/Align command, which brings up the Space/Align dialog box shown in Figure 7.13.

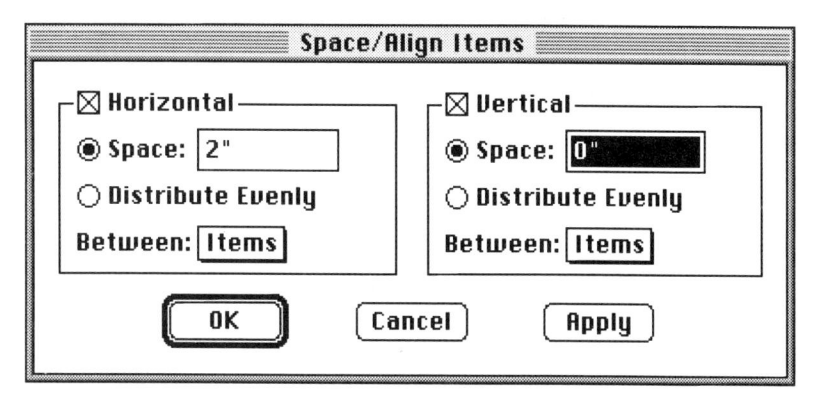

Figure 7.13. The Space/Align dialog box.

There are two sections in this dialog box; one is used to control the horizontal alignment of the two or more objects selected, and one to control the vertical alignment. You enable the desired section by checking the box next to the section label.

The first option in both sections is the Space check box and field. You may enter a value into this field in inches, picas, or whatever measurement you selected when you set the Preferences for the current document. You may also enter into this field a percentage between 0% and 1000%, in .1% increments. This will increase or decrease the space between items as a percent of the current space.

The last option in both sections is the Between pop-out list. Figure 7.14 shows the Between options for both horizontal and vertical alignment.

```
✓ Items
  Left Edges
  Centers
  Right Edges
```

```
✓ Items
  Top Edges
  Centers
  Bottom Edges
```

Figure 7.14. On the left are the horizontal alignment parameters. On the right are the vertical alignment parameters.

The middle option is the Distribute Evenly check box. Distribute Evenly places an equal amount of space between each object selected, without changing the position of the end objects in relation to the box that contains them. Figure 7.15 shows three boxes that have had the four Distribute Evenly options applied to their horizontal edges.

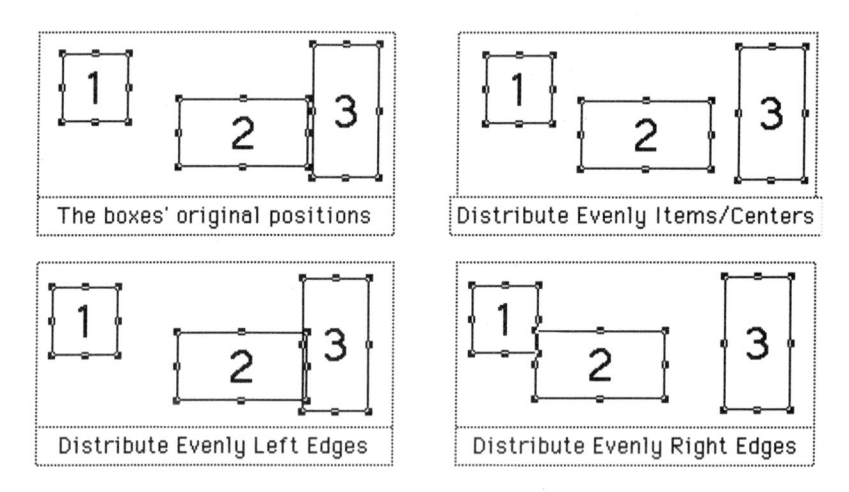

Figure 7.15. Distribute Evenly examples.

The top left example shows the boxes in their original positions. The top right example shows how they are distributed when Between Items or Between Centers is chosen. The distance between the right edge of box 1 and the left edge of box 2 is the same as the distance between the right edge of box 2 and the left edge of box 3; that is, the space between them is measured evenly from their centers. When there are more than three items, the same amount of space will be placed between the centers of all items, even if this causes them to overlap.

The examples on the bottom in Figure 7.15 shows the results of Distribute Evenly Between Left and Right Edges, respectively. In the example on the left, the same amount of space is placed between the left edges of each box; that is, the distance between the left edge of box 1 and the left edge of box 2 is the same as the distance between the left edge of box 2 and the left edge of box 3. In the example on the right, the space is divided evenly measuring from the right edge of each box.

When you apply the Distribute Evenly option for vertical spacing, the space between is measured from the tops and bottoms of the boxes rather than from their sides.

Space

You have just learned that the Space option can be used to place a specific amount of space between items, between their centers, or between their edges. The most common use of the Space option, though, is to align objects. This is done by entering 0" into the Space field and selecting the Between part that you wish to align. The Vertical section is used to align the tops or bottoms of objects. The Horizontal section is used to align objects' left or right edges. The centers of two or more objects can be aligned either vertically or horizontally, or can be centered over the same spot.

A Space/Align Example

Figure 7.16 shows four boxes that have been placed randomly on the page. We want to align the tops of these four boxes (vertical alignment) and place an equal amount of space between them.

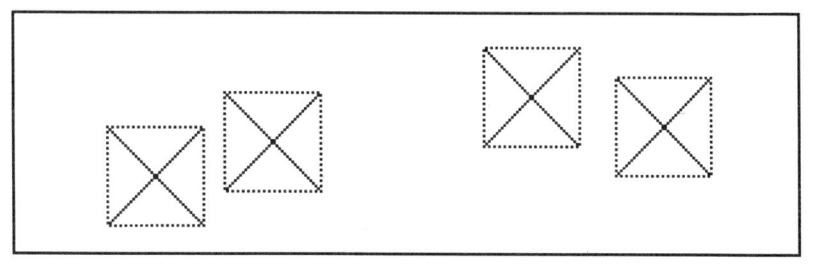

Figure 7.16. Four randomly placed boxes.

To do this all, four boxes must be selected by holding down the Shift key and clicking on each with the Item tool. Then the Space/Align function is selected from the Item menu to bring up the Space/Align dialog box. Figure 7.17 shows how the Space/Align dialog box must be set to cause the boxes in Figure 7.16 to be aligned vertically.

Figure 7.17. Space/Align in action.

The space between the items has been distributed evenly horizontally, and zero space has been placed between the top edges vertically. The result is shown in Figure 7.18.

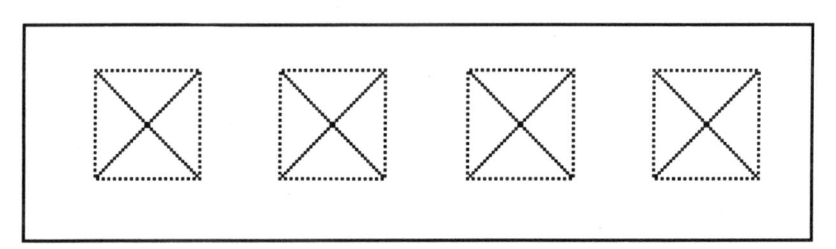

Figure 7.18. The tops of the boxes have been aligned, and all four have been evenly spaced.

Page Menu Extras

Master Guides

There is one option under the Page Menu that has not yet been discussed: Master Guides. Accessing this command brings up the Master Guides dialog box, as shown in Figure 7.19. However, you can access this command only when a Master page is displayed. Remember that you display a Master page by selecting its name from the Display pop-out menu under the Page menu, or by clicking on it in the Show Document Layout box. The values displayed in the Master Guides dialog box are those of the currently displayed Master page.

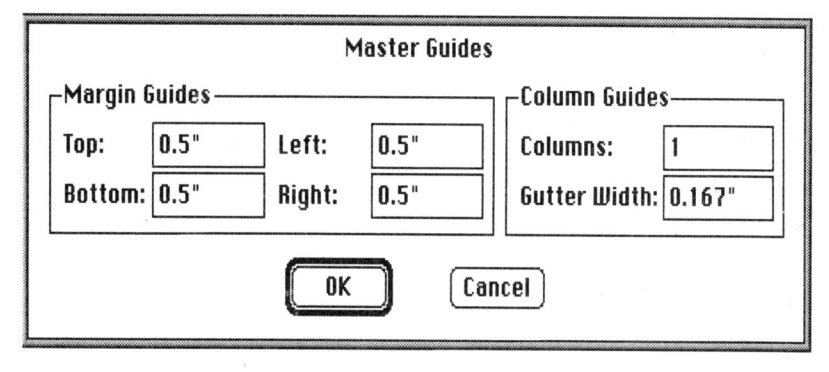

Figure 7.19. The Master Guides dialog box.

Through this dialog box you can adjust where the margin guides will appear on that Master page. You can also indicate how many Column Guides will display, and the amount of space that will be placed between them. Pages created based on this Master Page will display the same guides.

You cannot change the guides on an already created page. If you wish to change the guides, you must create a new Master page with the desired guides, insert a new page into the document based on that page, and copy the objects from the original page onto the new page. You would then delete the original page and place the new one in the proper order in the document.

▼ **NOTE** ▲ Remember that you must have the Item tool selected in order to be able to select multiple objects and to copy and paste objects. The Content tool can copy or paste only text in a text box or an image in a picture box.

View Menu Extras

At the bottom of the View menu are several commands that show and hide palettes other than the Tools, Measurement, and Document Layout palettes we have already discussed. These are the Style Sheets palette, the Colors palette, and the Trap Information palette.

The Style Sheets Palette

The Style Sheets palette shows the style sheets that are available for the current document; these are also shown in the Style Sheets pop-out menu under the Style menu when a text box is selected. Creating, editing, and importing style sheets is discussed in detail in Chapter 3.

Figure 7.20 shows a text box and the Style Sheets palette for the document that contains that text box. The cursor is in the first line of text, which reads "Heading One," and has been formatted as "heading 1,1." The "heading 1,1" style is highlighted in the Style Sheets palette.

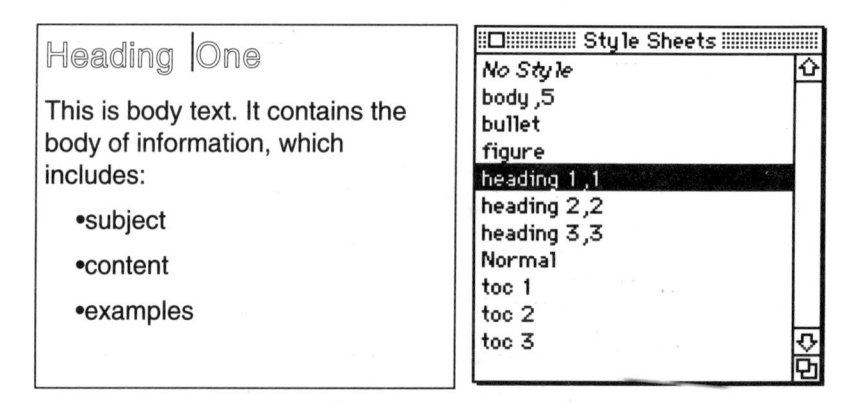

Figure 7.20. The Style Sheets palette reflects the style of the paragraph in which the cursor has been placed.

Remember that when you apply a style to text by selecting that style from the Style Sheets pop-out menu, that style is applied to the entire paragraph that contains the text insertion point or highlighted text. You can also apply styles by clicking on them in the Style Sheets palette. If you have enough space on your screen to leave the Style Sheets palette open, it can save time to select the styles from the palette rather than dropping down the menu to make your choice.

When the Style Sheets palette is shown, the View menu will display "Hide Style Sheets." Selecting this option or clicking on the close box in the upper-left corner of the palette closes the palette.

The Colors Palette

Selecting Show Colors from the View menu presents the Colors palette, as shown in Figure 7.21.

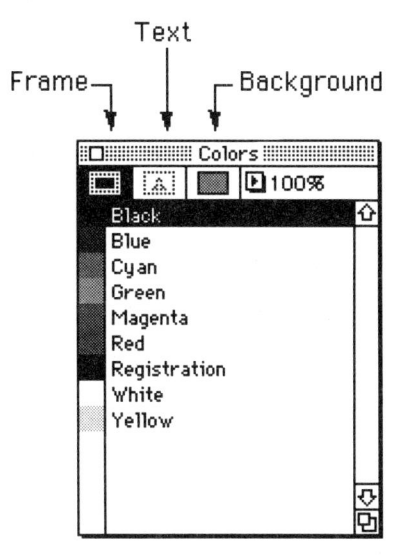

Figure 7.21. The Colors palette showing that the frame of the currently selected box is 100% black.

Beneath the title bar of the palette are three icons that determine whether the selected color will be applied to the frame, the text, or the background of a text or picture box. In this example, the indicated color, black, applies to the frame. Clicking on one of the other areas will control the color for that attribute. When a picture box is selected, the text attribute cannot be selected.

To the right of the background attribute area is a pop-out list that allows you to select a shade percentage for the currently selected attribute. The percentage shown in Figure 7.21 is 100. If you want a percentage other than those in the list, you can double-click on the percentage to select it, and type in the desired number. Clicking on the Return key applies that shade.

If you have not selected Frame from the Item menu and set a frame width larger than zero, then the color and shade changes you make in the Colors palette won't appear. But these parameters will be used if a frame is applied later.

When using the Colors palette to change the color of text, you must highlight the text that you wish to change before selecting a color. Only the selected text will be affected. If no text is highlighted, the color you select in the Colors palette will be used for text entered at the insertion point. A shade must also be set for the selected text color.

Remember that you must use the Color command from the Edit menu to add, delete, or edit colors in the Colors palette.

Blending Background Colors

As shown in Figure 7.22, when the Background icon is selected, the second bar in the Colors palette contains a pop-out menu that allows you to choose between a Solid and a Linear Blend background. Solid is the default setting, and it causes the background to be filled with a solid color. The second option, Linear Blend, allows you to fill the background of a text or picture box with a blend of two colors, or two shades of a single color.

When Linear Blend is selected, the third line in the Colors palette becomes active. This section contains two check boxes (actually circles) that allow you to set the two colors to be used in the blend. To select the first color, click on the check box labeled "#1" and select a color and shade percentage. Then click on the check box labeled "#2" and select the color and shade percentage to which you wish to blend. They don't have to be two different colors. Most blends are actually between two shades of the same color. Very seldom will you find that shading from one color to another is needed.

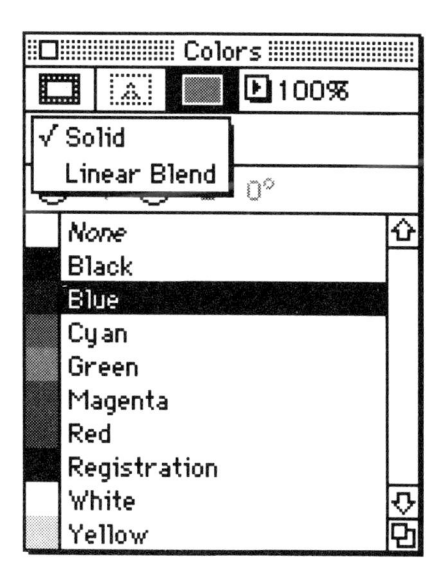

Figure 7.22. The Colors palette showing the pop-out menu with the two types of background fills available.

Next to the two check boxes is a field that contains the direction in which the blend will be made. The default angle is zero degrees, which causes the first color to be placed on the left side of the box and blend to the second color on the right side of the box. To indicate a different blend direction, double-click on the direction field and enter the desired angle. Figure 7.23 shows this effect and how other angles affect the blend direction.

▼ **NOTE** ▲ In order the see the effect of a linear blend, the box must *not* be selected with the Content tool. It either must be selected with the Item tool, or not selected at all. When a box with a linear blend is selected with the Content tool, the background will be shown as a solid fill using the first color.

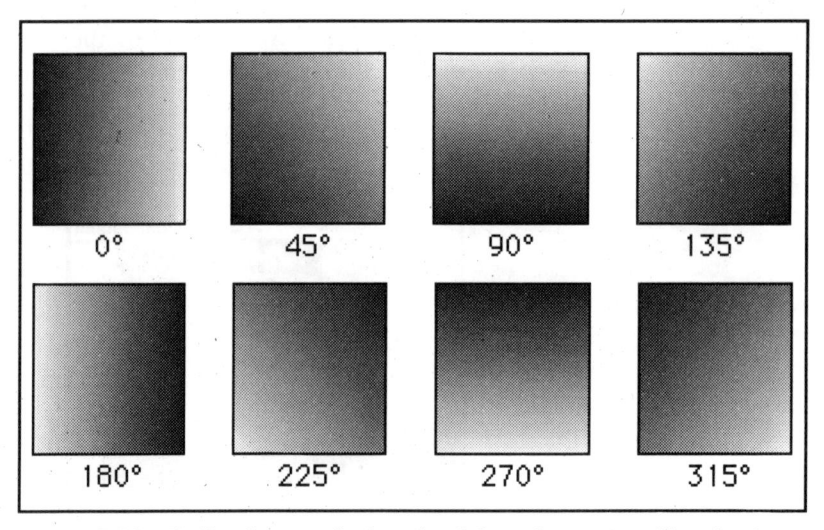

Figure 7.23. The background of each of these boxes is a blend using 80% black for the first color and 10% black for the second. The angle affects the direction of the shade.

When a box is rotated, the blend direction stays relative to the sides of the box. For example, if you had a box with a blend from blue on the left to red on the right, and rotated the box 90 degrees so that the left side was on the bottom, the blend would go from blue on the bottom to red on the top.

The Trap Information Palette

The Trap Information palette is accessed through the View menu, and its contents vary depending on the attributes of the selected item. Through this dialog box you can adjust all of the parameters that affect trapping. The default settings are the automatic trap parameters, and are usually adequate.

Trapping is affected as much by the type of printing equipment used as the design of the document. If you are printing a multicolored document, you should discuss trapping options with your printer.

Utilities Menu Extras

You can use the Check Spelling function under the Utilities menu to compare text in your document to QuarkXPress's standard dictionary. You can create specialized dictionaries that contain words you use often and are not contained in the QuarkXPress dictionary. QuarkXpress automatically hyphenates words, and can give recommendations for manual hyphenation. You can create specialized hyphenations and store them, and can also store groups of graphic images into files called libraries, making access easier.

Check Spelling

The Check Spelling function has three options. You can check the spelling of a single word, of all the words in a particular story, or of all the words in every text box throughout the entire document. Figure 7.24 shows the Utilities menu with the three spelling options.

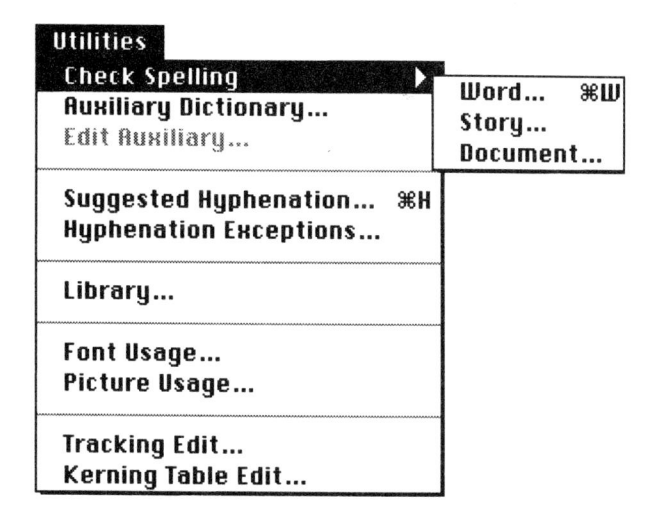

```
Utilities
Check Spelling        ▶   Word...     ⌘W
Auxiliary Dictionary...   Story...
Edit Auxiliary...         Document...

Suggested Hyphenation... ⌘H
Hyphenation Exceptions...

Library...

Font Usage...
Picture Usage...

Tracking Edit...
Kerning Table Edit...
```

Figure 7.24. The Utilities menu showing the Check Spelling function options.

When you select the Check Word option, the word following the text insertion point, or the word containing it, is checked against the QuarkXPress dictionary. You will then be presented with the Check

Word dialog box showing the suspect word. Below the suspect word is a field that will contain a list of possible alternatives. If the word is spelled correctly, you can click on the Cancel button to return to the document. If you click on one of the words in the list then click on the Replace button, the suspect word will be replaced with that word. Figure 7.25 shows the Check Word dialog box for a story that contains a misspelled word. Clicking on the Replace button in this example would change "benevilent" to its proper spelling, "benevolent."

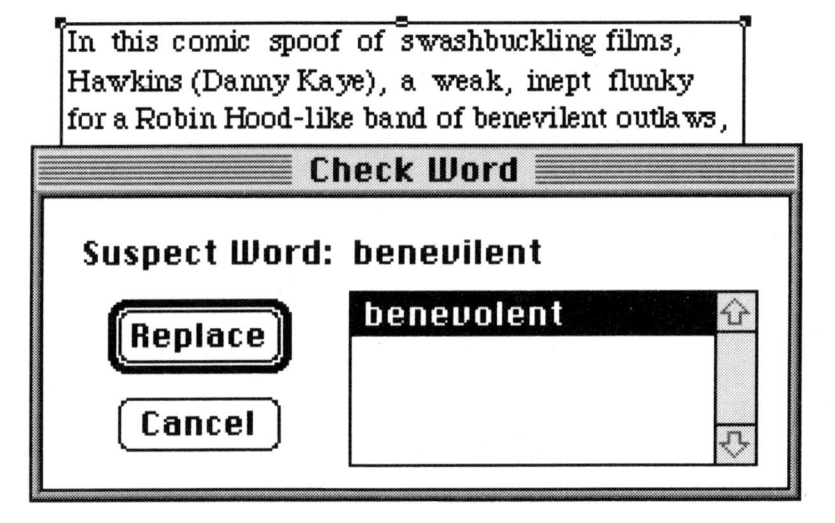

Figure 7.25. The Check Word dialog box.

    Choosing the Check Story option will compare the text in the currently active story (whether it's one text box or a set of linked text boxes) to the dictionary. Choosing the Check Document option will do the same for every word in every text box throughout the entire document.

    In either case, the total text, the number of unique words, and the number of words that don't match the dictionary are each counted. These figures are all presented in a dialog box like that shown in Figure 7.26. In this case, thirty-one words don't match any in the dictionary.

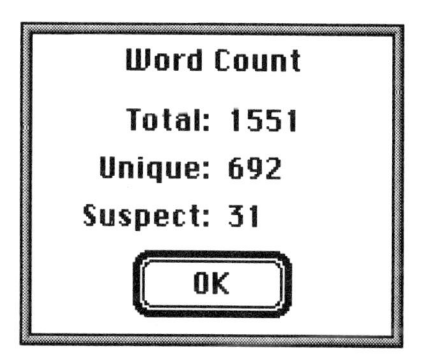

Figure 7.26. Before the Spelling dialog box appears, the text is investigated and the results presented in this dialog box.

When you click on OK, a spell checker dialog box appears. Figure 7.27 shows the Check Story dialog box, but the Check Document dialog box is identical. The first suspect word in the story or document is displayed. Clicking on the Lookup button displays a list of possible alternatives. You can click on the Skip button if the suspect word is in fact correct, or you can select a word from the list and click on the Replace button to replace the suspect word with the one selected. If the suspect word is incorrect but the correct word doesn't appear in the list, you can enter the correct word into the Replace With field, then click on the Replace button to replace it.

Figure 7.27. The Check Story dialog box.

Auxiliary Dictionary

In addition to the words in the XPress Dictionary, you can create auxiliary dictionaries and add words to them that can be used to check spelling. The Auxiliary Dictionary command brings up the Auxiliary Dictionary dialog box, from which you can open a previously created dictionary or create a new one. When you open an existing auxiliary dictionary and use the spell-check function, the text is checked against the words in both the standard dictionary and the auxiliary dictionary.

When an auxiliary dictionary is opened, you can click on the Keep button in the Check Spelling dialog box to add the suspect word to the currently opened auxiliary dictionary.

Edit Auxiliary

Selecting Edit Auxiliary from the Utilities menu accesses the dialog box shown in Figure 7.28, and allows you to edit the current Auxiliary Dictionary. The scrolling field contains the words in the current auxiliary dictionary; clicking on one of these words places that word in the lower field, at which point you can click on the Delete button to remove it from the list. You can add words to the list by typing them in the lower field and clicking on the Add button. Clicking on the Save button permanently changes that dictionary.

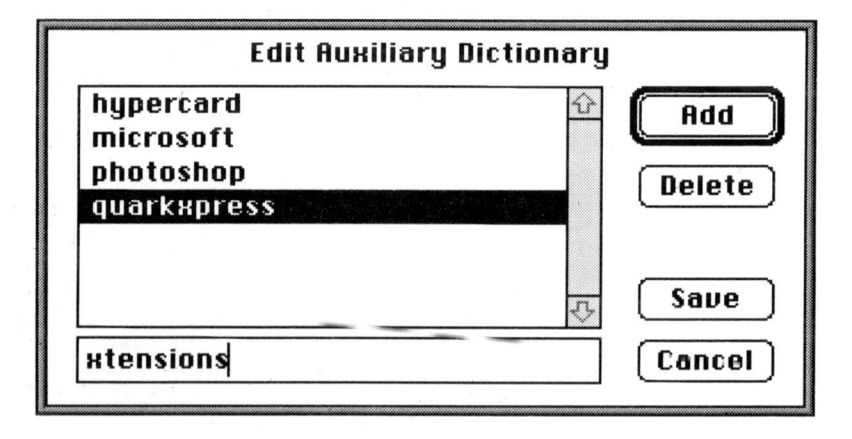

Figure 7.28. The Edit Auxiliary Dictionary dialog box.

Suggested Hyphenation

Choosing the Suggested Hyphenation command will bring up a dialog box like that in Figure 7.29. This dialog box will show the word that follows or contains the text insertion point, and suggestions about how it can be hyphenated.

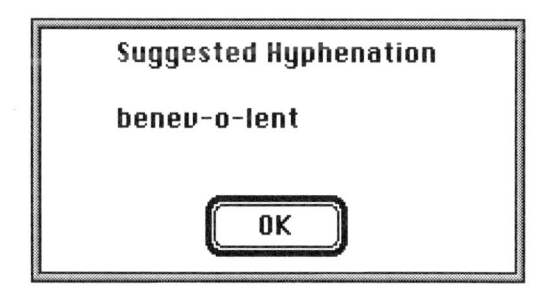

Figure 7.29. The Suggested Hyphenation dialog box.

Hyphenation Exceptions

The Hyphenation Exceptions dialog box, shown in Figure 7.30, can be used to change the way words are hyphenated.

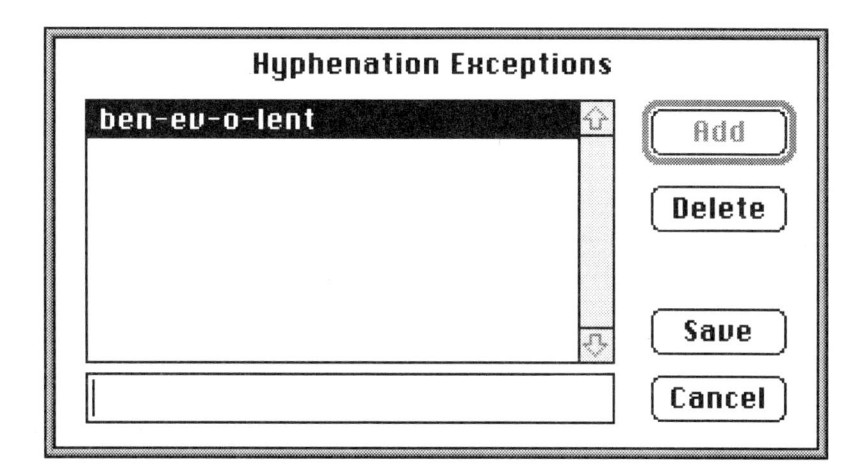

Figure 7.30. The Hyphenation Exceptions dialog box.

QuarkXPress uses standard rules of hyphenation to break up words at the end of a line. For example, in Figure 7.29 the word "benevolent" is hyphenated "benev-o-lent." This is the standard hyphenation for this word. In Figure 7.30, the Hyphenation Exceptions dialog box has been used to change the hyphenation to "ben-ev-o-lent." You can also use this dialog box to change previously added hyphenations, and to delete existing ones.

Clicking on the Save button saves the changes you have made since opening the dialog box. If you click on the Cancel button, the dialog box will be changed without recording any changes.

Library

QuarkXPress libraries are collections of objects that can be used in any document. You can save lines, text boxes, and picture boxes, and you can group any combination of these objects to be saved as a single object. Text saved as a library object retains all of its formatting and attributes, and picture boxes retain any style specifications that have been applied.

Libraries are opened or created by selecting the Library command from the Utilities menu. You can use this dialog box to open an existing library, or you can click on the New button to create a new library. When you click on the New button you are presented with a dialog box that can be used to enter a name and location for the new library. Once the library is created, its palette will appear next to the document. At that point you can use the Item tool to drag objects into the library. These objects aren't removed from the document; a copy is made in the library and a thumbnail is displayed on the palette. You can label each object in a library by double-clicking on it to open the Library Entry dialog box, shown beside a library in Figure 7.31. The labels for the contents of a library can be displayed by clicking and holding on the pop-out list icon at the top of the library palette. Selecting an objects' name from this list causes that object only to be displayed in the palette. When a library starts to get too large, it is often quicker to find an object by selecting its name from the label list than by scrolling through the thumbnails in the palette.

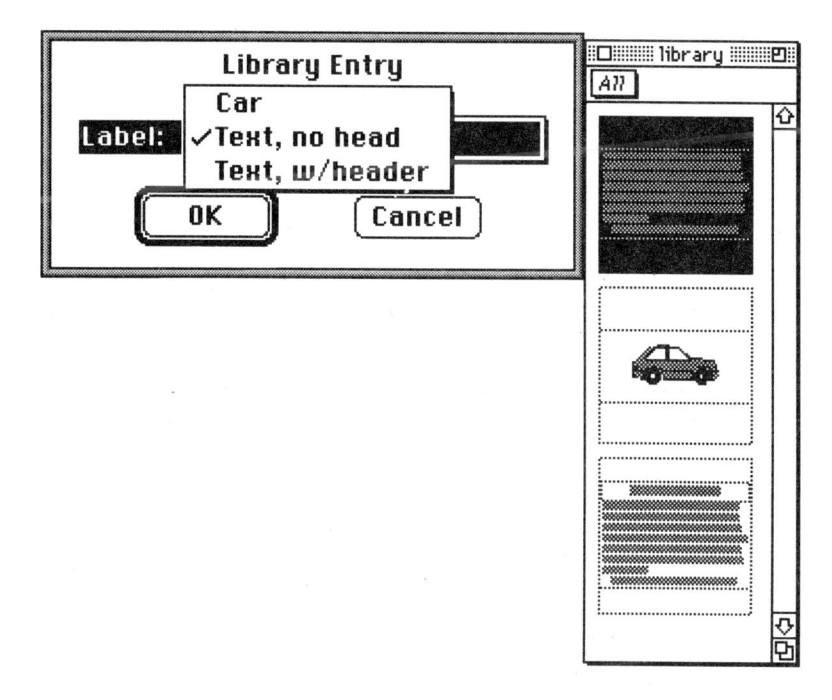

Figure 7.31. A Library Entry dialog box beside some library entries.

To place a library object into a document, use the Item tool to click and drag that objects' thumbnail from the library palette to the document. A full-sized copy of that object is created in that spot.

Highlighting an object in a library palette and selecting Cut from the Edit menu removes that object from the library and places it onto the clipboard. Changes are saved when you close the library.

Summary

▼ The text from a Quark XPress document can be saved for use in a word processor, or an entire page can be saved as an Encapsulated PostScript file.

▼ When using Apple's System 7, you can use the Subscribe To option to create a dynamic link to another document.

▼ The Find/Change command can be used to search for words, phrases, and special characters. Once found, these can be replaced with different text.

▼ The Hyphenation and Justification dialog box allows you to control where and how words are hyphenated and how space is allotted during text justification.

▼ Objects can be duplicated once or many times, and the position of the duplicated objects can be controlled with the Duplicate/Step and Repeat command. Objects can be deleted with the Delete command, as well as with the Backspace key.

▼ The Constrain command can be used to restrict the dimensions of objects within the object that contains them.

▼ The Space/Align command can be used to control how objects line up in relation to one another and to the page.

▼ A Master page's guides can be controlled with the Master Guides dialog box.

▼ In addition to the Tool Measurement, and Document Layout palettes, QuarkXPress can display a Style Sheets, a Trap Information, and a Colors palette.

▼ The spelling of a single word or all of the text in a document can be checked against either the QuarkXPress dictionary or against an editable dictionary that you create.

▼ The Suggested Hyphenation command will show you the recommended hyphenation for an individual word based on the current hyphenation rules and the exceptions indicated in the Hyphenation Exceptions dialog box.

▼ Groups of images can be collected and displayed in documents called *libraries* for easy access in future documents.

APPENDIX

```
⌘     Command
⇧     Shift
⌥     Option
⌃     Control
```

Keyboard Commands

The File Menu
New .... ⌘-N
Open .... ⌘-O
Save .... ⌘-S
Save As .... ⌘⌥-S
Get Text/Picture .... ⌘-E
Print .... ⌘-P
Page Setup .... ⌘⌥-P
Quit .... ⌘-Q

The Edit Menu
Undo .... ⌘-Z
Cut .... ⌘-X
Copy .... ⌘-C
Paste .... ⌘-P
Select All .... ⌘-A
Find/Change .... ⌘-F
General Preferences .... ⌘-Y
Typographic Preferences .... ⌘⌥-Y

Style/Text Menu
Next Larger Preset Font Size ..... ⌘⇧->
Next Smaller Preset Font Size .... ⌘⇧-<
Increase Font Size 1 Point ..... ⌘⇧⌥->
Decrease Font Size 1 Point ... ⌘⇧⌥-<
Other Font Size .... ⌘⇧-\

Type Styles:
  Plain .... ⌘⇧-P
  Bold .... ⌘⇧-B
  Italic .... ⌘⇧-I
  Underline .... ⌘⇧-U
  Word Underline .... ⌘⇧-W
  Strike Thru .... ⌘⇧-/
  Outline .... ⌘⇧-O
  Shadow .... ⌘⇧-S
  All Capitals .... ⌘⇧-K
  Small Caps .... ⌘⇧-H
  Superscript .... ⌘⇧-+
  Subscript .... ⌘⇧--
  Superior .... ⌘⇧-V
Horizontal Scale:
  Increase by 5% .... ⌘-]
  Decrease by 5% .... ⌘-[
Kern/Tracking:
  Increase by 10/200 em .... ⌘⇧-}
  Decrease by 10/200 em .... ⌘⇧-{
  Increase by 1/200 em .... ⌘⇧⌥-}
  Decrease by 1/200 em ...... ⌘⇧⌥-{
Baseline Shift:
  Move Up 1 Point .... ⌘⇧⌥-+
  Move Down 1 Point .... ⌘⇧⌥--
Character Format .... ⌘⇧-D
Alignment:
  Left .... ⌘⇧-L
  Center .... ⌘⇧-C
  Right .... ⌘⇧-R
  Justified .... ⌘⇧-J
Leading:
  Open Dialog Box .... ⌘⇧-E
  Increase by 1 Point .... ⌘⇧-"
  Decrease by 1 Point .... ⌘⇧-:
  Increase by 1/10 Point ..... ⌘⇧⌥-"
  Decrease by 1/10 Point ..... ⌘⇧⌥-:

Paragraph Format .... ⌘⇧-F
Rules .... ⌘⇧-N
Tabs .... ⌘⇧-T

Style/Picture Menu
Negative .... ⌘⇧-–
Normal Contrast .... ⌘⇧-N
High Contrast .... ⌘⇧-H
Posterized .... ⌘⇧-P
Other Contrast .... ⌘⇧-C
Other Screen .... ⌘⇧-S
Picture Size:
    Increase by 5% .... ⌘⇧->
    Decrease by 5% .... ⌘⇧-<
    Fit to Box .... ⌘⇧-F
    Fit to Box, Maintain Ratio ..... ⌘⇧⌥-F
Move Picture:
    Center in Box .... ⌘⇧-M
    Move Picture 1 Point .... Arrows
    Move Picture 1/10 Point ... ⌥-Arrows

Item Menu
Modify .... ⌘-M
Frame .... ⌘-B
Runaround .... ⌘-T
Duplicate .... ⌘-D
Step and Repeat .... ⌘⌥-D
Delete .... ⌘-K
Group .... ⌘-G
Ungroup .... ⌘-U
Lock/Unlock .... ⌘-L

Page Menu
Go To .... ⌘-J
Move To Next/Previous:
    Character .... Left/Right Arrows
    Line .... Up/Down Arrows
    Word .... ⌘-Left/Right Arrows
    Paragraph .... ⌘-Up/Down Arrows
Move To:
    Beginning of Line ... ⌘⌥-Left Arrow
    End of Line .... ⌘⌥-Right Arrow
    Beginning of Story ..... ⌘⌥-Up Arrow
    End of Story .... ⌘⌥-Down Arrow

View Menu
Fit in Window .... ⌘-0
Actual Size .... ⌘-1
Start of Document .... ⌃-A
End of Document .... ⌃-D
Scroll Up One Screen .... ⌃-K
Scroll Down One Screen .... ⌃-D
Hide/Show Rulers .... ⌘-R
Hide/Show Invisibles .... ⌘-I
Show Tools .... ⌘-Tab
Show Measurements .... ⌘⌥-M

Utilities Menu
Check Word Spelling .... ⌘-W
Check Story Spelling .... ⌘⌥-W
Suggested Hyphenation .... ⌘-H

Special Characters
Soft Return .... ⇧-Return
Nonbreaking Hyphen .... ⌘-=
Nonbreaking Space .... ⌘-Space
En Space .... ⌥-Space
Nonbreaking En Space ...... ⌘⌥-Space
Flex Space .... ⌥-Space
Nonbreaking Flex Space .... ⌘⌥-Space
Jump Line Characters:
    Previous Text Box Page Number ..... ⌘-2
    Current Page Number .... ⌘-3
    Next Text Box Page Number ..... ⌘-4
Find/Change Characters:
    Backslash .... \\
    Current Page Number .... \3
    Previous Box Page Number .... \2
    New Box .... \b
    New Column .... \c
    New Line .... \n
    New Paragraph .... \p
    Tab .... \t
    Wild Card .... \?

INDEX

▼ A

Accurate Blends, 158
All Caps, 39
Angle (linear), 22-23
Apple System 7, 174
Application Preferences, 145-152
ASCII text files, 31
Auto Constrain, 158
Auto Kern Above, 165
Auto Leading, 164
Auto Library Save, 150
Auto Page Insertion, 111, 152
Auto Picture Import, 155
Auxiliary Dictionary command, 200

▼ B

Baseline Grid, 63, 164
Bitmapped font, 35
Bitmapped graphics, 73
Bold type, 38
Borders, *see* Frames
Box Angle, 78
Breaking flex space, 165
Brightness, 147

▼ C

Capitalization, 39, 163
Character widths, 167
Check Spelling function, 197-199
Ciceros/cm, 156
CMYK color model, 128, 134, 135
Colors, 88, 146-148
    adding new to palette, 133-135
    background, 81-83
    blending background, 194-196
    deleting, 136
    duplicating, 135-136
    editing, 135
    from another document, 136
    manipulating, 132-137
    palette, 193-196
    trapping, 136-137, 148, 196
Color separation, 127, 137-140
    example, 138-140
Columns, 10, 191
Constrain function, 186-187
Content tool, 29-30
Contrast, 88-89
Control characters, 59-61
Control handles, 21
Copyfitting, 49-51
Corner Radius, 78
Cropping, 76

▼ D

Defaults, 145
Delete command, 185
Dialog boxes, 15
Dingbat font, 34
Dithering, 131, 158
Document Layout Palette, 115-118
    adding pages with, 117-118
    creating Master pages with, 117
    deleting pages with, 118
    moving pages with, 118
Documents, 8
    moving around in, 107
    searching entire, 177-178

viewing at different magnifications, 16-17, 18-19
working with, 15-24
Drop caps, 63-64
Drop-shipping, 126
Duplicate command, 184-185

▼ E

Editions, 175-176
Edit menu extras, 174-184
Em space, 44
Encapsulated PostScript, 74, 172-174
Endcaps, 23-24
EPS, see Encapsulated PostScript

▼ F

Facing pages, 154
File menu extras, 171-174
Files
    creating new, 9-12
    opening existing, 8-9
    see also Image files
Fill character, 67-68
Filters, 31
Find/Change command, 176-180
Flex space width, 165
Flowing, 108
Flush Zone, 183-184
Focoltone color model, 134, 135
Font outline, 35
Fonts, 34-42, 156-157
    proportional and nonproportional, 43
    searching for specific, 178-179
Formats command, 59
Four-color printing, 128
Frames, 83-85, 153-154
    color and shade, 85
    inside/outside, 85
    width, 85, 194

▼ G

General Preferences, 152-158
Go To command, 107
Graphics,
    adding, 73-87
    image formats, 73-74
    send to Back/Bring to Front, 79-80
    see also Picture boxes
Greeking, 157
Greyscale, 151
Grouping, 120-121
Guide colors, 146-148
Guides, 154, 191
Gutters, 10

▼ H

Halftone screening, 125, 129-132
    examples, 131-132
    manipulating an image's, 130-131
H&Js command, 180-184
Hanging text, 62
Horizontal alignment, 187-190
Horizontal Measure, 153
HSB color model, 134, 146
Hue, 147
Hyphenation, 167, 180-181
    characteristics, 182-183
    exceptions, 201-202
    suggested, 201

▼ I

I-beam cursor, 30-31
Ignore Attributes, 178-179
Ignore Case, 178
Image
    formats, 73-74
    importing an, 75-77, 155
    manipulating an, 77-79
Image files

missing, 91-92
  modified, 93
Imagesetter, 125, 126-127
Indentation, 61-62
Insert Pages dialog box, 112
Installation, 4-7
Invisibles, *see* Control characters
Italic type, 38
Item Coordinates, 154
Items
  aligning, 187-190
  constraining (*see* Auto Constrain; Constrain function)
  menu extras, 184-190
  moving and manipulating, 20-21
Item tool, 20-21

▼ J

Jump commands, 119-120
Jump line, 119
Justification, 180-181
  charcteristics, 183-184

▼ K

Kerning, 43-49, 52
  automatic, 165
  editing tables, 45-48
  saving/importing tables, 48-49
Keyboard equivalents, 12-14

▼ L

Laser printer, 125
Leading, 41-42, 52, 62
  automatic, 164
  maintain, 165-166
  mode, 167
Length (linear), 22-23
Library, 150, 202-203
Ligatures, 166

Linc indents, 61-62
Line space, *see* Leading
Lines-per-inch (lpi), 129
Line Style, 23-24
Line tools, 19-20, 162
Linking, 108-110
  automatic, 112
Live scroll, 107, 149
Location (linear), 22-23
Locking, 121
Low-resolution TIFF, 150-151

▼ M

Macintosh Color Picker, 146-147
MacPaint, 73
Maintain Leading, 165-166
Margins, 10, 154, 156, 191
Master Guides, 191
Master pages, 110, 191
  creating with Document Layout palette, 117
  items, 155-156
Measurement palette, 21-24
  for picture boxes, 86-87
  of text box, 51-53
Menus, 11-12

▼ N

Negative image, 88
Nonbreaking flex space, 165

▼ O

Object-oriented graphics, 73
Off-screen Draw, 150
Offset Across, 78
Offset Down, 78
Origin Down, 78
Orphans, 49
Orthogonal Line tool, 19

Outline, 38
Oval picture box tool, 74
Overprint, 136

▼ P

Page description language (PDL), 35
Page Grabber Hand, 150
Pages
    adding with Document Layout palette, 117-118
    automatic insertion, 111, 152
    deleting with Document Layout palette, 118
    facing, 154
    inserting and arranging, 112-115
    menu extras, 191
    moving with Document Layout Palette, 118
    size, 9-10
Pagination, 62-63
    automatic, 113-115, 119
    controlling, 114-115
Pantone color model, 134, 135
Paragraph
    alignment, 39-40, 64
    control characters, 59-61
    drop caps, 63-64
    formatting, 58-64
    line indents, 61-62
    line spacing, 62
    and pagination, 62-63
Pasteboard width, 148-149
PDL, *see* Page description language (PDL)
PICT, 73-74
Picture Angle, 78-79
Picture boxes, 74-75
    background, 81-83
    frames, 83-85
    height, 78
    Measurement palette, 86-87

    modifying shapes, 94-97
    polygonal, 95-97
    resizing, 75
    Specifications dialog box, 77-79
    suppressing, 86
    width, 78
Picture Box tool, 162
Picture Skew, 79
Picture Style
    commands, 88-89
    menu, 87-89
Picture Usage dialog box, 89-93
    missing image files, 91-92
    modified image files, 93
Pixels, 147-148
Plain type, 38
Plates, 125, 126
Points, 10, 156
Polygon
    adding handles to, 97
    deleting handles from, 97
    picture box tool, 74
    Reshape command, 95-97
Posterizing, 89
PostScript fonts, 35
Preferences, 145-167
    application, 145-152
    general, 152-158
    tool, 159-162
    typographic, 162-167
Previous Box Page Number command, 120
Printing, 125-140
    color separation, 137-140
    halftone screens, 129-132
    manipulating colors, 132-137
    multicolor, 127
    process, 125-126
    process versus spot, 127-129
    single-color, 126-127

Index ▼ 211

suppressing picture boxes, 86
traditional press, 126-129
Process color, 128
Program attributes, 11-15
Publishers, 174-175

▼ Q

Quark XTensions, 32
Quotes, 32-33

▼ R

Rectangle picture box tool, 74
Reference points, 22-23
Registration marks, 133, 149
Render Above, 156-157
Repeat command, 184-185
Reshape Polygon command, 95-97
RGB color model, 134
Rounded-corner rectangle picture box tool, 74
Ruler guides, 154, 156
Runaround options, 98-103
    Auto Image, 102
    Item, 100-102
    Manual Image, 102-103
    None, 99-100

▼ S

Sans serif, 34
Saturation, 147
Save Page as EPS function, 172-174
Save Text function, 171-172
Scale Across, 78
Scale Down, 78
Screen font, *see* Bitmapped font
Scroll bars, 107
    see also Live scroll
Scroll Speed, 151-152
Searching, 176-180
    documents, 177-178

ignoring attributes, 178-179
ignoring capitalization, 178
for Special Characters, 180
for whole word, 178
Sections, 113-115
    controlling, 114-115
    merging adjacent, 115
Send to Back/Bring to Front, 79-80
Serif, 34
Shade, 88
Shadow type, 38
Small Caps, 39, 163
Snap Distance, 156
Space/Align function, 187-190
Special Characters, 180
Spelling, 197-199
Spot color, 128
Step command, 184-185
Strike through, 38
Style sheets, 33, 53-58
    appending, 58
    creating new, 56
    deleting, 58
    dialog box, 54-56
    editing, 57-58
    importing, 56-57
    palette, 192-193
    saving, 58
Submenus, 14
Subscriber Options, 175-176
Subscribe To command, 174-175
Subscript, 39, 163
Superior type, 39, 163-164
Superscript, 39, 163

▼ T

Tabs, 64-68
    moving and removing, 68
    setting, 64-68

Tagged Image File Format (TIFF), 74, 150-151
Templates, 8, 110
Text
    automatic chain, 110-112
    changing color of, 194
    controlling with Measurement palette, 52-53
    entering and importing, 29-33
    flowing, 108-110
    highlighting, 30-31
    saving, 171-172
    within picture shapes, 103
    wrapping around images, 98-103
Text attributes, 33-51
    alignment, 39-40, 52
    kerning, 43-49
    leading, 41-42
    size, 40-41
    tracking, 49-51
    type fonts and styles, 34-42
    type width and spacing, 43-51
    see also Style sheets
Text boxes, 10-11
    adding/deleting text in linked, 109-110
    breaking links, 110
    linking, 108-109
    Measurement palette, 51-53
Text overflow indicator, 109
Text tool, 29-30, 160-161
Thumbnail, 76
TIFF, *see* Tagged Image File Format
Toner, 125
Tool palette, 17-20, 74
Tool Preferences, 159-162

Tracking, 43, 49-51, 52
Trap Information palette, 196
Trapping, 136-137, 148
Trumatch color model, 134, 135
Typefaces, *see* Fonts
Typesetter, 125
Type styles, 34-42
    basic, 36-37
    other, 37-39
Typographical effects, 49-51
Typographic Preferences, 162-167

▼ U

Underline, 38
Utilities menu extras, 197-203

▼ V

Vertical alignment, 187-190
Vertical Measure, 153
Viewing percentage, 16-17
View menu extras, 192-196

▼ W

Whole Word, 178
Width (linear), 23
Windows, 15-16
Word underline, 38

▼ X

XPress Dictionary, 200
XPress Preferences, 145

▼ Z

Zoom tool, 18-19, 159-160